Well-Being for Public Policy

Series in Positive Psychology

Series Editor
Christopher Peterson

Well-Being for Public Policy
Ed Diener, Richard E. Lucas, Ulrich Schimmack, and John Helliwell

Oxford Handbook of Methods in Positive Psychology
Anthony D. Ong

A Primer in Positive Psychology
Christopher Peterson

A Life Worth Living: Contributions to Positive Psychology
Mihaly Csikszentmihalyi

Handbook of Positive Psychology
C. R. Snyder and Shane J. Lopez

Forthcoming Books in the Series:

Handbook of Positive Psychology, 2nd Edition
Shane J. Lopez and C. R. Snyder

Well-Being for Public Policy

Ed Diener
Richard E. Lucas
Ulrich Schimmack
John F. Helliwell

OXFORD
UNIVERSITY PRESS

2009

OXFORD

UNIVERSITY PRESS

Oxford University Press, Inc., publishes works that further
Oxford University's objective of excellence
in research, scholarship, and education.

Oxford   New York
Auckland   Cape Town   Dar es Salaam   Hong Kong   Karachi
Kuala Lumpur   Madrid   Melbourne   Mexico City   Nairobi
New Delhi   Shanghai   Taipei   Toronto

With offices in
Argentina   Austria   Brazil   Chile   Czech Republic   France   Greece
Guatemala   Hungary   Italy   Japan   Poland   Portugal   Singapore
South Korea   Switzerland   Thailand   Turkey   Ukraine   Vietnam

Published by Oxford University Press, Inc.
198 Madison Avenue, New York, New York 10016

www.oup.com

Oxford is a registered trademark of Oxford University Press

Library of Congress Cataloging-in-Publication Data
Well-being for public policy / Ed Diener . . . [et al].
    p.   cm.
Includes bibliographical references and index.
ISBN 978-0-19-533407-4 (alk. paper)
1. Quality of life—Evaluation.   2. Well-being—Evaluation.
3. Economic indicators.   4. Social indicators.   5. Political
planning—Evaluation.   I. Diener, Ed.
HN25.W448 2009
320.6072'7—dc22

                                        2008035596

9   8   7   6   5   4   3   2   1

Printed in the United States of America
on acid-free paper

Acknowledgments

We are very grateful to a number of individuals and organizations who have made this book possible, and who have improved it immensely through their work in this area. We thank the John Templeton Foundation, the Positive Psychology Center at the University of Pennsylvania, the Gallup Organization, the Canadian Institute for Advanced Research, the Social Sciences and Humanities Research Council of Canada, and the National Science Foundation for the various types of monetary support they have given to our work in this area. Several scholars have given us detailed feedback along the way, and we are very appreciative to them: Paul Dolan, Daniel Kahneman, Martin E. P. Seligman, Chris Peterson, Robert Putnam, Chris Barrington-Leigh, Haifang Huang, Anthony Leigh, Rebecca North, Tessa Peasgood, and Andrew Clark. Other scholars have given us focused feedback on specific issues related to this work: Dan Haybron, Valerie, Tiberius, Felicia Huppert, George Vaillant, and Nic Marks. Our work has especially profited from the publications of Bruno Frey and Alois Stutzer, as well as Bernard Von Praag. These and many other leading thinkers have helped our work in so many ways. We also want to thank Katherine Ryan and Deborah Dexter, who provided valuable clerical and research assistance for the book.

Contents

Section I. Measuring Well-Being for Public Policy

1 Using Well-Being to Inform Public Policy   3

2 Defining Well-Being   8

Section II. How Well-Being Adds Information

3 Limitations of Economic and Social Indicators   23

4 Contributions of Well-Being Measures   46

5 The Well-Being Measures Are Valid   67

6 Issues Regarding the Use of Well-Being Measures for Policy   95

7 The Desirability of Well-Being as a Guide for Policy   119

Section III. Examples of Policy Uses of Well-Being Measures

8 Health and Well-Being: Policy Examples   133

9 The Environment and Well-Being: Policy Examples   147

10 Work, the Economy, and Well-Being: Policy Examples   160

11 The Social Context of Well-Being: Policy Examples   175

Section IV. Implementing the Measures

12 Existing Surveys   187

13 Conclusions   208

References   216

Index   236

Section I

Measuring Well-Being for Public Policy

Chapter 1

Using Well-Being to Inform Public Policy

Societies need subjective indicators of well-being to aid policy makers and ordinary citizens in making decisions. While various objective indicators, including gross domestic product (GDP), income, poverty rates, literacy rates, and longevity, provide valuable information which is currently used to gauge societies' and individuals' well-being, these measures also have a number of limitations. We demonstrate that subjective indicators of well-being, which reflect people's own evaluations of their lives, greatly augment the information provided by existing objective indicators of well-being. Therefore, we believe that accounts of well-being based on subjective indicators should be developed by national governments and international organizations, as well as by businesses and other more localized organizations. Not only will subjective indicators provide information that supplements data which are available through objective indicators, but they will also be valuable in and of themselves because they are more directly related to an individual's well-being when compared to objective indicators such as income. Importantly, these subjective indicators will not supplant existing measures, which also have their own strengths. Overall, accounts of subjective indicators of well-being will help policy makers make wiser decisions regarding policy alternatives and help citizens be better educated about the choices that affect their lives.

The major purpose of accounts of well-being, whether based on subjective or objective indicators, is to provide valid and useful information about the quality of individuals' lives. The subjective indicators described in this book provide information, but they will not replace other considerations that are important to policy makers or citizens. Achieving high levels of well-being is an important goal for individuals as well as governments, but it is not the only objective that determines actions. Moral considerations and the question of sustainability—the extent to which current decisions affect the well-being of future generations—should also influence government actions.

The purpose of this book is not to create policy guidelines. Rather, we propose that good government requires information about well-being to help formulate and evaluate such policies. Even when measures of subjective well-being reveal problems in society or in an organization, the measures themselves will not provide specific solutions or policy agendas. Rather, the measures can help to resolve long-standing puzzles about the relative importance of various factors that make lives more or less rewarding. In so doing, they may clarify the effects of past policy decisions and help predict the likely outcomes of various policy alternatives that might be put into place in the future.

In modern societies, progress is often gauged using economic indicators such as GDP and per capita income. In the absence of broader measures, national income, employment, and other measures of economic health are sometimes treated as if they were complete measures of national well-being. However, it is widely recognized that economic outcomes, though important, can tell us only part of the story about the quality of life for an individual or a nation. This is one reason that local and national governments also collect and pay attention to other indicators, such as life expectancy, education, and crime.

Where do subjective well-being measures fit into the broader collection of indicators? First, they can serve as a separate piece of information about the quality of life that a person or a population experiences. All indicators—including the social indicators described above—have shortcomings when it comes to fully capturing quality of life. Subjective well-being can add to the information that is available to guide policy decisions. In the same way that governments collect systematic measures on many aspects of the economy—ranging from employment to savings rates to growth—they should also collect a variety of measures reflecting individuals' subjective evaluations of their lives.

More importantly, subjective measures of well-being may be able to provide information about the relative importance of the various domains in people's lives—information that is crucial for making decisions that pit various policy goals against one another. For instance, policy makers might agree that it would be desirable to improve transportation, education, and health care within a particular city. Ideally, money would be spent to improve all three areas, but inevitably resources will be limited and decisions will need to be made regarding the focus of future policy initiatives. Because well-being reflects people's overall evaluation of their lives, measures of well-being should be sensitive to changes in the areas that are most important to the people. Thus, the same dollar amount invested in different areas might lead to different payoffs in terms of changes in well-being. Policy makers might want to consider these benefits to overall judgments of quality of life when deciding which policy to implement. Therefore, subjective measures of well-being provide crucial information regarding the relative importance of different domains that no other single indicator or collection of indicators could provide.

We admit at the outset of this book that it is will be a challenge to convince policy makers to consider the usefulness of well-being measures in guiding policy decisions. Many people—including some behavioral scientists who study such measures—have been skeptical about the quality and utility of such subjective assessments of the quality of people's lives. However, over the past hundred years, psychologists, economists, and other social scientists have accumulated a great deal of evidence regarding the reliability, validity, and sensitivity of such measures. We are now confident that such subjective evaluations are meaningful, and we strongly argue this point.

Overview

In this book we first discuss the nature of well-being. In Chapter 2, we make the case that people's subjective evaluations of the quality of their lives as a whole are central to the concept of well-being. In this regard, our definition of well-being is similar, if not identical, to modern definitions of well-being in economics, where well-being is typically called *utility*. Income and material resources may contribute to well-being; however, they are by no means synonymous with well-being.

Existing economic and social indicators shed important light on societal problems, and inevitably they will help determine what specific solutions to existing problems might be. But these indicators have important limitations and blind spots. We review these concerns with existing indicators in Chapter 3. In Chapter 4, we show the advantages that measures of subjective well-being have over other indicators, including a discussion of the specific information that they can provide that might be missed by the other indicators.

One concern with measures of subjective well-being is whether they are reliable and valid. In Chapter 5, we review the evidence showing that the measures do indeed possess considerable validity and are sensitive to important societal changes that affect quality of life. Although the measures of subjective well-being reflect aspects of quality of life that are also assessed by the economic and social indicators, they provide additional useful information on additional aspects of quality of life. For instance, well-being measures may reflect people's unique reactions to the conditions in their lives.

A number of issues have been raised about the adequacy and legitimacy of measures of subjective well-being, and we discuss these in Chapter 6. For example, we discuss the potential problems of adaptation to conditions, or "preference drift," as economists call it. We delve into the ticklish issue of paternalism, and whether measures of "happiness" necessarily will foster more paternalistic governments. A set of issues has been raised regarding measures of well-being, and we provide responses to these potential objections. Based on our conclusions, we then discuss the desirability of well-being as a guide for government policy in Chapter 7.

In order to illustrate how systematic measurements of subjective well-being can be used to inform policy, we discuss four different areas—health and medicine, the environment, the economy and work life, and the quality of community life—in Chapters 8, 9, 10, and 11. Within each of these four broad areas we discuss several specific issues. For instance, for the environment we discuss the things that measures of well-being can tell us about commuting, airport noise, the value of green space in urban areas, and air pollution. In the case of health and medicine, we discuss issues such as how well-being measures can guide decisions on how to distribute health research money. It is important to note at the outset that these examples are meant to reveal how accounts of well-being could inform policy if solid data were available. However, in many cases the data that are currently available provide an inadequate basis for enacting broad policies. Thus, these parts of the book should be taken as examples of ways that policy makers could use well-being information, rather than as recommendations for specific policy decisions.

Furthermore, in each of our examples we show how analyses that are based on measures of subjective well-being could help policy makers; but as will be seen, these findings rarely dictate the specific policies that should be adopted. For instance, commuting is a serious problem not only because of the time and resources it wastes and the air pollution it creates, but also because long commutes are associated with lower well-being. But this finding does not necessarily reveal the best solution to the problem of commuting. Various policies could be considered, including the implementation of fees for driving during peak hours, improvements in the quality of public transportation, or the reduction of urban sprawl. Importantly, each of these solutions may create their own set of problems, but these consequences could also be identified and tracked with systematic well-being measurements.

In Chapter 12, we describe the measures of well-being that are now in use, for example, in certain nations such as Canada and in ongoing longitudinal panel studies in nations such as Australia, the United Kingdom, and Germany. In some ways these assessments of well-being are laudable, but they usually do not form a comprehensive system of assessment that can be used to accomplish the goals set out in this book. Therefore, we describe what we recommend as ideal practices, including the specific measures that we believe should be included in any systematic accounting of well-being. Finally, we discuss the issue of when accounts of well-being should be put into place. We argue that although all of the research questions are not yet answered, the accounts should be implemented now, at least in rudimentary form.

Systematic programs to track well-being will not solve all of society's ills, nor will they lead to a dramatic shift in society's priorities. For instance, some might interpret our suggestion that economic indicators are imperfect to mean that we believe that material wealth is undesirable and that by focusing on well-being rather than income, people will become less materialistic than they currently are. We want to be very clear that we are not making such a claim and that a program of well-being measurement would not necessarily have this effect. In fact, we think that high well-being is already the goal toward which policy makers strive. However, the measures that are currently in place to gauge progress toward this goal are incomplete. Information about current well-being will allow policy makers to achieve their current goals more effectively and efficiently. Our suggestions are not radical, but we hope that they will have a substantial effect on our ability to achieve the goals that we, as a society, already hold dear.

Chapter 2

Defining Well-Being

Any proposal for a system of national accounts of well-being has the potential to be immediately derailed by misunderstandings about the precise definition of well-being that guides the endeavor. For instance, we would not be surprised if some critics quickly dismissed our proposal as a half-baked attempt to make people *happy* all the time. And by happy, critics might simply refer to a state of moderately aroused pleasantness. If that were our goal, it would not be difficult to shatter its foundations, as few would argue that being happy in this way should be the primary—or even a secondary—goal for society. It could easily be dismissed as a superficial and misguided attempt to distract people from more important concerns or to fool them into thinking that they should be comfortable with what they have, even when an objective look at their life conditions might suggest that other emotional reactions are in order. Laypeople and emotion researchers alike acknowledge that there is a place for feelings of anxiety, depression, and even anger at certain times in people's lives. Therefore, it is important to state at the outset that our goal for a system of national accounts is not to make people happy all the time—at least not in the way that the word happy is typically used.

This is also why, throughout the book, we focus on the term *well-being* rather than happiness. Happiness is a term that for psychologists and laypeople represents a state of contented pleasantness and is one of many specific emotions that people can feel in response to life events and daily experiences. Unfortunately, the term happiness is not always used in this precise manner. Instead, it can be used to mean something much broader, something closer to what we mean in this book by well-being. Precisely because happiness has both broad and narrow connotations means it cannot accurately convey the meaning of the construct that we believe should be assessed when guiding policy decisions. Instead, the term *well-being* is more appropriate for this task. Like happiness, well-being is a widely used term, and it too can potentially have many meanings. But for the most part, the various meanings that have been proposed come a little closer to the broad construct that we wish to assess than does happiness.

All definitions of well-being imply an evaluation. Well-being is good and desirable and ill-being is bad and undesirable. A crucial difference in definitions of well-being is the object of that evaluation. Some definitions focus on specific aspects of individuals' lives or abilities. For example, in health-related quality-of-life research, well-being is often defined as being healthy. In the economic realm, well-being is often defined as being wealthy. Most frequently, however, well-being is defined as an individual's global evaluation of his or her life across a variety of different aspects of that life. Thus, well-being refers to being well in general rather than within any specific area of life. In keeping with this relatively common usage, we define consummate well-being as an overall evaluation of an individual's life in all its aspects. Below we discuss the more precise components of this definition, focusing on debates that have emerged in past attempts to define well-being.

Subjectivity and Objectivity in Definitions of Well-Being

Sumner (1996) introduced an important distinction between objective and subjective definitions of well-being. This distinction concerns the perspective from which lives are being evaluated. Objective definitions require an objective point of view that is independent of an individual's own subjective values and norms. In other words, the definition would include features that would be considered to be ideal, regardless of how the individual who actually experienced those features evaluated them. In contrast, subjective definitions of well-being require a reference to the individual's own interests, needs, preferences, or desires.

Often the two definitions may be aligned. For example, many objective definitions of well-being include physical health as one important component (e.g., the Human Development Index). Health is argued to be objectively good, and it would be difficult to say a person's life is going well if he or she was bedridden or unable to care for him or herself . But health is also likely to play an important role in subjective definitions of well-being because most people prefer to be healthy. Despite this overlap, the distinction between objective and subjective definitions of well-being remains crucial.

Subjective definitions of well-being are aligned with the interests of the individuals whose well-being is being assessed. A life is going well only if the individual who lives this life endorses it as good and evaluates it positively. In this book, we adopt a subjective definition of well-being. It is important to note that our definition does not undermine the value of objective constructs such as human development, literacy, and physical health. National accounts of well-being will not replace accounts of other important aspects of human lives and activities such as life expectancy, infant mortality, literacy, gender equality, or crime rates. We simply propose that existing indicators fail to provide sufficient information about the quality of individuals' lives from their own perspectives.

We must also be careful to note that by suggesting that well-being should be measured, we are not proposing a form of utilitarianism. That is, we are not advocating the maximization of population levels of well-being as the primary policy goal (though future research might possibly bear this out as a reasonable one). There can be many good reasons why it might be important to pursue other policy goals. For example, it may be as important to maximize the potential for well-being of future generations as it is to increase well-being of those in the present. Another example is that it might be worthwhile to promote certain human rights regardless of whether they enhance subjective well-being on average. However, an analysis of any of these issues will benefit from an accurate assessment of well-being and its determinants.

It is important to avoid confusion between subjective and objective definitions of well-being and subjective and objective indicators (Sumner, 1995). For example, Aristotle suggested that "a happy life must include pleasure" (http://www.seop.leeds.ac.uk/entries/aristotle-ethics/). Most people would think of pleasure as something that is subjective because it involves an internal emotional experience. But Aristotle's definition of a happy life as one that includes pleasure is actually an example of an objective definition because it makes no reference to an individual's own interests, desires, or preferences. In other words, to be well according to Aristotle, an individual must have pleasure regardless of whether he or she desires it.

It is also possible for subjective definitions to include objective indicators. For example, a subjective definition of well-being could specify that the availability of food, water, and shelter is essential for well-being. This definition would be a subjective one if it specified that these objective indicators influence well-being because they affect individuals' evaluation of their lives. Thus, well-being definitions that focus on the satisfaction of basic needs are inherently subjective in nature—they imply that objective factors like food and water are components of well-being because everyone evaluates them as desirable.

Our definition of well-being, then, is clearly a subjective one. People have well-being only when they believe that their life is going well, regardless of whether that life has pleasure, material comforts, a sense of meaning, or any other *objective* feature that has been specified as essential for well-being. To be sure, any one of these components might turn out to be universally important because all or most people value it; but we do not take this as a given.

We should note in this context that our subjective definition of well-being is essentially identical to economists' concept of utility. As we discuss in more detail later on in this chapter, economists define utility as the satisfaction that a person experiences from the consumption of goods (Sumner, 1996). Like a subjective definition of well-being, utility is defined exclusively from the perspective of the individual. Economists tend to rely on the amount of money a person is willing to spend on a good as a useful proxy for the utility that he or she gets from that object. Furthermore, because of the links between money and the utility one gets from goods, the total amount of money that a person has available should be a useful proxy for the amount of utility he or she could potentially experience in life. Note that economists do not define well-being simply as having a lot of money. Indeed, standard economic theory assumes that well-being is achieved by spending money, not by accumulating it.

The Measurement of Subjective Well-Being

Our broad definition of well-being is not unique or unusual; many would agree with our broad starting point that well-being is a subjective phenomenon. But despite this agreement, there exist many different approaches to measuring subjective well-being. Each approach is based on a set of simplifying assumptions that could potentially create biases and errors in a national index of well-being. Thus, it is essential that we further specify the nature of the construct that we hope national measures of well-being could assess. We do this by reviewing various existing approaches to measuring well-being, pointing out the features that we think are most and least desirable within each approach.

Monetary Indicators of Preference Realization

We start with the oldest and most influential approach to the measurement of well-being within economics. In this approach, well-being is typically called utility. Although the term utility is also used more narrowly in applications of economic theory that are not concerned with well-being, economic theories of well-being equate well-being with utility (Sumner, 1996). One of the most widely discussed indicators of aggregate well-being is GDP, and changes in GDP are assumed to produce changes in well-being.

For those who are not economists, it may be surprising to learn that conceptualizing well-being in terms of wealth reflects a subjective definition of well-being; but this is in fact the case. This is because wealth is only a convenient objective indicator for the subjective construct of utility or well-being. Those who have large amounts of money can presumably buy whatever it is that they need to make their life a good one. And the subjective nature becomes apparent when we observe the vast differences that exist in the way that individuals spend their money. It is also important to emphasize that the focus on money is not a reflection of economists' materialism or their belief that the ultimate goal is to accumulate wealth. Indeed, the main assumption of economic theories of well-being is that people spend their money in exchange for market goods (objects, services, membership fees for organizations, health care) to realize their preferences. A billionaire who stuffs his or her billion dollars under the mattress (or into a stock portfolio) and lives like a homeless person would still have the well-being of a homeless person (plus any utility provided by having an available billion under the mattress).

Economists' reliance on wealth or income as an indicator of well-being is based on a theory that links money with well-being. The main assumption of the theory is that people are rational and that their choices maximize well-being. If an individual chooses option A over option B, economists infer that option A produced greater well-being than option B. This fundamental assumption implies that all individuals have the maximum level of well-being that is afforded by the options available to them. Importantly, this assumption does not imply that all individuals have the same level of well-being.

For example, an average New Yorker has the choice to drink water from the Hudson River, from a tap, or from store-bought bottles. Most New Yorkers choose not to drink water from a polluted river. In contrast, a poor child in a developing country does not have the same choices, and may be drinking polluted water because it is the only option available. The well-being of the New Yorker is higher than the well-being of the poor child because it is safe to assume that given the same choices as the New Yorker, the child would also drink purified water from a tap or bottle. Thus, a person's well-being depends on the range of options that is available to him or her. For marketable goods in a perfect marketplace, the range of options

Figure 2.1 A Model of Economic Behavior and Well-Being.

increases in proportion to an individual's wealth and disposable income. The wealthier an individual, the broader the range of available options. Thus, wealth is an indicator of well-being, but it is not the same thing as well-being.

Given this distinction, an important theoretical question concerns the strength of the link between the indicator (money) and the construct itself (well-being). As all economists know, this theoretical link will be weakened by violations of several assumptions of the theory. The causal model illustrated in Figure 2.1 shows the assumptions in terms of a model that links money to well-being.

An important link in the model is between options that are available and the well-being that a person experiences. The model assumes that well-being is equivalent to preference realization. But to realize preferences, it is not sufficient to have a range of options. A person must actually choose the correct one. Consumers face several problems when they have to choose among various options. Even with regard to a single consumer product—say a new television set—choosing the best option is often difficult, as the choices might vary along several dimensions. The choices become even more difficult when consumers have to decide how to allocate resources across several preferences. Is it preferable to buy a smaller house and a nicer car, or a bigger house and a less nice car? It would be foolish to assume that every purchase reflects an optimal allocation of money. It is equally implausible that people are entirely irrational in their purchases. Therefore, the truth lies somewhere between these two extremes, a fact that will affect the link between money and well-being.

If people are relatively bad at using money to maximize well-being (say, for instance, if their predictions about how much satisfaction they would gain from specific goods were inaccurate), the link between money and well-being would be quite weak. Unfortunately, without a complementary indicator of well-being, it is impossible to test whether the choices resulting from higher income actually do lead to well-being. This uncertainty creates ample room for dissent regarding the economic model. Not surprisingly, proponents of the model assume that most people use money rationally, whereas critics emphasize demonstrably irrational allocations of money that individuals sometimes make.

Another link in the model connects income and wealth to the range of options that are available to people. But again, there are several factors that can potentially weaken this link. Most importantly, not all preferences can be realized in the economic marketplace. This problem is well recognized in economics, but solutions to this problem are unsatisfactory (Dolan & White, 2007). Other problems are inefficient markets and the fact that some people may require different amounts of money to realize the same preference. For example, an individual with a disability may require more money for mobility than would other people. A farmer with a vegetable garden can have fresh organic produce for much less money than an individual who lives in Manhattan. Thus, a relatively straightforward theoretical link between income and options gets complicated by the realities of the market.

A final neglected aspect in the standard economic model of well-being concerns the link between work and income. According to the model, the only aspect of work that matters is the amount of wealth that it generates. However, people also have preferences about other aspects of their jobs. For example, autonomy in a job is often one of the strongest predictors of job satisfaction (Judge, Thoresen, Bono, & Patton, 2001). The realization of preferences about one's work is neglected in the standard economic model, which focuses exclusively on the role of individuals as consumers rather than the roles of producers or service providers in the economy.

The uncertainty about these three links creates uncertainty about the usefulness of money as an indicator of well-being. But there are additional concerns about the use of money in this way. Specifically, the assessment of wealth and income is not trivial. Although social scientists often take it for granted that reliable and valid measures of income are easy to obtain, these measures are often quite expensive and may sometimes be of questionable quality. For instance, at the national level, income is assessed with some reliability and validity, but this occurs only through a very extensive and costly assessment (http://www.bea.gov/). At the individual level, many studies use very simple self-reports of overall household income. And although the reports themselves seem straightforward, a careful examination of the underlying variable suggests that it may not be. Those individuals whose income comes entirely from a yearly salary might easily be able to provide this straightforward answer, but those who are self-employed or whose income comes from commissions or tips may not be able to accurately calculate their annual income. Factoring in taxes, nonwork income, savings, and accumulated wealth further complicates this task. Therefore, whether respondents are accurate when reporting what appears to be a straightforward amount remains questionable and compromises the validity of the measurement. Furthermore, even when more elaborate attempts to assess household income are used, these measures are not perfect. For instance, the German Socio-Economic Panel Study assesses household income using multiple questions about the various sources of income, yet Schimmack (2009) estimated the reliability of the household income measure in the German Socio-Economic-Panel at .80.

In sum, a number of assumptions are necessary to link income to well-being. The strength of these links in the causal theory is unknown, but it is likely that the actual relation between income and well-being is far from perfect. Thus, at a minimum, alternative measures of well-being can be used to test the underlying assumptions from the economic model. For example, a positive correlation between nations' GDP and subjective reports of well-being validates the claim of economists that GDP is an indicator of nations' well-being (Deaton, 2008). But more importantly, it is likely that these additional measures will provide valuable information beyond what imperfect indicators like income will be able to provide.

Affective Indicators

A second set of indicators consists of the affective responses that people experience in their day-to-day lives. Affect reflects the good and bad feelings that people have. Most theories of emotional states assume that emotions are elicited in response to a subjective appraisal of the environment (Lazarus, 1991). Thus, emotions should be responsive to whether or not the conditions in the environment match people's preferences. There is also evidence that the valence of the evaluation is the most important aspect for qualitative distinctions between emotions (Schimmack & Crites, 2005). Emotions of the same valence tend to be seen as more similar than emotions of opposite valence. Furthermore, distinct emotions that have the same valence (e.g., happiness and excitement) are more likely to be elicited simultaneously than those that have difference valences (e.g., happiness and anger) (Diener & Iran-Nejad, 1986). Given these two features of emotional experience, it may seem self-evident that broad measures of the pleasantness of one's emotional states would necessarily be good indicators of the concept of overall well-being.

Therefore, it might seem surprising that much more emphasis has been placed on income as an indicator of well-being in comparison to affect as an indicator of well-being (at least among economists). This emphasis on income can be traced partly to the rise of behaviorism in the 1930s. In psychology, several researchers were developing and testing affective theories of well-being in the first decades of the 20th century (Beebe-Center, 1932). Behaviorism ended this program of research, and the scientific study of feelings in psychology reemerged only gradually in the 1960s (Bradburn, 1969; Schachter & Singer, 1962; Nowlis, 1965). It was only after the *affective revolution* in the 1980s that psychologists rediscovered feelings as an important research topic (Bower, 1981; Frijda, 1986; Schwarz & Clore, 1983). Since then, the scientific study of feelings has increased dramatically. For example, the most widely used self-report measure of affective states has been cited over 3,000 times (Watson, Clark, & Tellegen, 1988).

Economists have been slower to recognize the importance of measuring people's feelings (Kahneman, 1999). Affective measures of well-being were initially discredited in an influential article by Robbins (1938), whose main claim was that it is impossible to say anything scientific about differences between individuals' feelings. One reason why this early opinion was not been challenged is that the concept of utility is not essential to many important economic problems. Even economists concerned with well-being in the branch of welfare economics have found ways to address their main problems without an explicit theory of well-being. Thus, economists felt little need to revisit Robbins' claim, and psychological research provided no compelling reason to revise economic theories of well-being. But now, 30 years after the affective revolution in psychology, a large body of evidence suggests that interpersonal comparisons of feelings are possible, and economists are recognizing the importance of studying human emotions (Kahneman, 1999).

It is important to examine the theoretical links that exist between feelings and well-being There are two processes that could potentially link the affect that people experience to their overall levels of subjective well-being. First, affective feelings might respond to the match between the actual conditions in a person's life and his or her preferences and ideals. Presumably, if a person achieves his or her goals and acquires the things in life that he or she desires (a nice home, a solid romantic relationship, a satisfying job), these matches will continuously provide positive emotional experiences. In contrast, someone who does not achieve these goals would experience negative feelings when thinking about this mismatch.

If all affective feelings resulted from the subjective evaluation of the conditions in a person's life, then these feelings would provide excellent indicators of overall well-being. However, the link between evaluations and emotions is not always straightforward. For instance, some feelings may be elicited by causal factors other than the realization of preferences. The most obvious example is that people can—and do—alter their affective experiences by taking drugs that directly influence the neurological processes that produce experiences of pleasant feelings in the brain. These changes in emotional states are not produced by actual changes in people's lives, and therefore they do not reflect a person's overall well-being (unless the person's only preference in life was to experience positive feelings).

This concern raises a broader issue regarding the nature of affect. Psychologists distinguish between two types of affective experiences (Schimmack & Crites, 2005). Emotions are intentional states that are directed at an object (I am happy about my life). In contrast, moods are not directed at specific objects (I simply feel happy). Using this distinction, emotions reveal the fulfillment of desires, but moods do not. To the extent that affective indicators tap moods rather than emotions, they might be considered to be imperfect indicators of well-being. For example, mood disorders (e.g., depression, anxiety) could weaken the link between well-being and affective indicators of well-being.

But this concern leads to the second process through which affective experiences—including moods—could serve as useful indicators of overall well-being. People have a desire to feel good, and therefore pursuing positive emotions and avoiding negative emotions is an important goal in itself (Schimmack, Radhakrishnan, Oishi, Dzokoto, & Ahadi, 2002). Thus, the emotions that a person experiences may directly affect well-being regardless of whether those feelings resulted from a subjective evaluation of the conditions in the person's life. In fact, as was noted above in the example of the person who takes drugs to experience pleasant feelings, such feelings could potentially be a sufficient indicator of well-being. This would occur if the desire for pleasant feelings was the only desire that a person had. Although it is unlikely that many people pursue a purely hedonistic existence in which feeling good is the only goal that they pursue, most people do report that feeling good is one of many important goals. Thus, the contribution of moods to overall affect balance is not a serious problem for affective indicators of well-being.

Another problem with affective measures of well-being is that some evaluations of one's life may not elicit an affective response. Instead, some evaluations may be purely cognitive. A large body of research in psychology has shown that evaluations vary along a hot–cold, cognitive-affective dimension. Evaluations of some attitude objects (e.g., foods) are primarily affective, whereas others (e.g., political candidates, policies) are primarily cognitive (Eagly, Mladinic, & Otto, 1993). Affective measures of well-being are based on the assumption that ideals that elicit stronger affective responses contribute more to overall well-being. However, this assumption is problematic because the affective system is historically older and evolved primarily to solve problems that most humans encountered in their ancestral environment (Frijda, 1986). Thus, the affect system may be biased toward problems that were historically essential, and it may fail to respond adequately to newer concerns and problems that require more complex cognitive evaluations.

Take cheesecake as an example. From an evolutionary point of view, cheesecake—with its high sugar and fat content—is exceptionally good at fulfilling the basic need of nourishment. In an environment with scarce resources it would be foolish not to eat as much cheesecake as possible. Not surprisingly, the affect system evolved with an innate preference for sweet taste (Fox & Davidson, 1986). However, in today's affluent societies where caloric resources are not scarce, many people have other concerns (e.g., the desire to maintain a low body mass index (BMI)) that might conflict with the desire to eat copious amounts of cheesecake. These additional desires might not be built into an ancient affect system that evolved over hundreds of generations, and thus they might not be associated with a strong affective response. If not, then it is possible that individuals who give in to their desire to eat large amounts of cheesecake might experience more pleasure than individuals who successfully maintain their low BMI, even if the strength of the actual desire (eating cheesecake versus maintaining a low BMI) is identical.

The asymmetry in affective response results from the fact that some desire fulfillments have a stronger impact than others on the affect system that produces feelings of pleasure. This would be a problem for affective measures of well-being because the theory introduces an objective aspect into what is supposed to be a subjective evaluation process. Well-being would no longer be based on an individual's opinion about what is good for him or her. It would now be based on the processing of information in the human affect system. Such a model would ignore the possibility that additional information processing systems that evolved later may lead to a different evaluation of what is good for the individual.

Humans are probably the only beings who can transcend the evaluation of their lives on the basis of their feelings. This does not mean that their feelings are unimportant or should be ignored. Rather, it means that humans can pursue desires that are independent from—or at least more loosely connected to—the affect system. Thus, hedonism could be argued to neglect the uniqueness of humans. This uniqueness requires an assessment of human well-being that goes beyond affective responses because people may prefer outcomes that they believe are incompatible with the maximization of feelings of happiness and pleasure.

As a final note on the utility of affective indicators, we would like to acknowledge that at least for contemporary psychologists, our distinction between affect and cognition and between ancient and modern brain systems may appear overly simplistic. In the brain, everything is connected and cognitive processes (thinking) and affective processes (feeling) are intertwined. There are primitive cognitive processes (recognition) as well as complex and sophisticated feelings (guilt, compassion). We acknowledge that this is the case. However, we also believe that there remain some fundamental differences between cognition and affect that can create biases in evaluations that influence our well-being. It is an empirical question as to whether these biases undermine the usefulness of affective measures of well-being.

Evaluative Judgments of Life

A final type of indicator that we consider consists of the evaluative judgments that individuals can make about their lives. These indicators, which emerged when social scientists first created social indicators of well-being (e.g., Cantril, 1965; Andrews & Withey, 1976), are commonly referred to as life satisfaction or global happiness measures. These measures usually require respondents to explicitly consider the features of their lives and evaluate them. This evaluative component might take the form of self-reported feelings of satisfaction. Or, alternatively, the measures might ask respondents to indicate whether the conditions of their lives match with their ideals. For example, one commonly used measure, the Satisfaction with Life Scale, includes a satisfaction question ("I am satisfied with my life"), as well as an item that is explicitly evaluative in nature ("My life is close to my ideal").

The appeal of using evaluative judgments as indicators of well-being is that there is a very close link between the indicator and construct itself— global evaluations are conceptually identical to the construct of well-being. Therefore, the only link that creates potential problems for the measurement of well-being is between the evaluation itself and a person's *judgment* of that evaluation. Critical perspectives on these evaluative judgments focus on people's ability to provide adequate reports of their well-being (Kahneman, 1999; Schwarz & Strack, 1999).

Biases may occur at various stages during the complex task of integrating information about many aspects of one's lives and the match to one's ideals. Examining and reducing the presence of biases is a challenging task. A large portion of this book is devoted to the examination of the large body of evidence on this issue. In this introductory section, it is sufficient to say that it is possible to examine biases in judgments of well-being empirically by means of a process called construct validation. To validate a measure of well-being, or several measures of well-being, it is important to use the measure in empirical studies. It then becomes possible to see whether the measure produces results that are consistent with theoretical expectations. No single finding is able to demonstrate validity, but a body of empirical findings can provide increasing amounts of support for the validity of a particular measure. The evidence reviewed later in this book shows that subjective indicators are sufficiently valid to provide unique and valuable information about well-being. This does not mean that they are perfect, but in many ways, they are as good as widely accepted measures in other domains.

In short, we have defined well-being as a life that matches an individual's own ideals. We think of income, affect, and well-being judgments as alternative indicators of well-being. These indicators reflect well-being for different reasons and they have their own biases and measurement problems. By integrating the information across different indicators, it is possible to obtain a better impression of individuals' and societies' well-being.

Section II

How Well-Being Adds Information

Chapter 3

Limitations of Economic and Social Indicators

Economically developed nations have many indicators in place to track quality of life in their societies. In addition, individual states, cities, and business organizations often measure important aspects of life in order to give leaders information that can be used to make wise decisions and to improve the quality of life. In this chapter we describe two sets of measures—social indicators and economic indicators—that are typically used for these purposes. Both provide important insights into how organizations and societies are functioning. These indicators can also provide specific guidance on how to improve organizations and societies. However, both types of indicators have limitations—limitations that can often be rectified by collecting and attending to subjective measures of well-being.

Social Indicators

Much information that is relevant for policy making comes from what are labeled *social indicators, key national indicators*, or *quality-of-life indicators*. These indicators assess diverse areas ranging from infant mortality, to sulfur dioxide in the air, to the amount of land that is devoted to national parks. The idea that guides the use of these indicators is that they assess societal circumstances that are important for making better lives for citizens. As Dolan and White (2007) have noted, the social indicators approach reflects an objective model of well-being because it presumes that one can generate an adequate list of the characteristics that are necessarily required for a good society. Nations, states, cities, and regions should then be able to accurately measure those attributes and base policy decisions on the components that are lacking.

Different approaches have been used to identify comprehensive sets of social indicators. One approach is to solicit opinions from a wide range of individuals who have knowledge about diverse areas of life. For example, the United States General Accounting Office (GAO), along with the National Academies' Institute of Health, brought together scholars and leaders to formulate a list of core national indicators that could be used to provide a systematic account of the nation's well-being (Forum on Key National Indicators, 2003). The group listed about ten indicators in each of eight areas. Examples of the broad areas that the forum participants considered were crime, the environment, education, and governance. The specific indicators primarily consisted of objective measures such as life expectancy, but the group also suggested that subjective indicators should ultimately be included. For instance, forum participants suggested that it would be worthwhile to know whether people think the nation is "on the right track." Table 3.1 presents selected indicators that were proposed by the group.

An alternative approach is to identify sets of indicators using theoretical ideas about the objective factors that are required for individuals to experience well-being. In his groundbreaking work on poverty, Sen (1990) suggested that poverty cannot be defined simply in terms of money and that progress cannot be judged solely in terms of economic growth. Instead, he presented an approach in which quality of life consists of having the capabilities needed to pursue important human functionings. For example, education and health are needed to pursue important goals such as providing for one's family. Regardless of the amount of money that

TABLE 3.1.   Selected Measures Proposed by the Forum on Key National Indicators

Violent crime rate
Level of sulfur dioxide in the air
Participation in organized sports
Rates of volunteering
Attendance at performing arts
Home ownership
Enrollment in science and engineering
Adolescent birth rate
Labor force participation
Proportion of children receiving child care
Percent afraid to walk alone after dark
Per capita water consumption

people have, they also need education and health to be fully functioning humans.

Based on these considerations, the United Nations created the Human Development Index to track and compare the well-being of nations. This index incorporates national per capita income, but it also includes additional social indicators including those related to education and health. Similarly, in a proposal for cross-societal indicators of well-being that are based on capabilities, the Oxford Poverty and Human Development Initiative (OPHDI) suggested adding subjective well-being and other related constructs to the capabilities indicators derived from Sen. In Table 3.2 is a list of quality-of-life indicators derived from the OPHDI list.

Sen's work, and the applied efforts that are based on it, focuses on promoting capabilities. But this is not the only theoretical basis that could be used to guide the selection of social indicators. Diener (1995) suggested that a value-based method for identifying indicators would provide a useful tool for assessing the overall quality of life within societies. Specifically, he borrowed from the work of Schwartz (1992), who suggested that there are universal values that people hold to some degree across all cultures. According to Schwartz, values can be placed into seven categories including mastery, happiness, intellectual, equality, harmony, social order, and wealth. Diener identified existing indicators that capture progress in each of these seven areas.

Importantly, because the amount of variance that exists in these indicators differs for rich versus poor countries, Diener developed separate sets of indicators for nations that were more or less economically developed. Although all of the indicators are desirable, some of them differentiate better among poor nations whereas others differentiate better among rich nations. For example, the percent of eligible students attending college is more sensitive to differences among rich nations than among poor countries. Table 3.3 shows several of the measures Diener identified.

TABLE 3.2. Internationally Comparable Indicators

Domain	Indicators
Material	Food, housing, income
Health	Longevity
Productivity	Work
Security	Safety
Intimacy	Friends and family
Community	Education, neighborhood, ability to help others
Spiritual	Well-being from religion, spirituality, or philosophy
Subjective well-being	Life satisfaction, happiness, domain satisfactions
Psychological well-being	Autonomy, competence, relatedness, meaning

TABLE 3.3. Social Indicators

Basic need fulfillment (Clean water, food, and shelter)
Physicians per capita
Suicide rate
Literacy rate
College attendance
Human rights violations
Income equality
Deforestation
Environmental treaties
Homicide rate
Savings rate
Per capita GDP

Much work went into the formulation of each of the lists described above, and there is no doubt that the indicators that have been included provide important information about the well-being of specific societies. Furthermore, there is a considerable amount of overlap across the various lists that exist. This means that regardless of what method is used to identify the indicators, there are some domains that repeatedly emerge as important. This is encouraging because it means that there is agreement regarding at least some of the components that are required for a life to be considered a good one.

Yet despite the important contributions that social-indicator-based approaches have made, they are not without limitations. These limitations generally fall into one of two categories. First, the fact that systems based on social indicators reflect objective approaches to well-being means that some individuals or groups of individuals must decide which domains are most important. And this leaves room for disagreements. Second, although the measurement of social indicators often appears to be straightforward, a close examination shows that measurement is often more complicated and more problematic than it might appear to be at first glance. We discuss these two categories of concerns in the following sections.

Which Domains Should Be Included and Who Should Decide?

Objective list approaches to the measurement of well-being posit that there is some finite set of domains that contribute to overall well-being. Unfortunately, the domains that should be included within that set are not obvious, and therefore someone must identify the domains that should be measured. Regardless of whether this is done through an inclusive brainstorming approach (like that of the GAO) or through a more deductive theory-driven approach (like those of Sen and Diener), potential for disagreement exists.

To the extent that the final list is flawed, the picture of well-being that emerges from these indicators will be incomplete or inaccurate. A number of specific concerns about objective list accounts fall under this broader point.

First, and most importantly, it is not clear whether the domains that tend to be included on existing lists are all necessarily important for overall well-being. For instance, *number of hobbies* is included in the Living Conditions Index of the Netherlands (Boelhouwer & Stoop, 1999), but is its inclusion justified? What about people who love their work so much that they do not have time for hobbies? What about people who spend time in other meaningful activities (e.g., volunteering or even just playing with their children) that don't technically count as hobbies? Although there are certainly domains that most would agree should be included on any comprehensive list, the number of such domains is small relative to the large number that has been suggested for the various list-based approaches that exist today.

The flip side of this problem is that it is not difficult to think of domains that have been omitted from any particular list. For instance, immunizations are often listed in national indicator programs, but periodic medical exams for children and the elderly are often not. Enrollment in science and engineering might specifically be noted, but not training in psychology, dance, or history. Who decides which indicators are needed and which can be ignored?

Even if broad agreement can be reached that a certain domain—say access to the arts—is important, questions come up about which activities within this domain should count toward the overall index. Certain lists might suggest that the number of venues for performing arts within an area or city is important, but other criteria including the number of cinemas might not be. Who decides which activities count and which do not? Should the demolition derby or professional wrestling count as performing arts? Who is to say that watching ballet is more important and more desirable for a society than watching professional basketball? It could be argued that many lists are composed by ivory-tower scholars who neither understand nor represent the values of the rest of the population. Although many of us might prefer the symphony to professional wrestling, this subjective preference is a weak criterion for including any social indicator in a comprehensive system that is supposed to reflect an objective account of well-being.

We do acknowledge that the examples above might seem somewhat superficial. One might argue that we could avoid such debates if national systems for assessing well-being were restricted to the small number of domains that have wide support. Or alternatively, if some agreement about the underlying theoretical premises that guide conceptualizations of objective well-being could be developed, then the domains that were important could be derived deductively. But whether a list of domains is composed by a group of experts or by scholars working in a systematic way from a conceptual framework like Diener's proposal or the OPHDI measures, the objective list approach will inevitably have this inherent limitation— the indicators reflect a set of values of those who compose the list, in terms of either the starting assumptions or the final domains that are selected.

Furthermore, the debates about which domains to include are not limited to areas that could be dismissed as trivial. For instance, nowhere on the list of the U.S. Forum on Key National Indicators do religion and spirituality appear. Yet, religious participation is associated with a host of positive outcomes including lower crime rates and less delinquency. And perhaps more importantly, a majority of people in the United States (along with many other societies) believe that religion is desirable and important. Similarly, the list does not include the percentage of children who live in two-parent families even though these family structures are associated with many desirable outcomes. A cynic or a motivated critic could argue that these omissions reflect a liberal bias on the part of those who create lists. And although such omissions may instead reflect a relatively benign fear of offending certain constituencies who would consume the information provided by the indicators, the disagreements that will inevitably occur have the potential to derail any systematic attempt to assess the well-being of societies using objective list accounts.

One might respond to this concern by noting that each specific indicator that is included is a proxy measure for a broader underlying construct. For instance, if access to the arts is important, it might not be necessary to assess every opportunity to enjoy artistic endeavors that exists within a city. Instead, a small sample might be examined, and this sample might correlate with and serve as a proxy for other instances within the broader domain. Thus, even if the number of venues for performing arts is the only art-related indicator that is assessed, this indicator may reflect a community's overall investment in the arts and thus provide a useful index. The cities with many centers for performing arts may also have many art museums, cinemas, libraries, and even sports arenas. Thus, we may never have a perfect list, but through careful consideration, a *good enough* list of proxy variables could be obtained.

There is certainly some degree of truth to this response, but it also raises a second concern about the social indicator approach—where does one stop when collecting indicators? How much information should be obtained before we really understand the well-being of a nation, state, city, or organization? It will surely be the case that more information is better than less, but how much is good enough? Subjective well-being measures can help to answer this question. There needs to be some well-being criterion that can be used to determine whether the additional information that is available does a *good enough* job assessing well-being. Even if well-being measures do not replace objective lists (and we are certainly not arguing that they should), they may be able to answer fundamental questions about which objective domains are most important.

A final concern regarding the specific domains that are included within an objective list account relates to the fact that there will likely be differences—both within and between cultures—in the value that individuals place on any specific domain. For instance, Becker, Denby, McGill, and Wilks (1987) discuss the fact that in systems designed to rank the quality of life in distinct geographical areas, climate is often included. Cities whose temperature hovers around 21°C (70°F) tend to be seen as most desirable, whereas those that experience temperatures far above or below that mark are considered too hot or too cold. This would mean that places like Alaska and Helsinki would be seen as too cold, whereas places like Arizona and Alice Springs would be too hot. Yet, many individuals flock to these locations and profess to enjoy such extreme climates.

Not all people will value safety, social contact, formal education, spirituality, or the arts to the same degree. If these cultural and individual differences are substantial, then the results that one gets from systems of national or regional indicators will not actually reflect the well-being of the population. This is a problem inherent in all objective list approaches. We want to be clear that we are not suggesting a purely relative model where there are no universal values or desires. Indeed, we think that some preferences are likely to be very close to universal, if not completely universal. However, this is unlikely to be true of all the indicators that are typically included in existing systems. And thus, the problem of individual differences in preferences is likely to be substantial with any reasonably large and comprehensive list of the social indicators that could conceivably affect quality of life.

The concerns listed here are not fatal flaws for objective-list-based systems of national social indicators. Instead, they are limitations that will hinder any attempt to gauge the well-being of a population using objectively defined criteria. The information that can be provided by such systems is clearly useful, but problems emerge when deciding which specific information to assess and how to integrate that information. As noted earlier, and as discussed in more detail in Chapter 4, some additional criterion is needed to answer the questions that these limitations raise. We believe that subjective well-being measures can provide this criterion.

Thus, such measures will not only supplement existing list-based accounts, they will also make them more useful.

Measurement Problems with Social Indicators

The attempt to identify sets of objective indicators that can be used to gauge the health of a nation results in part from a degree of skepticism about subjective measures in general. Those who want to assess the quality of life of a population may distrust subjective reports and may want to turn to something more objective that can be clearly observed and empirically verified. And, in fact, the objectivity of most social indicators is an important strength. The assessments that make up these indicators are based on data that in principle can be observed by all. Yet it is important to acknowledge that this qualifier *in principle* is needed. A close examination reveals that the numbers that are actually used for these social-indicator-based indexes are not always accurate. Many factors involved in data collection can have negative effects on their validity.

For instance, some concepts that might seem straightforward are in fact quite difficult to define and/or measure. Take suicide, for example. Suicide can be clearly defined as an event in which a person takes his or her own life. Suicide rates should be relatively easy to calculate, as modern technology provides sophisticated (and objective) techniques for determining the cause of death. Yet, if the availability of these technologies varies across or within nations, then the accuracy of suicide rates may vary. And more fundamentally, doctors in some cultures might be reluctant to pronounce the death a suicide because of the stigma that is involved. In such cultures, clear cases of suicide may be labeled as death by accident. Thus, it is not always easy to determine which deaths are suicides, and measuring suicide comparably across societies is rarely a simple matter (Rockett & Thomas, 1999).

The suicide rate is an example of an indicator that is easy to define but potentially difficult to assess. The measurement problems that are associated with social indicators are exacerbated when even the definitions are difficult to pin down. There are certain cases where the definition might be clear within a culture, but may shift subtly across cultures. For example, homicide is defined differently in various societies, and therefore homicide rates might not be directly comparable. Death is objective, but whether a killing counts as manslaughter, justified homicide, an accident, or first-degree murder varies according to the laws and customs of nations, states, and municipalities.

Other indicators may appear to be quite similar across cultures, but the specific meaning of the objective characteristics that are assessed may vary. Take education, for example. Although it is straightforward to count years of schooling and calculate average years of schooling in nations, the content and quality of schooling vary enormously across and even within nations. The actual amount of learning that a high school graduate has received, for example, not only varies across individuals, but also differs substantially among nations. Not only do some nations require more hours and days of school per year than other nations, curricula might be much more rigorous in some nations than they are in others. Even among wealthy nations, standardized testing shows that there are vast differences in the knowledge that students have acquired during the same number of years of schooling.

Furthermore, different nations or regions may have similar scores on an index, but they may arrive at these scores in different ways. A single indicator could conceivably capture either low or high quality of life. For instance, having a strong, well-funded police force could potentially result from a high crime rate (which would be negatively associated with quality of life), a well-organized government (which might be positively associated with quality of life), or a strict focus on law and order (which might be positively or negatively associated with quality of life depending on the values of the individuals who live in the society). Similarly, most people would want easily accessible, high-quality health care. But an index that is based on the number of hospital beds, ambulances, and doctors could reflect a strong investment in health care or it could reflect the fact that many people are unhealthy, perhaps due to behaviors such as smoking and reckless driving.

A third measurement issue concerns the fact that it is not always obvious what the optimal level of some indicators really is. For instance, longevity is desirable, and average life expectancy is often used as a proxy measure for the health of a nation. But should longevity be increased by spending enormous amounts of money on medical care to keep people who are in extremely poor health alive? There are certain indicators where more is almost always better; just about everyone would agree that zero violent crime is the ideal. However, for other indicators the ideal level is unknown, and there would undoubtedly be widespread disagreement. For example, how many people should own their own homes or attend the performing arts? How many people should be doing volunteer work and how much should they do? As measures get more precise, such questions become increasingly important. It is not enough to just add up all the scores on indicators that are generally defined as good. As the above examples show, much more interpretation—subjective interpretation—is required to distill the useful information from these objective indicators.

A final measurement issue concerns the sensitivity of these indicators across the full range of reporting units. Ideally, there should be no floor or ceiling effects, and the indicators ought to reveal movement when progress is made. Diener (1995) noted, for example, that wealthy nations pile up very close to one another on the Human Development Index. This is due to the fact that these nations do not differ that much on the factors that contribute to the index, including longevity, education, and income. This is especially apparent when considered against the backdrop of the variability that exists across all nations. The small differences might be important ones despite their small size, but the nations might differ more on other meaningful indicators such as income equality, or university attendance, where ceiling effects are less pronounced.

How Should the Information Be Integrated?

The issues with selecting domains for inclusion and accurately assessing these domains are probably the most pressing concerns that confront programs for collecting broad ranges of social indicators. However, another issue that might potentially limit the social indicator approach is that even if an acceptable list of indicators can be developed and assessed, some weighting scheme must be developed to integrate the information that is obtained. Few would argue that each indicator is equally important. For instance, one might argue that indicators that relate to basic human needs (the need for food, water, and adequate shelter) are more important and thus should be weighted more heavily than indicators that relate to higher-level pursuits. But beyond this basic rule, coming to any agreement on the importance of various other domains will be difficult if not impossible. Which is more important for a society—its savings rate or the percentage of people who attend college? Even if we could obtain a relatively long list of indicators to assess, new problems will be created. The more complete the system of national indicators becomes, the more difficult it will be to aggregate across the various components using weighting schemes that reflect the values of the population that the measure is attempting to describe.

A study by Becker and his colleagues (1987) is informative in this regard. Becker et al. examined the quality of life in 329 metropolitan areas. They showed that how one weights the components that make up an overall index will have a strong influence on the aggregated ranking. In fact, 59 of the 329 regions could be ranked anywhere from first to last, depending on the weights that are given to the specific social indicators. Thus, one person's weighting of the various indicators might lead to completely opposite assessments of the quality of life in a city compared to another person who had very different weights. The Becker et al. study is instructive because it illustrates why some individuals might hate a city while others might love it. Some citizens may crave museums and professional sports, while others prefer quiet and peace. Thus, some might love a small town in the Midwest whereas others prefer New York. Which city provides a higher quality of life? The disagreements that people have about this question likely reflect the fact that individuals use very different weights when considering the various social indicators that could be used to evaluate an area.

The problem of weighting shows how difficult it is to aggregate across various domains. But some scholars argue that any form of aggregation is inadvisable. By combining scores from many different domains, dissimilar items will inevitably be added together. Thus, two different nations might receive similar scores for overall quality of life, but they could obtain these scores in very different ways. Aggregation necessarily removes information, and potentially inappropriate conclusions could result. But aggregation is inevitable. After all, even single indicators are really aggregates. For example, homicide rates could be further divided into specific categories that provide unique information about the quality of life of an area. Homicide by an unknown assailant, for example, might mean something very different than homicides that occur when the victim knows the killer. Which is the proper level of measurement that should be considered for a system of social indicators? Should it be overall crime rate, homicide rate, or homicide by unknown assailants? One can imagine a useful purpose for each, but the idea that all aggregation is bad brings those who wish to use the information to an impasse. It is certainly good to know how many people die from bacterial diseases, even if the numbers are not broken down by type of bacteria. It is also good to know how many people die from contagious diseases, which is an even more global aggregate. Thus, aggregation is unavoidable, but it certainly raises the issue of which level of analysis is most useful.

Summary

Social indicators provide useful information, but they have inherent limitations. For one thing, they emphasize the values of those compiling the list. In addition, these indicators inevitably omit important characteristics that can potentially influence quality of life. Indicators have various problems related to aggregation and level of analysis. Finally, the optimum level of all indicators is not clear. Because of these limitations, subjective indicators are needed. For one thing, subjective indicators such as life satisfaction can be used to give an overall picture of quality of life. Exhaustive lists of potentially important domains in life need not be identified to use subjective well-being measures because anything that is important should ultimately be reflected in the subjective measure. Furthermore, as we have argued above, subjective well-being measures can provide the weights necessary to convert diverse indicators into a coherent aggregate measure of the quality of life.

Some have championed social indicators because these measures are objective—they provide concrete numbers from observable behavior. When just the numbers themselves are examined, this is certainly true. But numbers alone are of little use, and all numbers must be interpreted. The interpretation that is required to use social indicators often adds a degree of subjectivity that potentially exceeds the subjectivity involved when using subjective measures of well-being. Thus, social indicators are important and valuable, but not because they are objective.

It is also important to note that in many ways, subjective well-being measures allow for a diversity of opinions about what makes a life worth living, and this is a goal for national systems that assess quality of life, especially in democratic nations. For instance, the U.S. Forum on Key National Indicators called for citizen participation in creating the list of indicators. But unfortunately, it is not clear exactly how citizen participation might be accomplished. What seems most likely is that indicators would be added to represent the values of various interest groups. In contrast, the subjective indicators taken from representative samples of the population are inherently democratic, reflecting the views of the entire population and capturing the factors that influence the feelings of well-being of all citizens.

By pointing to problems with social indicator measures, we do not mean to suggest that they should not be used. Of course they should; they provide valuable information to policy makers and laypeople alike. Hagerty et al. (2001) list a number of criteria that can be used to evaluate social indicator measures, and using these can help to improve the indicators. What we wish to emphasize, however, is that social indicators, no matter how extensive, cannot fully capture the quality of life in a society.

Economic Approaches to Quality of Life

An alternative to social indicators can be found in the broad range of measures that are used to assess the pace and structure of economic activity. As noted in Chapter 2, these measures are typically assessed because lay theory and economic theory alike link income and wealth to the underlying construct of well-being. The strength of these theoretical links is demonstrated in the vast number of indicators that are typically examined and the great expense that is required to collect them. In Table 3.4 we list just a small sample of the economic indicators that are typically collected within

TABLE 3.4. Selected Economic Indicators

GDP per capita	Stock prices	Inventories
Savings rates	New orders	Exports and imports
Interest rates	Retail spending	Price levels
Inflation rates	Money supply	Labor force participation
Currency values	Housing starts	Productivity
GDP growth	Consumer sentiment	Purchasing power
Unemployment	Bankruptcies	Consumer debt
Capacity utilization	Average work hours	Jobless claims
Profits and wages	Median incomes	Income distribution
Foreign exchange reserves	Balance of payments	Poverty rates
Foreign debt	Terms of trade	Tax rates
Employment	Output by industry	Price/earnings ratios

a nation. Many of these indicators are published yearly or quarterly, but some are issued daily or even tracked continuously throughout the day (as is true of broad indicators of the performance of various stock markets).

It would be an understatement to say that considerable resources are used to generate these economic measures. The time, money, and effort that are expended to acquire them means that they must provide information that is quite valuable. In other words, those who are paid to make economic and policy decisions would not bother with the effort and expense if these indicators did not actually aid decisions. However, it is important to realize that not all indicators that are in use now were always thought to be useful. Instead, the information that is collected varies over time and across cultures and contexts, and the value that people attach to any specific economic indicator depends on the extent to which the data that the indicator provides are thought to support better decisions. As we shall see, beliefs about what information is needed evolve over time.

National accounts of income and expenditure are now routinely calculated for all nations. They are collected using increasingly standardized rules established by international expertise and agreements. However, the systematic nature of these assessments has existed for less than a century. Importantly, the specific indicators that are assessed (and the specific methods by which they are collected) do not necessarily reflect the one true picture of economic health of a nation. Instead, they provide snapshots of distinct areas of the economy that are thought to be particularly important for the decisions that are most pressing at that moment. For instance, Perlman and Marietta (2005) traced the development of national accounting systems in Germany, the United Kingdom, and the United States. They showed that development resulted from various political imperatives of the time, ranging from the coordination of industrial and military production in times of war (in Germany and Great Britain) to attempts to understand and improve social welfare (in the United States during and after the Great Depression in the 1930s). Thus as Keynesian macroeconomics came to stress the separate but linked determinants of consumption, investment, income, and employment, there was a corresponding need for full accounting of both the expenditure side and the income side. Gross domestic product (GDP) emerged as a compromise between the separate estimates available for the two sides of the accounts.

The complicated and indirect process through which indicators of national income and expenditure were developed is helpful in showing that these accounts were adopted and subsequently adapted in response to changing needs for information and changing theories about how the level of national income is determined. Furthermore, they illustrate that there are often no simple answers when it comes to defining the state of the economy. For instance, if we want to know about the overall economic productivity of a nation, should we focus on GDP or gross national product (GNP)? GDP is based on what is produced within the national borders, whereas GNP is based on what is produced by the citizens of the nation, regardless of where that production takes place. For the purposes of estimating the determinants of domestic economic activity, GDP is the more relevant concept. But GNP is the better measure of income available to domestic residents. These complicating factors show that GDP is not a uniquely defined measure of the value of national production. The complications get even greater when the critical adjustments are made to remove the effects of price-level changes to produce measures of real expenditure and GDP.

One further point about the national accounts of income and expenditure is worth making. The official indicators are mainly derived from representative surveys rather than a complete accounting of incomes and expenditures. A variety of census benchmarks are then used to convert from survey estimates to national totals. Indeed, one of the major forms of technical assistance that industrial countries provide to the transition economies is help in moving from inefficient systems in which everything is counted to the design and management of credible survey methods to establish national accounts. We make this point here because national systems for assessing subjective well-being will also depend on well-designed, nationally representative surveys. Indeed, perhaps the most cost-effective way of collecting life satisfaction data would be through the addition of a few key questions to surveys already required for the production of the national accounts. These would include surveys of employment, surveys of consumer finances, and selected waves of census-based surveys, such as the U.S. Current Population Survey.

Despite their importance to societies, national accounts of income and expenditure suffer from a number of important limitations, at least if they are going to be used as a proxy for national well-being (Diener & Seligman, 2004). Specifically, concerns can be raised about what is included in these indexes, what is excluded, and whether the weights represent the contribution of distinct types of spending to overall well-being. For example, some of the most important aspects of life lie outside of the scope of the national accounts of income and expenditure. Diener and Seligman (2004) noted that love, social capital, environmental pollution, fair and effective governance, virtue, and spirituality usually cannot be incorporated into national economic accounts. Societies differ in income, but they also differ in other ways that heavily influence the quality of life in them. This is one primary reason why social indicators were developed to supplement what is assessed through economic indicators alone. But this is also a place where subjective measures of well-being can play a role.

Although it is clear that constructs like virtue and spirituality cannot be included in national economic accounts because a monetary value cannot be assigned to them, there are other activities that may have economic value but are still not included in GDP. For instance, activities such as housework, hobbies, and volunteer work are not included in the national accounts unless they involve some form of commercial transaction. This causes problems for two reasons. First, if the activity has value but is not counted in a system of national accounts, then the picture of economic activity that one gets from these accounts will be inaccurate. Second, subtle shifts in the nature of the underlying activity can lead to changes in whether it contributes to the national indexes. This could lead to misleading conclusions about change in economic productivity over time. For instance, some have noted that there have been recent increases in the economic size of the so-called voluntary sector. However, these are due in part to the increasing use of commercial organizations for fund raising within nonprofit organizations. The use of paid employees instead of volunteers creates a new addition to GDP, even though the same activity (which, presumably, has similar value) is being accomplished.

Thus, the same goods and services can count or not count in the national accounts of income and expenditure, depending on who performs them and in what manner. For example, if a person gives homemade gifts such as jam to his or her neighbor, and the neighbor returns the favor by house sitting while the person is away on vacation, the effort these people put into making these goods and delivering these services does not enter the national accounts. If these same goods and services were purchased, the national accounts would show this as a rise in output and income. The shift over recent decades from home production to market production of everything from childcare to meals to entertainment and fitness has raised GDP and shrunk the importance of home and neighborhood production.

Does this reflect a real change in productivity? Has the change been good or bad for welfare? There are certainly arguments on both sides of this issue. Our point in this book is that measures of well-being can provide fresh primary data to help show which of these many changes have improved or decreased the quality of life. What is clear is that the growth of measured national income is only a part of the story, because it does not reflect the value of the diminished home production and neighborhood contacts.

Other forms of economic activity that might not be reflected in national accounts include *gray market* and *black market* goods and services. These are not reported to the government in order to avoid taxes or because they are illegal. In some cases these activities, sometimes labeled as the *shadow economy*, represent a large percentage of the total economic activity of a society. Some systems of national accounts attempt to make estimates of and allowances for this shadow economy. But for obvious reasons, most criminal activity, especially relating to drugs, fraud, extortion, and theft, is not easily counted. Furthermore, if national economic accounts were to be used as a proxy measure for national well-being, questions could be raised about whether such activity *should* be included in the overall index. It would be hard to see how the labor put into extortion and the extortion payments themselves could reflect utility, well-being, or quality of life, even if they are forms of economic activity.

A related concern about economic measures is that some goods and services become part of the national accounts for reasons that might reflect a lowering of well-being, rather than an increase. For instance, some of nature's most valuable resources have been so plentiful that little effort and often no economic exchanges were needed to acquire them. Clean air, clean water, and even some food sources provide key examples. But as populations grow, scarcity of all these resources becomes more likely. Thus, it can take more effort to acquire the same real standard of living. Because national accounts measure the costs of production and not the value attached by consumer to what is produced, increasing pressures on natural resources tend to be matched by increases in GDP that are not matched by corresponding increases in utility. Again, the gains in GDP that co-occur with these changes would not accurately reflect any true change in the quality of life that occurred as once freely available resources were commoditized.

Many economic activities also have consequences for those not directly involved in the production, exchange, or consumption of the primary good or service. For instance, manufacturing processes may create air or water pollution that affects people who never buy or sell the product being produced. Rude behavior in traffic or other shared public spaces also creates negative externalities, as both parties go home less happy. Benevolent behavior, on the other hand, might create positive effects, with both the donor and the recipient of kindness experiencing increased positive affect. These secondary effects, called *externalities*, are rarely completely accounted for in national economic indicators. Some externalities relating to common property resources do end up indirectly affecting the national accounts, such as when wild stocks of fish are overfished and subsequently replaced by farmed fish; but many others are missed. Economists are aware of these issues and have developed alternative techniques for assessing the value of these externalities. But most standard national measures simply cannot incorporate an accurate accounting of these secondary effects.

It is important to note that the idea of externalities can be extended to nature as well—to animals, plants, and the environment. If a human activity harms a significant part of the ecosystem, this can be seen as a negative externality even if the economic activity does not directly affect other humans. Similarly, externalities might be felt by future generations. So even if some national indicators can take account of externalities that occur close in time and to proximal individuals, it may not be possible to capture the broad range of externalities that exist.

Each of the above concerns relates to the economic activities that may be related to utility (and, hence, well-being) that might not make it into national economic accounts. However, additional concerns can be raised that reflect questions about the theoretical links between the economic indicators and well-being. As noted in Chapter 2, the extent to which money can be used as an indicator of well-being depends on the theoretical model that underlies this link, along with the validity of some assumptions that are required for the model to work. But a close examination of the types of specific components that are assessed in economic indicators leads to additional questions about these links.

For instance, economic measures do not distinguish between the production and exchange of beneficial products and the production and exchange of detrimental ones. Societal ills may force people to spend money on ameliorative measures, yet this would still be reflected in an increase in GDP. Prisons certainly contribute to the economic accounts, but does an increase in the number of prisons that is necessitated by rising crime rates really reflect a gain in well-being? A society with legal prostitution, heroin, and gambling might have a large reported income based on economic exchanges for these items. In these circumstances, it is tempting to think that luckier or better-managed communities might be able to achieve more security with smaller armies and fewer prisons, freeing up resources for the achievement of other needs. To assess these possibilities, one needs a measure of well-being that takes into account the quality of the social fabric, and not just what is spent to keep it in reasonable repair.

Many have argued that it is presumptuous to second-guess other people's choices. Perhaps we should assume that governments and individuals will spend their money in ways that best reflect the utility that they could potentially receive. We agree that people are likely not wholly irrational with the choices that they make. But if there are any systematic errors in judgment— and the psychological literature suggests that there may be many—then the economic decisions that people make, and the money they have, may not be perfect indicators of the well-being that they experience.

The final concern is one that relates to the values that are promoted by the intense scrutiny that economic measures receive. Because so many economic indicators are published, and because these indicators receive so much attention from politicians and policy makers, significant ongoing attention is drawn to material aspects of life. People think about the things that happen to be the current focus of attention, and thus information about our economic well-being will continually be at the forefront of our thoughts. We hesitate to suggest that things would be different if attention were drawn elsewhere, as the importance of economic concerns may truly be driving the emphasis on these indicators. But it might be useful to consider what would happen if every week a tally appeared in the media on how many people attended church, did a good turn for a neighbor, or exercised. Such accounts might increase these behaviors by making them more salient and by reinforcing the message that they are desirable. Although we do not know of any evidence showing this to be true, the current emphasis on economic indicators could conceivably make people more materialistic and less attentive to other important areas of life. Advertising has a special role here, as most advertising is explicitly intended to encourage the idea of a good life as being one involving more consumption, whether a bigger house, foreign travel, a more expensive car, or more stylish clothes.

In describing the limitations of economic measures we do not mean to imply that they are without merit. Like the social indicators described above, economic indicators provide society with important information. The long list of shortcomings that we present is simply meant to show that we need more than economic accounts to measure the well-being of society. There are inherent limitations in these measures, and increasing refinements will never produce perfect indicators of national well-being. Something more is needed to address these limitations and measures of subjective well-being are a strong contender in this respect.

Valuing Nonmarket Goods

Before parting from the topic of the limitations of economic measures, it is necessary to acknowledge that economists themselves have recognized many of the issues that we have described above. In fact, economic tools have already been developed to address some of them. These novel approaches tend, however, to work from the same assumptions that guide the more standard economic indicators that we have already described, and thus they may ultimately have similar flaws. For instance, these alternatives often assume that individuals will make rational economic decisions about the value of the goods and services that they exchange. Thus, the value of resources that do not have prices can be determined by examining the value of the things that people would be willing to give up to acquire them.

For instance, one externality that is often discussed is the environmental damage that results from manufacturing certain products. This pollution is not typically included in the cost of the product itself. A *revealed preference* approach has been developed to evaluate the cost of this environmental damage. In the case of air pollution, the value of clean air has been assessed by comparing housing prices in locations that have different amounts of air pollution. Of course, such analyses require quite a few assumptions, and it is often very difficult to hold constant all of the other factors that might also influence relative housing prices in these areas with differing levels of air pollution.

One could then ask whether it is possible to modify the revealed preference approach in various ways to estimate the value that people place on a variety of intangible resources. For instance, one might estimate the value of trust in one's neighbors by assessing average levels of trust and then comparing the prices of similar residences that are located in areas where trust in one's neighbors is high versus low. Or an alternative approach might be to assess the amounts that they are willing to spend on burglar alarms and theft insurance (items that compensate for a lack of trust). But we argue that such attempts will likely not capture the effects on well-being that these intangible goods really have. As we shall argue, trust means much more than just protection against the loss of goods from theft. Trust is a positive feature of life, with well-being consequences that are likely greater than what can be bought through insurance or extra security. Hence, what people are willing to pay for insurance and security is likely to understate the value to them of living in a community where security fences would be irrelevant.

Because of the limitations of the revealed preferences method, economists have invented several additional approaches to valuing goods and services that do not have explicit, identifiable value within the marketplace (see Adler, 2006, for a review). For instance, one way to evaluate these goods and services is simply to ask people how much they would be willing to pay if money were required to get them. These *contingent valuation* or *willingness-to-pay* methods use simple survey techniques to estimate the value of goods and services that typically do not have a cost. A similar method is to present people with *standard gamble* hypotheticals in which they are given a choice between two alternative possibilities, each of which has distinct outcomes and probabilities.

These procedures are often used to determine the value that people place on various aspects of health. For instance, a person might be given a choice between two treatment alternatives related to a serious disease. Alternative 1 might be a treatment that would have a 75% chance of resulting in full recovery and a 25% chance of resulting in death. Alternative 2 might be a treatment that keeps the patient in a wheelchair but otherwise healthy for a 25 more years before he or she dies. The features of the two alternatives can be varied (e.g., likelihood of success in the first alternative, severity of the condition, or the length of time in the second) until a point is reached where the respondent finds the two alternatives to be equally desirable. Through various calculations, the precise value of the medical condition (or the cure for that condition) can be obtained. Similar techniques ask respondents how many years less they would be willing to live without a specific health problem relative to living a specified number of years with the problem. An additional related method is to calculate Quality Adjusted Life Years, *QALYs* (Dolan, 2000), by asking people to rate health states on a nonmonetary scale from 0 to 1, where 0 is death and 1 is perfect health.

The methods above are not simply used in research; these approaches are also used to guide policies and to determine regulations. For example, the contingent valuation method is used in the United States by the Environmental Protection Agency, the Army Corps of Engineers, the Forest Service, and other agencies (Adler, 2006). The technique is used to evaluate environmental hazards and risks, as well as to evaluate the impact of specific policies regarding safety and health. For example, the U.S. Food and Drug Administration relies on QALY evaluations to translate health states into dollars in order to calculate cost–benefit analyses for treatments. These methods are also used by various agencies in the United States to evaluate the damage done to the environment by natural disasters and by human activities such as landfills. Thus, the alternative methods devised by economists to assess the value outcomes have an important impact on policy (see Adler, 2006, for a review).

Because these alternative approaches to identifying the value of various goods and services play a significant role in the formation of policy and regulations, they need to be evaluated carefully. Virtually all of the alternative methods for valuing outcomes are based on hypothetical choices and responses. Thus, they depend on people's motivation when answering these questions and their ability to truly understand what living with and without specific attributes would really be like. Questions can be raised about people's ability to accomplish this task. For example, can respondents truly imagine what it is like to be blind? Can they really understand how the loss of a limb affects day-to-day activities and the quality of life that results? Can people envision the difference in their lives if a landfill were located a mile from their homes or if the length of their commute were cut in half?

When confronted with questions about hypothetical states, respondents must imagine what the states would entail. But when talking about major life changes, this task is likely to be quite difficult. Therefore, respondents are likely to use quick heuristics to respond to the question. For example, when asked a standard willingness-to-pay question regarding the amount they would spend to avoid paraplegia, respondents may quickly call to mind a set of activities that would differ if they did not have the use of their legs. However, the life of paraplegics is much more intricate and complex than this, and will include many pleasant moments that the respondent is unlikely to consider. Thus, willingness to pay to avoid the state might yield a poor estimate of the quality of life of a person with paraplegia. Gilbert, Pinel, Wilson, Blumberg, and Wheatley (1998) demonstrate that people underestimate the adaptation that is likely to occur following negative events. Thus, when people are asked to respond to questions about hypothetical negative situations, they might believe the state is worse than it might actually be.

The alternative methods are known to show certain anomalies that call into question the validity of the results (Adler, 2006). For example, people may profess a willingness to pay an infinite amount to correct a problem. In addition, people seem to be relatively insensitive to the scope of the problem or the outcome. For instance, respondents profess the same willingness to pay for an outcome that affects just a few thousand people as they would for an outcome that affects many thousand people. Some studies have shown that estimates from willingness-to-pay hypotheticals seem to be relatively unaffected by the degree of risk or by the probability of the state. In other words, they might be willing to pay the same amount to prevent a relatively unlikely negative outcome as they would pay to prevent a more likely outcome, even though this is not a rational response.

In addition, research shows that tasks like the standard gamble can be influenced by the ordering and mode of administration of the task (Brazier & Dolan, 2005). Also, Beatty et al. (1998) found that in studies evaluating accident prevention programs, people sometimes give quite different values for the same outcome (e.g., death) depending on the context in which that outcome occurred. In other words, people varied in the amount that they were willing to pay to prevent a death depending on whether that death resulted from a traffic accident, carcinogen exposure at the job, or a malfunctioning cribs for young children. Furthermore, in a set of empirical studies that examined the thought process underlying such judgments, Beatty et al. found that willingness-to-pay judgments were usually not made in accordance with the underlying theory. Specifically, all safety improvements were seen as a good thing, and willingness-to-pay judgments were not sensitive to the risk reduction that was involved. Instead, the amount that respondents reported being willing to pay was often the amount of money that for them would not seriously alter spending patterns. The authors state that their set of findings "clearly casts doubt on the reliability and validity of willingness-to-pay based monetary values of safety estimated using conventional contingent valuation procedures" (p. 5).

Another question about the alternative methods is who should serve as respondents in the surveys. Should the studies include a representative sample of the citizenry, or only those who might be possibly affected? For example, in valuing environmental changes in parks, should only people who regularly visit parks be used as respondents? In the case of health, where average people might have little insight into a particular disease and its symptoms, should only medical experts be used, or perhaps only those who actually have the disease that is being evaluated? If laypeople are used, then what type of information should be given to respondents before they give their estimates? For instance, if respondents are asked to evaluate the value of a cure for paraplegia, what should they be told about the condition of paraplegia itself? Should the pleasures that paraplegics experience be mentioned or only the difficulties? The information given to respondents necessarily focuses their attention on certain aspects of the state, but the information that is provided does not always reflect that which is most salient to those who actually experience the state.

When answering questions about health states, people tend to focus on the state itself, not on the additional characteristics that will also exist in a person's life. In other words, when asked to think about what life would be like after becoming the victim of a crime, the person might imagine himself or herself as a "full-time victim" and not just as a person with a complicated life who has happened to have experienced a crime (Dolan & Moore, 2007). This means that other domains of life, including domains that are unaffected or even enhanced by victimization, are not considered. For example, a person answering a question about being burglarized might not consider the social support he or she would be likely to receive following the event. Dolan and Moore (2007) reviewed evidence showing that people predicted that certain health problems, such as HIV or not receiving a needed kidney transplant, would be much worse than they actually turned out to be.

So again, the measures discussed in this section go beyond traditional economic indicators by attempting to derive values for goods, services, and states that are not exchanged in the marketplace. These measures certainly address some shortcomings of existing measures, but for the most part, the cognitive processes that are required to complete these measures are complicated and may not lead to meaningful results. Indeed, many reviews of the techniques used in these areas suggest that substantial problems exist.

Summary

We hope that the basic message of this chapter is clear. We do not believe that the sets of measures discussed in this chapter—social indicators, traditional economic accounts, and novel economic measures for evaluating less tangible goods—should be ignored. In fact, we do not perceive these measures and the subjective measures of well-being that are the focus of this book as competitors. Instead, they are best seen as complementary pieces of information that together permit a better understanding of how people are faring in their lives. When considered in combination, these various indicators should provide guidance on what can be done to improve people's well-being. Social and economic indicators and accounts measure crucial aspects of life for individuals, groups, communities, and nations. As we hope to show in the rest of this book, subjective measures of well-being not only provide additional information about these lives, but they also offer an appealing way of estimating the relative importance of different aspects of life, and hence of permitting more effective use of the social and economic measures. Ultimately, this should lead to better decisions by families, firms, communities, and governments.

Chapter 4

Contributions of Well-Being Measures

In the previous chapter we described the limitations that social and economic indicators have when they are used to map the quality of life of societies. In this chapter we outline the value that well-being measures have in this regard, and we discuss how they can complement economic and social indicators. Although subjective well-being measures have their own limitations, these limitations are often different from those of economic and social indicators, and therefore the subjective measures are able to provide additional useful information for decision makers. Subjective measures, and the research results that flow from them, can provide valuable information for government, business, and other organizations, as well as for individuals and families.

Subjective assessments of well-being are important because they capture people's experiences and evaluations. Thus, they are potentially much broader than economic and social indicators because they are not limited to an evaluation of those aspects of life that are observable to others. Observable life conditions provide incomplete information about quality of life because the same conditions can be valued differently by different individuals. Furthermore, perceptions of specific conditions vary depending on culture, values, and goals. Quality of life is in part a subjective concept, and subjective measures are required to fully assess it.

People's subjective reactions to events are also relevant to policy because these reactions affect people's future behavior. People who are satisfied with their jobs are likely to stay in these jobs; people who are dissatisfied with their spouses are likely to leave these spouses. And as we discuss in more detail later on in this book, there is good evidence that broader feelings about the quality of one's life (including judgments of life satisfaction) also motivate a broad range of important behaviors and life decisions. Thus, by understanding how subjective reactions affect behavior, policy makers can use information about these reactions and the factors that affect them to help guide societies toward desirable futures.

One strength of subjective measures is that they can be assessed using representative samples of entire populations. This accords with the desirable features of democratic governance by giving equal weight to the rich and the poor, the young and the old, with no one group in the position of saying what is best for the others. Furthermore, the measures reflect not just people's conscious (and perhaps inaccurate) ideas about what is important for quality of life, but all the factors—both recognized and unrecognized—that influence the desirability of people's experience. And because well-being is an overall evaluation of life, its measures reflect an integrative weighting of how various societal circumstances interact with culture and values to influence quality of life. Alternative approaches—including the social indicators approach discussed in Chapter 3—inevitably reflect the values of those who select the specific domains to be measured.

The subjective measures also have another strength—they provide a common metric that can be used to compare outcomes across domains. Because they are broad assessments, they can be used to derive comparable values for disparate consequences. For example, legislatures might be faced with trade-offs when deciding whether to promote advances in health or encouraging growth in the arts, or when specific policies pit improving safety against increasing costs. A city official might be faced with the decision of whether to spend more on parks or on transit buses. A business leader might be forced with a difficult choice of providing employees with more vacation time, better dental insurance, or a more generous retirement plan. Each of these benefits would be costly, and the CEO should want to know how much job satisfaction would be enhanced by each alternative. Although measures of well-being cannot provide absolute answers to these important questions, they can provide information about the relative effect of improvements in each domain, and this information will be relevant when comparing the alternatives.

One might argue that subjective measures of well-being do reflect important conditions in people's lives, but that the information that they provide is mostly redundant in the light of what can be obtained through other means. The extent to which the measures provide novel information is certainly an important criterion by which they should be judged, and research evidence suggests that although subjective measures do correlate with alternative indicators, they can also tell us something new.

For instance, well-being measures often show considerable convergence with economic and social indicators. We examined the correlations of nation-level well-being in the Gallup World Poll. We found that national per capita income and national average longevity both correlated very strongly with national levels of the *Ladder of Life* scale, a form of global life evaluation. This is as would be expected, and a complete lack of association between well-being and intuitively appealing predictors like health or income would cast doubt on the validity of the measures. But it is also clear that life evaluation measures tap into many other aspects of life. For example, estimates of national happiness are quite similar across different studies (including the Gallup World Poll, the World Values Survey); those nations that are identified as being particularly happy in one study are also quite happy in the other. But more importantly, this correlation holds even after the correlation between income and life satisfaction has been removed (Helliwell, 2008). This means that the measures capture something beyond the wealth of the nation, and whatever this additional component is, it is reflected in the well-being estimates from two different studies.

Similar results emerge when distinct predictors are examined. For example, in the Gallup World Poll we found that an indicator of national longevity predicted the global well-being measure even when national income was controlled. Other predictors, including the amount of corruption in the nation, were strong predictors of the average levels of positive emotions that are experienced across nations. In a related investigation, Verme (2007) found that measures of freedom of choice predicted greater life satisfaction in nations, even after controlling for gross domestic product (GDP) and many other societal characteristics. Thus, subjective well-being measures are associated with objective characteristics of societies, but they are not completely in conformance with those measures. In the following sections, we describe specific functions that measures of well-being could serve that could help leaders and citizens make better decisions.

Enhancing Economic Analyses

Assessing the Externalities of Economic Activities

Dolan and White (2007) suggested that even if policy makers do not value subjective well-being as an end in itself, well-being measures could be used to make better decisions in the economic realm. For example, well-being measures can help society value the *externalities* of economic activity. The production and exchange of market goods and services can affect quality of life for those not directly involved in the transaction. Analysis using measures of subjective well-being can help to attach values to these external effects. This, in turn, can help to inform cost–benefit analyses involving the activities that lead to these externalities.

Most economists recognize the need for some method of evaluating externalities because such valuations are often relevant to policy decisions. However, no completely satisfactory method has been developed for doing so, in part because virtually every human activity has some nonmarket effects on other people's behavior (Hunt & D'Arge, 1973). Their very pervasiveness makes them difficult to quantify within the classical economic model. Measures of well-being can be used to evaluate the importance of some identifiable externalities, as well as those of other noneconomic aspects of life, by calculating what are known as *compensating differentials* (e.g. Helliwell and Huang 2009). As pointed out in earlier chapters, well-being scales can be used to evaluate the impact of circumstances such as air pollution and traffic congestion that influence quality of life. By comparing the life satisfaction effects of some identifiable externality (such as aircraft noise levels, e.g. Van Praag and Baarsma 2005) with the effects of income on life satisfaction, it is possible in some circumstances to estimate the values of the externalities in terms of equivalent changes in income, thus providing a way to assess their relative importance.

Valuing Nonmarket Goods, Services, and Costs

Many other factors that influence the quality of life are not evaluated by the economic market in terms of cost. For example, societal characteristics such as national security, air pollution, law enforcement, terrorism, and traffic accidents are likely to influence the quality of life of individuals and societies, yet their value or cost is not fully captured by standard economic measures. For this reason, policy makers cannot easily compute cost–benefit analyses when it comes to policies pertaining to these public goods. Frey, Luechinger, and Stutzer (2004) suggested that subjective well-being measures could be used to evaluate them.

Frey et al. (2004) illustrated their approach with the issue of terrorism. Although terrorist activity is obviously undesirable, questions inevitably arise about how much resources should be spent to prevent terrorism. Money spent on homeland security cannot be used for research on cancer, to improve schools, or to build parks. In order to evaluate the impact of terrorism on well-being, Frey et al. examined life satisfaction data in multiple areas within Europe that varied in prevalence of terrorism. Even after controlling for economic conditions, terrorist activities were associated with lowered life satisfaction. For example, the influence of terrorism in France was estimated to be approximately 1/7th the size of effect of being unemployed (which is one of the larger effects in the literature on well-being). Importantly, the impact of terrorism was spread across all citizens within affected areas, whereas the impact of unemployment was only for those who actually experienced unemployment. Thus, when the number of people who were affected is taken into account, the impact of terrorism was quite large. These values can then be compared to alternative techniques for assessing the value of reducing terrorism. For example, willingness-to-pay techniques have been used to assess people's valuation of terrorism in Ireland. Willingness-to-pay estimates for eliminating terrorism were extremely high, with people saying that they would be willing to pay 41% of their total income to eliminate terrorism. Obviously, much more work is needed to compare the willingness-to-pay method with the subjective well-being method. Nonetheless, this research demonstrates how values might be imputed from the well-being figures.

It is also likely that the well-being approach to valuing nonmarket goods may have advantages over the willingness-to-pay or contingent evaluation approach. In fact, Dolan and Peasgood (2006) argued that the subjective well-being approach is superior to that offered by the contingent valuation method because people have difficulty imagining how good or bad specific life circumstances will really be. For instance, the harm to quality of life caused by airport noise could be assessed either by examining the subjective experience of those living in the paths of runway flight-ways or by asking these people how much they would pay to have the effects of the noise eliminated. The willingness-to-pay method suffers from the fact that respondents are really just guessing as to whether or not aircraft noise will bother them in the long run. Or, if they have lived near the airport for a long time, they may be misremembering how satisfied they were in the past, which might lead to an underestimation of the cost of living near the airport.

Even the economic method of *revealed preferences* suffers from the fact that prospective buyers do not know how much the noise will bother them when they decide how much a residence near an airport is worth. Furthermore, there might be restrictions in the housing market that lead to it not being *in equilibrium*. Factors such as older owners' unwillingness to move could mean that the market prices of homes are difficult or impossible to calculate using the standard revealed preferences account. In addition, it might be impossible to know which other homes without aircraft noise are identical in all respects to those with the noise. These comparable homes provide a basis for the revealed preference calculation. Thus, the well-being approach can be used to calculate the impact of public nuisances such as waste sites or power plants, as well as the value of public benefits such as parks.

Compensating for Government Actions that Unevenly
Affect Citizens

One reason to assess the value of nonmarket goods is that the government
must sometimes compensate citizens for harm that is done. Some citizens
must take the brunt of certain government actions—like the construction of
airports or landfills—whereas other citizens are spared from these unpleasant circumstances. If those affected will receive compensation, how can
the proper amount be calculated? Sometimes the market can provide values for compensation. For example, zoning regulations might affect the
value of an owner's land, and in many cases this effect can be judged by
changes in market values. However, in some cases, existing methods cannot provide a fair value, and in these cases effects on well-being can be
used.

Another instance of policies that may unevenly affect the quality of life
of citizens is the case of taxes that differentially affect different income
groups. For example, progressive taxes are designed to most heavily tax
the rich. This policy is based, in part, on the belief that wealthy people can
afford to give more money to public services without it affecting their well-
being than can individuals with lower incomes. Not only can this be tested
with the well-being measures, but the loss of well-being can be calibrated
for different levels of taxation.

Other types of taxes, for example, those on food, may disproportion-
ably affect the poor, who spend a much larger percentage of their income
on necessities than do the wealthy. In some localities food is not taxed,
whereas in others, the standard sales tax is imposed, making it a regressive
tax that takes a greater portion of poor people's incomes. Is the well-being
of poor people affected in areas with regressive taxes versus in areas without them? Although well-being measures cannot provide definitive answers
to whether such taxes are desirable or fair, they can help provide an answer
to questions regarding the tax structure that maximizes overall feelings of
quality of life.

These are not the only examples of policy decisions that involve nonmarket goods that can be evaluated using well-being measures. For example,
if there is a trade-off between inflation and unemployment, how are these
two to be valued in terms of quality of life? Whereas unemployment might
rob some people of self-respect and resources, inflation can rob those who
have carefully accumulated savings. If we can use measures of subjective
well-being to calculate the effects of unemployment and inflation on quality of life, we can then determine the total effects of the two by weighting
them by the numbers of people they affect. In such a way policy makers
can better determine what types of trade-offs harm the fewest people, and

the degree to which various demographic groups are harmed or benefited by different policies.

Evaluating and Improving Public Goods and Services

Many public goods and services have been identified as having significant effects on life satisfaction beyond the effects that flow through economic channels. For example, community investments such as improved street lighting, better roads, recreation leagues, senior centers, health services, after-school programs, and mass transit systems are all thought to affect the quality of life of citizens. The effectiveness of the design and delivery of these goods and services can all be evaluated using subjective well-being. Specifically, well-being can be measured in communities that differ in the characteristics of interest and the different communities can be compared. If enough communities are available for analyses, alternative explanations of any differences that exist between communities with and without the services in question and the effects on happiness can be determined.

Such evaluations are important to policy makers who face difficult decisions about spending priorities. Furthermore, the well-being measures can help policy makers determine the optimal amount of public goods, the point at which only small increments in well-being are brought about by further spending. For example, how much park space is *enough*, after which few gains in well-being are seen? By calculating well-being curves for varying amounts of a public good, the declining marginal utility of nonmarket public goods can be judged, thus helping to establish spending priorities. Currently such decisions are often based on the hunches of policy makers and the influence of political pressure groups. The well-being measures provide a more systematic and perhaps fairer method of allocating public resources.

Setting Fines and Compensation for Lost Welfare

Imagine the case of a drunk driver who harms another person in an automobile accident. In such instances criminal penalties are often imposed. In addition, the victim might sue the perpetrator for damages. But how much should be awarded to the victim? In some cases lost wages might help set the compensation. But in others, where the victim can still perform his or her job, this method of determining compensation is not possible. Consider the following injuries:

- The loss of an arm
- The loss of taste

- The loss of sexual ability
- Exposure to carcinogens
- Brain damage resulting in loss of sexual desire
- Brain damage resulting in difficulty with numbers
- Chronic back pain
- Loss of vision or hearing

How might a jury or judge set damages for an injury where another person or organization is at fault? Some damages are meant to be preventive or punitive, but many damage awards are designed to compensate the injured party for his or her loss. Loss of well-being could be used as an alternative to lost wages when determining damages.

There are important advantages to using lost well-being in addition to lost wages as a method of calibrating damages or worker's compensation claims. One advantage is that an award can be determined even when the outcome that resulted does not interfere with work. Another advantage is that some disabilities can cause a greater loss in well-being than might be intuitively obvious, and well-being measures can reveal this discrepancy. For example, deafness might result in a greater loss of well-being than blindness, but this might not be self-evident to people, such as jurors, and lost compensation due to lower wages might not mirror the differences in well-being. Third, well-being measures can provide a basis for compensation even for those who do not work. In these situations, no wages are lost, and therefore if wages were the only factor used to determine awards, then the victim would get nothing. Homemakers and retirees might lose substantial amounts of well-being without losing any wages, and the well-being accounts could yield evidence that would justify specific damage amounts. In this way, systematic accounts of well-being, including figures for lost well-being due to various conditions, could help courts and organizations set compensatory awards. On the other hand, the fact that the life satisfaction effects of income are small relative to many of the other consequences of disability suggests that larger monetary compensation may be inferior to a variety of measures that might make it easier for victims to build and use their capacities for engagement.

Loss of well-being might also be used to set fines for misconduct. Many behaviors are not serious enough to warrant detention in jail. In these cases, illegal behaviors may be punished with fines of varying amounts. How are such fines determined? Intuitively, one might set fine amounts by evaluating the cost that the illegal behavior had for society. But in cases where crimes involve damages whose cost has not been set or evaluated by the market, alternative strategies are required. One approach is to set the fine at a sufficient level to discourage the illegal behavior, but not so high that public sensibilities are offended. Another approach would be to set the fines so as to create the maximum revenue for the public coffers—optimizing the point where the law is broken sufficiently frequently to produce the most income, and not so high that the revenue-producing behavior is eliminated (of course, this approach is in conflict with eliminating the behavior altogether for the betterment of society). In order to balance these two approaches—one designed to allow some of the behavior and one designed to eliminate it altogether through harsh penalties—subjective measures of well-being could be used. For example, fines for littering could be based on the effects of litter on people's feeling of well-being, as well as on the effects of strict police enforcement on their well-being. A dirty society might be an unhappy one, but a society that is fearful of the police and nervous about committing even the slightest infraction might also be less than ideal.

Fines for many behaviors—from parking infractions to making too much noise, from skateboarding in public places to jaywalking—might all be set by taking relevant well-being findings into account. In this case, proximal measures of well-being that focus more precisely on people's satisfaction with specific domains or the effect that they feel at particular moments might be used instead of global measures of life satisfaction. For example, littering might have a slight effect on life satisfaction but a larger effect on people's moods in a littered environment or on satisfaction with the environment and neighborhood. These empirical findings regarding the effects of specific factors on well-being outcomes could help policy makers determine whether a real problem exists without relying on intuitions alone. The well-being accounts could also help analyze and justify fines and other measures designed to prevent certain behaviors that only some segments of society consider undesirable.

Improving Governmental and Organizational Effectiveness

Evaluating Trade-offs and Integrating Multiple Factors

It is obvious that policy decisions become quite difficult when resources are scarce or problems are severe. It may be impossible to find enough money to cover all the costs involved with a specific problem, and therefore policy makers must determine how to get the most bang for the buck. But these problems are exacerbated when—as is almost always true in the real world—decision makers are not just dealing with one problem but with many. And in most cases, these problems occur across many different domains, some of which are difficult to compare directly. Devoting resources in one area will take away from the resources that are available elsewhere; but how can the effects be compared when the domains cannot be evaluated using a common metric?

Measures of well-being can help solve this *apples versus oranges* problem that policy makers constantly face when comparing alternatives from different domains. For example, city planners may face choices between economic growth and increased air pollution. Certain political ideologies call for an emphasis on economics, whereas other ideologies call for an emphasis on other factors such as equality or environmental conservation. How can a policy maker weigh alternatives in a systematic way, and move beyond a total reliance on intuition and ideology? Broad measures of well-being can provide a valuable source of information because they can reveal how people's well-being is affected by the various policies under consideration. Research might show, for instance, that environmental degradation would have more of an effect on well-being than would a corresponding increase in economic growth. Well-being measures provide a method for evaluating the trade-off between improvements in these separate domains.

Identifying Characteristics of Desirable Places to Live and Work

Subjective measures can be very helpful in determining how to improve goods, services, working conditions, and the quality of communities. But these measures can also be used to guide decisions in smaller organizations. In a world in which there is increasing competition for workers, customers, and tourist dollars, subjective measures can be extremely helpful in guiding leaders. For example, business executives want to attract and retain the best and brightest workers. Thus, employee happiness and satisfaction are concerns that are relevant to the bottom line. Business leaders can use well-being measures to determine how the units of the company vary in terms of worker satisfaction. This information can also be used to determine the factors that are associated with these differences in satisfaction, which can help identify a course of action to improve well-being. Ultimately, by improving productivity and reducing turnover, attempts to maintain and increase worker satisfaction can have tangible economic benefits for the company.

Various types of satisfaction reports can be useful to business leaders. For example, the well-being of employees can lead to higher customer satisfaction and, ultimately, even to higher profits (Harter, Schmidt, & Keyes, 2007). Those workers who have lower job satisfaction are the most likely to be absent from work frequently and to change jobs often (Clark, Georgellis, & Sanfey, 1998; Frijters, 2000; Pelled & Xin, 1999). Because employee hiring and training are costly, especially for professional and other highly skilled workers, it is sensible to monitor the well-being of workers and take steps to keep it high. Furthermore, people higher in well-being at work are more likely to show *good citizenship* behaviors such as voluntarily helping other workers (Crede, Chernyshenko, Stark, Dalal, & Bashshur, 2007). There is also evidence that satisfied and happy workers are more productive (Judge, Thoresen, Bono, & Patton, 2001). Although these effects were originally considered to be too small to be meaningful, more recent evidence has shown that they are substantial enough to make noticeable differences in profits. Thus, the well-being of workers on the job can provide very useful information both to business executives and to societal policy makers.

Although companies routinely conduct cost–benefit analyses in all phases of operations from manufacturing to transportation to sales, rarely do they measure and evaluate the costs and benefits of policies designed to increase worker engagement and morale. The subjective measures can provide insights that otherwise might escape business executives. Satisfied employees are valuable, and factors beyond salary can help attract and retain them.

Similar considerations can guide the policy makers of cities and states. For example, in an increasingly mobile world, how does a city attract a highly educated and able citizenry? What urban factors are likely to lead to the positive experience that will induce educated people to move there and remain there? What types of experiences convince tourists that they should visit (and perhaps return to) a city or region? What mix of museums, shopping, historical spots, and restaurants leads people to evaluate their tourist experience in positive terms? The subjective measures can give insights that supplement the conclusions that are drawn from other sources.

Many community leaders currently take steps to improve their communities, and occasionally these efforts include the collection of survey data to determine what aspects of life within a community are most and least desirable. The ideas that we propose in this book would provide a systematic accounting of factors across cities and regions that lead to higher feelings of well-being. In the absence of such measures, leaders are left guessing based on unsystematic observations. Systematic data collections can show where problems are most acute and where communities are flourishing. This information can then help identify factors that contribute to these differences.

Community leaders are able to use measures to guide their decisions in many areas of life. Consider for a moment how crime statistics and educational test data give leaders feedback about where to deploy resources and where changes are needed. How could traffic engineers create safer roads without systematic data on when, where, and why accidents occur?

In the absence of measures, leaders are left with vague impressions about where problems lie. These impressions can be biased by lobbyists, news reports, and other unsystematic sources of knowledge. Systematic well-being assessments will allow local and regional leaders make better decisions about improving quality of life in their jurisdictions.

Setting and Justifying Policy Default Options

Policy makers often want to give people choices, and not thrust specific options on them in a paternalistic way. One method of giving choice, but also of assuring that the choice associated with higher long-term well-being is selected more often, is to set default choices that can easily be changed (Thaler & Sunstein, 2003). By studying how option presentation affects the choices that people are likely to make, those who manage the system can make the most desirable choice more likely to occur. For example, when employees are asked to enroll in specific health insurance programs, they might be given different choices with varying long-term benefits. Having choice allows people to tailor their program to their specific needs, but many people do not want the choice and would be happy to go with whatever option was provided. Furthermore, many people may not consider their options and may actually select programs that are not ideal.

To ensure that the most desirable choice gets chosen most frequently, it can be listed first, which might make it more likely to be chosen by more people (Dolan & White, 2007). Similarly, if a society wants people who die in automobile accidents to donate organs so that others might live, the default option can be set such that people are assumed to have given consent to donate unless they opt out of this choice. Default options often could be justified by reference to data on subjective well-being showing that people are happier in areas where organ donation occurs, that organ donors are happier, and that people who receive needed organs, as well as their families, are much happier than those who do not receive them. In countries where organ donation at death is the default choice, organ donation rates are quite high, as high as 90%. But in those countries where the default option is not to donate and people must opt into an organ-giving program, rates of donations tend to be low, even as low as 20% (Dolan & White, 2007). Thaler and Sunstein (2003) have labeled the approach of setting defaults within the overall approach of citizen choice "Libertarian Paternalism," because it has the paternalistic element of guiding choices but yet leaves the final choice to citizens.

Ultimately, if a system of libertarian paternalism were put into place, those who set default choices would require some guidance about the specific decisions that they should make. Evidence about effects on well-being could be used to guide these decisions. If certain options are associated with higher well-being, then all else being equal, those options should be made the default. Of course, there may be additional concerns that override the focus on well-being, but when these alternative concerns do not point to an obvious choice, then well-being should provide a reasonable criterion for deciding among alternatives.

Helping Resolve Difficult Debates

Oftentimes, reasonable arguments can be made on both sides of policy debates. Any single policy will have multiple consequences, and reasonable minds may differ regarding which are more important to consider. In such cases, well-being measures can potentially swing difficult decisions in one direction. For example, reasonable arguments can be made for and against the legalization of prostitution or gambling. This is why some states and cities allow such activities, whereas others do not. In these cases, knowing how well-being is affected by the various alternatives can prove helpful in choosing the more desirable course of action. Does well-being suffer in communities that allow gambling, or are any negative consequences offset by the positive effects of economic growth? Is depression more prevalent when gambling is allowed? Arguments about these activities often refer to assumptions about well-being effects; research that directly assesses these associations could inform these debates.

Hate crime legislation is another example of an area of criminal law that has caused heated debate in the United States Hate crimes are those in which a person is robbed or attacked because of his or her membership in a specific group. For example, if a person was assaulted specifically because he or she was a member of an ethnic minority, then the perpetrator could be convicted for violating hate crime laws. Proponents of hate crime legislation argue that added penalties are needed when crimes are motivated by prejudice, because such crimes are pernicious and tear at the fabric of society. The opponents of hate crime legislation argue that criminal activities are already punished by the law and that the motivation for committing crimes does not affect the seriousness of the act itself. They argue that the illegal action is equally detrimental to the victim whether it is motivated by personal animus or prejudice toward a group. In such debates, measures of well-being might provide useful information. Do minorities feel more secure where hate crime legislation is in place? Do people feel more positive toward minority groups after hate crime legislation is enacted? Does life satisfaction increase or decrease, or remain unaffected? Although measures of subjective well-being might or might not provide decisive information in any particular policy debate, it does have the potential to provide useful information.

In some cases, well-being measures can be combined with experiments and quasi-experiments to evaluate the impact of potential legislation. For example, a policy could be instituted in randomly selected neighborhoods, communities, or regions, and subjective measures could be collected before and after the implementation. In this way the subjective measures could provide insights into how change affects citizens. For example, some municipalities require that people clear snow from the sidewalks in front of their homes and businesses. This makes it easier for pedestrians, but can be a hardship on those required to do the clearing, especially if they are in ill health. Further, citizens might perceive a requirement for snow clearing to be an undue imposition on them, or something that should be done by the government. Do the benefits of policies such as this outweigh the costs? Is well-being higher in communities where snow removal is required, and do citizens evaluate the quality of their physical communities higher in such districts? Snow removal is of course a minor aspect of quality of life in most communities, but many policies taken together can add up to substantial differences in the experience of quality of life. Thus, systematic assessment of well-being can give community leaders information about the most desirable measures for their regions.

Identifying Groups in which Misery Exists

A major function of government is to eliminate the misery of its citizens. Reducing or eliminating causes of suffering such as starvation, epidemics, and violence has been seen by most governments in modern times as essential to their success. How better to calculate levels of misery than to directly measure them through national well-being assessment systems? After all, such assessments can not only yield a global view of the misery level in a society, but they can also determine the groups or regions in which misery is most prevalent. Furthermore, the subjective measures do not prejudge what circumstances are most associated with feeling miserable, or what threshold levels of circumstances are required to move people out of misery. By directly assessing misery, the well-being and ill-being accounts pinpoint the groups in which misery needs to be addressed and the conditions that led to this distress.

Existing research already points to some groups who are known to experience lowered well-being. For instance, previous research shows that the unemployed are much less satisfied with their lives than are employed people, and even less satisfied than would be predicted from their lower-than-normal incomes. Researchers also know that illegal sex workers (at least those who have been surveyed so far) tend to report very low levels of well being. Thus, well-being measures can help identify pockets of unhappiness, whether they are defined by occupation, geographic area, or other attributes. This can help to direct more detailed research into the likely causes of these differences, and to suggest how conditions might be improved.

We have analyzed the Gallup World Poll and World Values Survey data (Helliwell and Huang 2008; Helliwell, 2008) and discovered certain characteristics that tend to exist in societies that have high well-being. These societies tend to be economically developed, to have effective governments with low levels of corruption, to have high levels of trust, and to be able to meet citizens' basic needs for food and health. None of these findings are surprising, but they do point to the fact that characteristics beyond economic development do influence people's feelings of well-being. Although some might argue that it is not the role of the government to make people happy, the actions of most governments (and the rhetoric that politicians rely on) belie this critique. It seems even less debatable that societies should work to reduce misery, and the accounts of well-being will be very helpful in identifying unhappy groups.

Advancing the Definition of the Good Society

Thus far, we have discussed the practical benefits of assessing and attending to well-being measures. But these measures can also serve more abstract and philosophical goals as well. For instance, well-being measures might provide insights about the general characteristics of a good society. Consider for a moment the structure of society. Although most people reading this book would agree that democracy, equality, and freedom are some of the most important values that a society can pursue, it is not always clear that more of these characteristics is necessarily better. For instance, in the United States there are debates about the use of ballot initiatives, which reflect a more direct form of democracy than the procedures of representative democracy through which most laws are typically made. Similarly, questions inevitably arise about the relative importance of freedom versus security—the policies that promote one value often interfere with the other. So although democracy, equality, and freedom are desirable, there must be some optimal level of each for the ideal functioning of a society. Well-being measures can help assess the policy alternatives that promote optimal functioning and thriving societies.

It will also be possible to explore other societal characteristics that lead to high well-being. In the *culture wars*, one group may argue for the importance of fine arts while they decry the degradation of the society that results from materialistic values. On the other side, proponents of more *lowbrow* forms of entertainment might argue that the government should not intervene either by restricting or by supporting specific types of entertainment. Digging deeper, well-being data and research can suggest better ways of providing leisure activities, and managing public spaces, so as to increase the extent and quality of the all-important social interactions that can occur there. For example, there are now research efforts under way to examine how museums, whether public or private, can be better used as shared spaces.

One role of the well-being measures is to help judge outcomes in an *experimenting society*. Policy makers often engage in protracted debates about how to solve specific problems and how to enhance quality of life. Fortunately, because distinct cities and states are free to set policies and even some specific laws, these different regions can be thought of as informal experiments that test the effects of various policy decisions. If well-being was tracked in regions with differing policies and over time as policies change, then the effects of these policies could be determined and could inform future debates. As it stands now, debates often continue for decades because reasonable arguments can be made on both sides and little evidence is available to evaluate their effects. Societies that take advantage of naturally occurring experiments (including those that result from policy differences across different cities and states) might over time arrive at the highest level of quality of life.

We suggest that even if well-being measures cannot completely resolve disputes about the nature of the *good society*, they yield an additional perspective on these debates. For example, are people happier in regions where the arts flourish, or is well-being equally high where these forms of entertainment are much less common? After all, if the arts are important enough to deserve government support, they should produce positive and measurable outcomes. At an even broader level, the well-being measures can shed light on whether more authoritarian or more libertarian societies experience the highest well-being. And of course, if these effects depend on cultural values, well-being measures should be able to reveal this too.

One critical area where such debates become particularly relevant concerns the degree of social security that governments should provide for their citizens. Conservatives often argue that people are responsible for their own welfare, and the government should intervene only in rare cases. Liberals, on the other hand, argue that governments have a responsibility to help people through their most troubled times. The debate about this issue often revolves around philosophical issues, although the economic behavior likely to be fostered by the two approaches has also been central to the debate. One overlooked perspective concerns the type of society that is most likely to foster the experience of well-being in the long-run. It is likely that conservatives assume that the society with little government intervention is likely in the long term to be the happiest because people are better off when they are responsible for the outcomes that affect them. Conversely, liberals are likely to assume that people will be happier if they feel secure about retirement and when they get needed help after experiencing unemployment or disability. In this debate, systems for measuring well-being can offer instructive insights and can help mold effective policies about optimal levels of welfare assistance.

Large-scale experiments can be used to evaluate whether factors such as green space in civic centers can increase quality of life in them. Cities can be randomly assigned to conditions and well-being outcomes measured (similar to what is already being done in small-scale studies). It can be argued that in the long run, such experiments will save societies money. The major cost occurs in the data collection phase, but many cities might be interested in the interventions even in the absence of the study, making these studies somewhat more feasible. The cost of the collection of well-being data will usually be trivial compared to the intervention itself. Furthermore, the experiments can save societies from investing heavily in interventions that do not produce effects. In this way, an experimenting society can systematically learn how to enhance the citizens' well-being.

Refining Policy Concepts

Policy rests ultimately on shared ideas. In each society there are ideas and concepts that become concretized in the law. Justice, crime, and fairness are all concepts. But even more concrete terms such as poverty, unemployment, and disability are ultimately also concepts, and their character changes depending on how they are defined and measured. Although concepts such as poverty or empowerment are often defined in objective terms, there is usually an internal and subjective component to these concepts as well. Crime and punishment are often defined not only by the act committed, but also by the degree of forethought, and the intention and motivation involved.

Subjective measures can, for example, help to define the concept of poverty. Income alone is not enough to define poverty because people may live in communities or contexts where they require more or less income, and family support and potential earning power can mitigate some of the effects of low income. Furthermore, people can be poor in spirit—feeling powerless. In contrast, people with little money might have an education, valuable job skills, and confident and optimistic attitudes that make their low income less dire. If poverty is defined as people's inability to meet their basic needs, subjective measures can be helpful in identifying the destitute. People who lack optimism and feelings of empowerment might require more assistance to obtain work, for example, and therefore people's mental state can help in identifying and defining concepts such as poverty.

Helping Citizens Make Better Personal Choices and Informed Voting

Once the parameters of a happy society are mapped, one important way that the findings can be used is through better education. As citizens and policy makers alike learn of the findings, they will be better able to make good decisions regarding well-being. Well-being findings can help people make better choices regarding their future quality of life because these people will come to understand the factors that are generally associated with well-being. People will also come to understand (and ideally prevent) the errors that people typically make when predicting how various life conditions will make themselves feel.

Because the science of well-being will be aided by the findings that result from national systems of well-being assessment, people's education should become increasingly sophisticated. Even in the economic realm, people can be educated about well-being findings, and thereby make better choices. For example, they can learn of the dangers of materialism (Kasser, 2002), the influence of comparisons on making purchases versus the later enjoyment of the item at home ("joint versus separate evaluation," Hsee & Zhang, 2004), and the errors people sometimes make when they forecast their future happiness in various circumstances (Gilbert, 2007). They may also take account of the experimental evidence showing that pro-social behavior increases the life satisfaction of the givers, and by more than they expect (Dunn, Aknin, & Norton, 2008).

In conclusion, policy makers often rely on personal hunches and intuitions about the causes of well-being. They may argue for certain legislation based on broad values and ideology, but there is little doubt that they also use implicit theories of the good life to guide their opinions. Why, for example, would leaders support the building of parks, universal education, or ideas about welfare if it were not for the belief that these enhance people's quality of life? National systems for assessing well-being are likely to make these theories of well-being more explicit and sophisticated. Over time this should lead to better policy decisions.

Subjective Well-Being as a Goal in Itself

In an article entitled, "Beyond money: Toward an economy of well-being," Diener and Seligman (2004) argued that there is more to quality of life than money alone. They suggested that well-being measures are in a privileged position to reveal variation in quality of life that extends beyond economic wealth. Subjective well-being is an important goal in itself because it is likely to enhance the success and effective functioning of that society. A society high in well-being is likely to function better than a society in which people are chronically depressed, angry, fearful, and distrustful. It is not just that high well-being feels pleasant and low well-being feels unpleasant, but that people usually function better when they are not chronically in a negative state. People who are above neutral in well-being are likely to be better citizens and employees, and to live longer and healthier.

In support of these ideas, Fredrickson (2004) proposed the "broaden-and-build" theory of the function of positive emotions. She suggested that the purpose of pleasant moods and emotions is to help people build their resources for the future. A person who feels *happy* usually does so because of the perception that things are going well, that there are no imminent dangers or threats. Thus, the person who is feeling positive is in the fortunate circumstances of being able to build resources that might not be needed immediately, but which could be vital in the future. Thus, *happy* people often feel playful and curious, leading them to learn new skills and information. Similarly, people in a positive mood tend to feel social and therefore build strong connections to others that could be essential to success and survival in the future.

In support of the broaden-and-build model, Lyubomirsky, King, and Diener (2005) found that happier people were on average more successful in terms of health, income, work ratings by supervisors, and social relationships. In a longitudinal study that controlled for a number of possible confounding factors, Graham, Eggers, and Sukhtankar (2004) found that happy people earned more money and were in better health five years later. Oishi, Diener, and Lucas (2007) found that happy people were more sociable and successful in achievement domains than were unhappy people. Boehm and Lyubomirsky (2008) found that happy people perform better in work settings than do unhappy people, and that at least part of this association reflects a path from well-being to work performance.

Happier people tend to be healthier, and longitudinal research suggests that individuals high in subjective well-being tend to live longer than do those low in well-being (Pressman & Cohen, 2005). For example, they are less likely to be involved in traffic and other fatal accidents (Kirkcaldy & Furnham, 2000; Koivumaa-Honkanen, Honkanen, Koskenvuo, Viinamaki, & Kaprio, 2002 and are more likely to perform a number of healthy behaviors such as exercising and using sunscreen (Grant, Wardle, & Steptoe, 2007).

Thus, measures of subjective well-being can be used to help predict future outcomes in society, much as measures about economic optimism help predict the future course of the economy. They can also be used to point to places where subjective well-being is a worthy policy goal. For example, if happier people recover more quickly in hospitals, and are discharged sooner, relatively inexpensive measures might be introduced to increase feelings of well-being of patients.

One concern is whether happy people are so positive that they ignore problems and are satisfied with conditions that should actually be altered. Little research has been conducted on this question, although there are several relevant considerations. One is that by being positive, a person might actually make a situation better. For example, social relationships are rarely all positive or all negative; they tend to be some mix of interactions along the pleasant–unpleasant dimension. However, happy people are likely to perceive the relationships as more positive than are unhappy people, and are more likely to react to the other person in positive ways. Thus, there is a chance that the relation will actually be more positive because of these perceptual effects.

At the societal level there are some indications that happy individuals as compared to their less happy counterparts might not be prone to overlook bad conditions in their societies. For one thing, people's political attitudes and feelings cluster separately from their feelings about their lives (Andrews & Withey, 1976), suggesting that people can be satisfied with their lives but dissatisfied with their societies or government or vice versa. Second, there is evidence that happy people do approve of their societies considerably more than unhappy people when conditions are good, but that this effect is reduced when conditions are bad (Tov, Ng, Diener, Kesebir, & Harter, in press). For example, as Figure 4.1 shows, people who

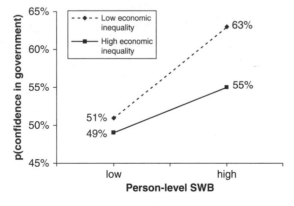

Figure 4.1 Well-Being and the Perception of Societal Characteristics.
Expansion for SWB in figure 4.1 is Subjective Well-Being.

report high evaluations of their lives have greater confidence in government when income equality is relatively high, but not much more confidence than dissatisfied people when income equality is low.

Thus, initial evidence does not indicate that people high in well-being are indiscriminate in their judgments.

Mental Health

An important facet of public health is mental health. Those who suffer from mental health problems are very frequently unhappy. Indeed, one of the major groups of unhappy people in developed nations consists of individuals suffering from diverse mental illnesses and addictions. The World Health Organization (2008) estimates that in the decades ahead depression will become the second most frequent cause of disability in the world, exceeded only by AIDS. The national accounts of well-being provide a major way of tracking the well-being of this important population and the effectiveness of interventions to help them. Furthermore, societies with accounts of well-being can more effectively evaluate the effects of other types of legislation, for example, workplace and welfare laws, on mental health.

Some have pointed to a *psychological Heisenberg principle*, the idea that measuring something often changes what is measured. If a society begins measuring well-being, it might or might not increase well-being. However, it is very likely that published measures of well-being would lead to more attempts to increase it, and of course, better information on whether these attempts are successful. If societies have national accounts of well-being, more attention and weight will be granted to it.

Conclusions

National accounts of well-being will help leaders and ordinary citizens more carefully evaluate their choices in reference to the desirability of the experiences they produce. In many areas, assumptions are made regarding the effects that policy decisions will have on well-being outcomes. But evidence rarely exists for these hunches. National systems for tracking well-being will allow societies to make better decisions by revealing which circumstances truly are associated with higher well-being. Not only do all people want to experience high well-being, but societies are likely to function more successfully when this occurs. Furthermore, even when well-being is not considered a goal in itself, the accounts of it can help make more effective decisions in arenas ranging from economics to health to welfare.

Chapter 5

The Well-Being Measures Are Valid

One of the common criticisms of the use of well-being scales for policy purposes is that the measures are based on self-reports that cannot be verified. Because these self-report scales refer to internal psychological states, there is no way to determine whether the reports themselves reflect something real within the person. People could lie about their well-being, they could lack insight into their well-being, or they might be unable to translate a valid internal feeling into a numbered response in a systematic manner. If so, the specific numbers that researchers obtain from a self-report of well-being would have little use, particularly in policy settings.

The concern about the extent to which well-being can be observed ignores the fact that all measures—whether they are self-report measures of psychological constructs or seemingly *objective* measures of easily observed characteristics such as height and weight—must be empirically validated to determine whether they are good measures. Fortunately, there are widely accepted procedures for conducting such evaluations, and regardless of the type of measure that is being assessed, the process is exactly the same. To determine whether a measure is useful, one must conduct empirical tests that examine whether the measure behaves as would be expected given the theory of the underlying construct. Anytime we find evidence that the measures behave as would be expected, this provides evidence that the measures are, in fact, of high quality. The more evidence that exists, the more confidence one can have in the measures.

It is easy to forget that this process of assessing the match between empirical observations and underlying theories occurs with all measures.

People might ignore the fact that the scales that they use to determine whether they have gained a few pounds must pass a series of empirical tests before they can be shipped from the factory to the store where they bought it. And it is only when the scale starts failing their own empirical tests that they start to realize that it is time for a new one. For instance, when a person finds that their weight fluctuates by 50 pounds from one day to the next, they are likely to assume that the scale is wrong, not that their weight really has changed that quickly. Similarly, when a scale reports that a three-foot-tall two-year-old weighs more than a six-foot-tall adult, it is more likely that existing theories about how weight is associated with age and size are correct and that the scale must be broken. In each case, confidence in the measure is influenced by the match between the observation and the knowledge of how the underlying construct should behave. Furthermore, measurement in all areas, even sophisticated domains in the physical sciences, started at a relatively crude level and became more sophisticated over time (Campbell & Fiske, 1959). Think of early measures of time or heat, for example, and then consider the dramatic increase in validity of the measures that we have today.

Furthermore, many of the most important entities in sciences such as physics cannot be directly observed. Instead, they must be inferred from indirect measures. For example, subatomic particles, planets outside our solar system, and black holes have not been directly observed and measured, but can be assessed by interlocking measurements built on theories of the phenomena involved. In this chapter, we use measurement principles and procedures for evaluating measures to assess the quality of reports of subjective well-being. In general, there are two broad characteristics that must be evaluated: reliability and validity. Reliability refers to the extent to which a measure yields consistent results. Validity is more complex, but in general, it refers to the extent to which a measure actually assesses what it is supposed to assess. We discuss these two characteristics in turn.

Reliability

A key requirement for any measure is that it is reliable. As noted above, a reliable measure yields consistent results. For example, a thermometer is reliable if it gives the same reading in repeated assessments of body temperature within a short retest interval that does not allow for actual changes in body temperature. A weight scale is reliable if it gives the same result when the same person steps on the scale twice and two scales ought to give the same reading when the same person steps on them. An unreliable scale that reads 100 kg on the first occasion and 150 kg just minutes later would be useless to assess weight. Similarly, a well-being measure that reports both high and low levels of long-term well-being over the course of an hour would provide little useful information about the state of a person's life.

A well-being measure can be highly reliable and still fail to measure well-being. In other words, it might be reliable, yet not valid. For example, a scale may provide a stable and consistent estimate of a person's weight, but the score that we could get from that scale would be an invalid measure of that person's well-being (under the plausible assumption that simply being heavier is not a valid indicator of higher or lower well-being). Nevertheless, reliability is important because low reliability limits the validity of well-being measures. If we never got the same answer twice from the same measure of well-being, then this measure cannot produce valid results because the information is inconsistent. Low reliability occurs when the measure in question contains a relatively high proportion of random error variance. Random errors can occur when people mistakenly check the wrong number on a paper and pencil inventory, when they misread or mishear the question that is being asked, or give wrong responses through any number of other random processes that affect how respondents answer.

It should be noted, however, that the influence of random error variance on aggregated ratings of well-being is, in practice, relatively benign. First, random error variance does not distort the direction of the relation between well-being measures and other variables. For example, if unemployment had a negative influence on well-being, random error variance would attenuate the correlation between unemployment and a well-being measure, but the well-being measure would still be negatively related to unemployment (Schimmack, Schupp, & Wagner, 2008). Random error will not turn negative correlations into positive correlations or vice versa. Thus, if we are attempting to identify the factors that are related to well-being and the relative importance of several factors, the unreliability of well-being measures is not a serious problem.

Second, strategies can be used to counteract the effects of random error variance. For instance, random error variance can be reduced by aggregating over several measures of well-being. In small-scale, inexpensive studies, researchers often include several well-being questions for this purpose. For example, psychologists often use a five-item scale to assess life satisfaction (Diener, Emmons, Larsen, & Griffin 1985), and such scales are more reliable than the single items of which they are composed (Schimmack & Oishi, 2005). For the large-scale surveys that would be required for a system of national indicators, this multiple-item approach to improving reliability might be too costly. Thus, many large-scale surveys often include only a single item to assess each aspect of well-being. This is still not a problem because large sample sizes compensate for low reliability. For example, the precision of an estimated level of well-being for a perfectly reliable measure in a sample of 100 respondents is the same as the precision of a mean estimate for a measure with a reliability of .5 in a sample of 200 respondents. Thus, national indicators based on a single item can still provide valid information for subgroups (e.g., men and women), even if they are too unreliable to measure well-being of a single individual. Psychologists are often more concerned about reliability than are other behavioral scientists because psychologists tend to focus on individuals rather than groups or populations.

Although random measurement error can be a relatively benign error, it can be costly to ignore its influence altogether (Schmidt & Hunter, 1996). For example, behavioral geneticists use correlations between monozygotic twins to make inferences about genetic influences on well-being (Stubbe, Posthuma, Boomsma, & De Geus, 2005). A correlation of .38 across monozygotic twins suggests that 14% (= .38*.38) of the variance in well-being is due to inherited variability in respondents' DNA.[1] This finding would suggest that the remaining 86% of the variance would be due to environmental factors (e.g., unemployment). This inference is correct only for perfectly reliable measures of well-being. If the well-being measure had a reliability of only .50, the finding would imply that genetic influences explain 28% of the variation in well-being, whereas the true effect of environmental factors would reduced to 72%.

Another reason why it is important to estimate reliability of well-being measures is that reliability can distort the comparison of effect sizes across studies. For example, a study that includes a single well-being item may find a small correlation between unemployment and well-being. It might then be tempting to compare this correlation to associations with other variables that have been found in other studies. If the measures that are used in these additional studies differ in reliability (and this difference is ignored), however, inappropriate conclusions may be drawn. For instance, a separate study that uses a multiple-item measure of well-being may find a stronger correlation between well-being and a personality trait than the correlation between well-being and unemployment in the original study. A direct comparison of the observed correlations across these studies might lead the researcher to inflate the importance of personality traits relative to the effects of unemployment. In reality, the difference in correlations might be due to the differences in reliability.

---

[1] The correlation between MZ twins shows the joint effect of genes on the phenotypes of each twin. The square root of the correlation reveals the effect on the phenotype of a single twin. As the square of this effect is the amount of explained variance, r is a direct estimate of the amount of variance that is explained by genetic variation.

To illustrate the effects of unreliability, we can examine how a true correlation between unemployment and well-being would change when well-being measures that differed in their reliability were used. First, let us assume that a single-item measure of well-being has a reliability of .60 (which means that 60% of the variance in the measure is well-being true-score variance and 40% of the variance is random measurement error). The corresponding reliability of a multiple-item scale that is made up of five items, each with individual reliabilities of .60, is .89. Thus, the error variance is reduced to just 11% of the total variance. If the true correlation between unemployment and subjective well-being is .30, then unreliability in the well-being measure would attenuate this effect to $r = .23$ for the single-item measure and $r = .28$ for the five-item measure. Thus, not only would the correlation look smaller than it actually is, but it would vary across studies simply because of the differences in the measure. It is important to note that random measurement error does not distort comparisons of effect sizes of two measures with equal reliability, which is the case if effect sizes are compared within the same study using the same well-being indicator. However, for all other comparisons, effects should be compared on the basis of adjusted effect sizes that control for random measurement error.

Examining reliability is relatively simple, and the reliability of well-being measures has been assessed in numerous studies using a variety of different paradigms. The most direct approach is to ask respondents the same well-being question twice within a single interview (Andrews & Withey, 1976; Headey, Veenhoven, & Wearing, 1991). Unfortunately, estimates of reliability using this approach may be distorted by several processes, for example, the desire to be consistent and the ability to remember the previous response (Saris, Van Wijk, & Scherpenzeel, 1998). Participants may simply be able to remember and report the response they had just provided, which would mean that the process that the respondent went through to come up with the response would be very different at the first and second occasions. In addition, because people may feel compelled to provide consistent reports, they may provide the same number as they did during an earlier assessment, even when the underlying process would have led to a different outcome on the second occasion. Either of these effects may lead to an overestimation of reliability. In contrast, respondents might feel that the researcher expects a different response in light of the interviewing questions, and this could lead to an underestimation of reliability.

A second method for determining reliability is to examine the internal consistency of multiple-item Subjective Well-Being scales (Eid & Diener, 2004). Like the approach described above, this method is susceptible to memory effects. On the other hand, the multiple-item technique may underestimate reliability because individuals may be motivated to respond differently to questions with slightly different wording. That is, respondents may exaggerate the difference between a satisfaction item and a happiness item because they assume that the questions must have different meanings if the researcher is asking both of them (Schwarz & Strack, 1999). A third approach to estimating reliability is to examine the retest correlations over longer time intervals. If a suitably long interval is chosen, this should eliminate memory effects (and this assumption can be tested explicitly). The main drawback of this approach is that the longer the time interval, the more likely it is that true changes in well-being will occur. These true changes would lead to an underestimation of the reliability of the measure.

Because each technique for estimating reliability has limitations, it is best to compare the results that are obtained when different procedures are used. Fortunately, the different methods produce fairly consistent estimates of reliability. Broadly speaking, the reliability of a single well-being item is about .6. This estimate is based on several research findings. First, retest correlations of the same item within a single interview tend to range from .6 to .7 (Andrews & Withey, 1976; Headey et al., 1991; Schimmack & Oishi, 2005).[2] Similar estimates are obtained when a single item is correlated with a multiple-item scale within the same survey (Wanous & Hudy, 2001), or when correlations among individual items of a multiple-item scale are examined (Schimmack & Oishi, 2005). A meta-analysis by Saris et al. (1998) found an average retest reliability of $r = .55$ for a single life satisfaction item presented alone in the survey. The six-week retest reliability in a German national representative sample was also .55 (Schimmack, Wagner, Krause, & Schupp, in press). Reliability estimates based on panel studies yield higher values in the .6 to .7 range (Ehrhardt, Saris, & Veenhoven, 2000). The higher reliability in these studies is due to practice effects, as revealed by increasing reliabilities over time (Ehrhardt et al., 2000; Schimmack et al., 2007).

Because the processes that are required to answer well-being questions might vary across different types of well-being measures, reliabilities might vary too. One hypothesis is that global life satisfaction judgments are less reliable than affect measures or domain-specific satisfaction judgments. Schwarz and Strack (1999) argued that because global satisfaction

---

[2] The test-retest correlation provides an estimate of the amount of reliable variance that exists in each measure. The square root of this correlation reveals the effect of the underlying latent variable on each observed score. Because the square of this effect is the amount of explained variance, the correlation between the two observed measures provides a direct estimate of the amount of variance in each measure that can be explained by the underlying latent trait.

judgments are necessarily broad, they require memory and aggregation across many different types of information. The processes of remembering and aggregating can be influenced by various contextual effects, which would mean that the reliabilities of global satisfaction judgments should be lower than reliabilities for more concrete judgments of domain satisfaction or affective reactions. Empirical evidence provides mixed support for this hypothesis.

For instance, Saris et al. (1998) found substantially lower reliability for global life satisfaction judgments in one study, but a meta-analysis showed relatively small differences. Similarly, Alfonso, Allison, Rader, and Gorman (1996) compared the internal consistencies (Chronbach's α) and two-week retest correlations of the five-item Satisfaction with Life Scale with similarly worded five-item scales of domain satisfactions in nine life domains. The most reliable domain satisfaction measure was satisfaction with sex life ($\alpha = .96$, retest $r = .87$), which was only slightly more reliable than global life satisfaction ($\alpha = .89$, retest $r = .83$), and global judgments were more reliable than judgments of some domains. A comparison of the reliabilities of life and domain satisfaction items in the German Socio-Economic Panel with the global life satisfaction item also revealed no systematic differences, with some domain satisfaction ratings having higher reliabilities and others having lower reliabilities (Schimmack & Lucas, 2008).

Systematic comparisons of the reliabilities of cognitive well-being (e.g., life satisfaction) and affective well-being (AWB) measures are rare. Eid and Diener (2004) compared the reliability of the five-item Satisfaction with Life Scale with reliabilities of four-item affect scales for a variety of affects and found very similar results. Using the Spearman–Brown formula, the average reliability of a single life satisfaction item was .64 compared to an average reliability of .60 for a single affect item. These results are consistent with an unpublished study by Schimmack et al. (2007) that compared short-term retest correlations (1–2 months) of 12 life satisfaction items and 18 affect items. The average retest correlation for life satisfaction was slightly higher, $r = .56$ (median $r = .57$), than the average retest correlation of affect items, $r = .49$, (median $r = .50$). Overall, the content of well-being measures has surprisingly little influence on the reliability of well-being measures.

One aspect of well-being measures is the number of response categories that respondents can use to record their rating. Too few categories may lower reliability because respondents with different levels of Subjective Well-Being are forced to use the same response category. Furthermore, a low number of response categories make it less likely that ordinal responses approximate the properties of an interval scale. Saris et al. (1998) found that 10-point scales were much more reliable (20 percentage points) than scales with four or five response options. Too many response categories or continuous rating scales may increase error because respondents find it difficult to choose a response category.

An experiment with random assignment of respondents to a 7-point scale and an 11-point scale revealed higher reliability for the 11-point scale (Kroh, 2006). Thus, the evidence suggests that, at least in the range from 2 to 11 response categories, more response categories produce higher reliability. It is therefore unfortunate that one of the first well-being measures had only three response categories (Gurin, Joseph, & Feld, 1960), which led to the use of three-point or four-point scales in numerous studies. Other measures sometimes include multiple items that respondents answer using a true/false response scale. This multiple-item approach is relatively costly, and it is often more efficient to have a smaller number of items or a single item with more response options. We strongly urge researchers to use scales with more response options and to phase out measures with three or four response categories that are still in use.

A few studies have examined the effect of the data collection procedure on reliability. The most relevant distinction is between interviews and self-administered questionnaires. It is possible that respondents might be more careless when recording their own responses using paper and pencil self-administered questionnaires than when responding to an interviewer. Or alternatively, the interaction with an interviewer might result in a greater influence of transient contextual factors. However, reliability does not appear to be affected by these procedural differences (Kroh, 2006).

In summary, reliability reflects the amount of systematic variance that exists in a measure and it is inversely related to the amount of random measurement error in the measure. Reliable measures result in consistent responses, and thus reliability can easily be assessed, usually by administering the measure repeatedly over time. Both multiple-item and single-item measures of well-being contain substantial amounts of reliable variance. The large surveys that will be required to develop national indicators of well-being will likely require short scales, and sometimes even just a single item. Existing empirical evidence suggests that even a single item has sufficient reliability for the purposes of creating national indicators.

Validity

According to Messick, "Validity is an overall evaluative judgment of the degree to which empirical evidence and theoretical rationales support the adequacy and appropriateness of interpretations and actions on the basis of test scores or other models of assessment" (1995, p. 741). The fact that validity is an *evaluative judgment* rather than a single number makes it less straightforward to evaluate validity than reliability. But it is important to note that this does not mean that validity cannot be assessed and evaluated. Researchers must carefully consider the theory that underlies the construct they wish to assess and then determine whether the empirical evidence supports the idea that the measure really does assess that construct. In short, the question of validity as it applies to well-being is a question of whether a well-being measure actually assesses well-being. Scientists use what is known about the correlates of well-being measures to address this question.

Validity is crucial to any program of national indicators. Early on, economists rejected subjective measures of well-being because they assumed that subjective measures are invalid. It is important to note that this rejection was based on *assumptions* about the measures, rather than on failed empirical tests of validity. At the same time, economists assumed that income is a valid indicator of well-being, but few studies have systematically tested this assumption. The lack of empirical validation research on income or gross domestic product (GDP) as a valid indicator of well-being may account for the strong impact of articles that have challenged this assumption (Easterlin, 2003). From a validity perspective, this controversy boils down to conflicting claims about the validity of GDP and subjective well-being ratings as indicators of societies' well-being. If we assume GDP is a valid measure, well-being in the United States increased over the past decades. If we assume happiness ratings are valid, it did not. It will be impossible to answer these fundamental questions without examining the validity of both well-being measures. Unfortunately, researchers have a tendency to assume that their measures have perfect validity. This is unlikely. Thus, it is equally questionable to reject subjective measures out of hand as it is to simply assume that they are perfect measures of well-being.

There are many reasons why subjective measures of well-being could be invalid representations of experienced subjective well-being. First, people may simply say that they are happy without feeling or being happy. This could occur for a number of reasons, including the desire to mislead or the inability to accurately reflect on internal states. In this case, the subjective report is not a valid reflection of the subjective state. It is also possible that people are correctly reporting on something subjective, but that the subjective state that they are describing does not reflect what scientists and policy makers mean by well-being. For example, if a person accurately reports on a subjective feeling about his or her life, but that feeling is determined entirely by the mood he or she is in at the time of judgment (rather than by the stable circumstances in his or her life), then we might reject the validity of this measure as an indicator of an overall state of well-being. Finally, verbal reports could be invalid because of difficulties in translating judgments into the verbal labels and numbers used in the scale.

Before we examine the relevant findings in the well-being literature, it is important to make a few general remarks about validity. First, validity is not a dichotomous, either/or construct. It is a quantitative construct that can hypothetically range from no relation between a measure and the actual construct that it is designed to measure to a perfect relation between a measure and the construct it is intended to measure. Thus, a single demonstration that a well-being measure is systematically biased (e.g., higher ratings on sunny days) does not imply that these measures are useless because the bias may be too small to undermine the validity of a well-being measure.

Second, validity is a characteristic of a particular measure. Demonstrating validity for one subjective measure of well-being does not imply that all subjective measures are valid. Thus, it is inappropriate to make statements about the validity of subjective measures in general. Some subjective measures may be more valid than others. That being said, it is impossible to provide a detailed review of each measure that exists in this book, and so some amount of generalization across similar measures will be required. Our conclusions should be seen as educated guesses about the validity of similar measures. The ability to generalize across measures depends on the similarity of the measures and the potential threats to validity. For example, it is fairly safe to generalize from a 7-point global happiness rating to a 10-point global satisfaction rating, but it is less clear whether the validity of ratings of one's feelings in response to a specific stimulus can be generalized to ratings on one's average level of affect in the past month.

Third, validity can only be examined for a construct with a precise definition, and not all constructs that we would like to measure have such definitions. For instance, some indicators are simply useful because they help to predict things. This would be true even if we did not know what the underlying construct was that the measure assessed. For example, public opinion researchers regularly track consumers' confidence in the economy. The indicator that results is used to predict other economic outcomes. But it is relatively unimportant whether an index of consumer confidence really measures confidence. The index is only relevant because it is a valid predictor of economic behavior in the near future (if people say they are less likely to buy a car in the next three months, they actually buy fewer cars in the next three months). In contrast, a national account of well-being is not designed to predict the future. It is designed to examine current well-being or well-being in the recent past. It can be designed to evaluate the effectiveness of policies after they have been implemented. It may also be used to make predictions, but this is not its primary purpose. Thus, it matters whether an indicator of well-being really measures well-being. In psychology, this type of validity is called construct validity. When we ask whether a well-being measure has construct validity, we ask, "Does a well-being measure really measure well-being?" To answer this question, it is important to define well-being. We have defined well-being broadly as a favorable evaluation of a life by the individual who lives this life. To examine the validity of a specific well-being measure, we need to examine whether the measure behaves in accordance with theoretical assumptions about well-being.

The construct validity process is an iterative one. The first steps of validation are to test hypotheses that are derived from core assumptions about the construct under investigation. If a measure fails to conform to predictions based on these core predictions, it raises doubts about the measure. Once a measure passes several tests of core predictions, it is possible to test more peripheral hypotheses. At this point, it is possible that predictions are not supported. For peripheral hypotheses, it is no longer clear whether disconfirmed predictions reveal validity problems or whether the new findings suggest that the original theory needs to be revised. Thus, from a validity point of view, it is more important to demonstrate the obvious. For example, it may be obvious that people in a prosperous and peaceful country like Norway are happier than people in a poor and violent country like Zimbabwe, and this finding is unlikely to make the headlines in the news. But from a validity point of view, it is crucial that a well-being measure shows this difference. If it does not show this difference, the most plausible inference would be that the well-being measure was invalid. The alternative inference that well-being in Zimbabwe is really as high as in Norway would require a radical revision of the most essential assumptions about well-being. For example, we would have to explain why thousands of happy Zimbabweans are leaving their country, while Norway has more immigrants than emigrants. Similarly, if people in a psychiatric hospital reported higher life satisfaction than people without mental problems, the measure would be suspect.

Different Types of Validity

The first way to assess the validity of a measure is through an examination of *face validity*. Face validity refers to the extent to which a measure looks like it measures what it is supposed to measure. For instance, the question "Is your life close to your ideal?" appears to measure the construct of well-being if that construct is defined as a life that matches a person's preferences. In contrast, few people would be willing to accept a measure of well-being that simply measures the distance from a person's head to his or her toes. There is simply no reason to assume that this indicator would tap into the underlying construct of well-being. Most subjective well-being measures have high face validity because the content of the question maps closely onto the construct that the measure is intended to measure.

Face validity is desirable, but is a weak validation criterion. There are many reasons why a face-valid measure may fail to be a valid measure of well-being, and there are good reasons why a measure with low face validity may be a valid measure of well-being. For instance, economists often use money as a measure of well-being, and they may encounter the criticism that this measure lacks face validity. Conceptually, it is not hard to argue that the construct of money is distinct from the construct of well-being, and therefore a measure that asks about a person's income would lack face validity as a measure of well-being. However, if money were, in fact, strongly correlated with well-being, the amount of income that a person has would be a reasonable indicator of his or her well-being. Although the money measure lacks face validity as an indicator of well-being, it could nevertheless be valid because the construct that it does assess (money) is closely linked with well-being. In this way, money would be a valid but indirect measure of well-being. Therefore, face validity is useful to consider, but it is neither necessary nor sufficient for a measure to be valid.

Content validity refers to the extent to which the content that is actually assessed by a measure reflects the breadth of the content that is assumed to exist in the underlying construct. The importance of content validity varies for different well-being measures. Global indicators, whether objective (GDP) or subjective (global life satisfaction), have no sampling issues. It is assumed that all relevant information is reflected in a single global indicator.

In contrast, other well-being measures assess a collection of more specific content areas that are assumed to be included in a life that is evaluated favorably. These may include specific life domains, specific emotions, or specific preferences that could potentially be satisfied. Again, there are both objective and subjective measures that have this characteristic. For example, the Human Development Index assesses health, education, and income separately before integrating this information into a single index. The content validity of this measure depends on the ability of this measure to represent all objectively desirable aspects of lives. Content validity is also an issue for multiple-item scales with heterogeneous content. An example is the Oxford Happiness Scale, which is widely used in well-being research (Hills & Argyle, 2002). Items in this measures include "I am always laughing," "I always have fun with other people," "I love everybody," and "I think I look extremely attractive." The content of this scale raises questions about its validity as a measure of well-being. For example, a person may still believe that he or she looks extremely attractive even after losing his or her house and family in a fire, although the latter events should presumably lower well-being. In contrast, a person might be very happy and yet not laugh a lot.

Content validity is a particularly important issue when developing AWB indicators (Schimmack, 1997; Schimmack, 2003). It is important to ask whether all affective states are equally important for well-being and whether some affects are more representative of overall affect than others. For example, Bradburn's (1969) seminal affect measure included the item "on top of the world." But it is not clear that peak experiences like feeling on top of the world contribute to overall well-being. Instead, it appears that the frequency of more mundane levels of positive emotions is more important (Diener, Sandvik, & Pavot, 1991). Many contemporary studies use an affect measure that includes the items *determined* and *ashamed* but does not include the items *happy* or *sad* (Watson, Clark, & Tellegen, 1988). Some affects like anxiety and hope are based on people's beliefs about the future. As such, they are less able to reflect well-being in the past. Decisions about which affect items to include will influence the content validity of the overall measure.

Content validity is also an important issue in studies that examine satisfaction with life domains. Again, the number of life domains is infinite and researchers often choose only a limited number of domains that seem important from the infinite universe of domain satisfactions (Cummins, 1996). The rationale for including or excluding certain domains is often based on the researcher's own opinion about which domains are most important. However, this means that to other researchers, the choices may seem arbitrary. Furthermore, some domains may be excluded because they are deemed irrelevant in a certain population, and domains that are included but are not applicable to a large number of participants create problems with missing data. For example, how should a respondent who is not in a romantic relationship answer a question about satisfaction with romantic relationships? The person may be legitimately dissatisfied with the lack of an important relationship, but if he or she responded to the question, does that change the meaning of the item? What of items inquiring about work satisfaction for those who do not work at a paying job?

Another issue is whether items are truly subjective. For example, an item "How good is your dwelling?" is ambiguous because it can be answered in an objective manner and in a subjective way based on individual's preferences. Based on our definition of well-being as subjective, an item that clearly assesses subjective evaluations would have higher content validity (e.g., "I am satisfied with my dwelling" or "My dwelling is close to my ideal dwelling") than one that could be interpreted as reflecting an objective report on the domain (e.g., "My house is large").

A final aspect of content validity concerns the focus on ongoing experiences versus enduring dispositions. Many psychological measures are designed to assess internal dispositions rather than manifest levels of well-being. Self-esteem, optimism, and cheerfulness measures often ask participants to rate their general tendencies. In most cases, these measures are not designed to measure well-being. If these measures actually assessed what they were intended to assess, they should be relatively independent of actual changes in people's life circumstances, and therefore they would be unable to track well-being. The content of AWB measures should focus on actual experiences rather than internal dispositions.

In conclusion, the content of well-being measures is important and is likely to have an influence on the validity of a well-being measure. Most well-being measures that have been used tend to have reasonable content validity, although our discussion highlighted some possible problems. Broadly speaking, measures with slightly different content provide relatively similar information (Andrews & Whithey, 1976). However, for the creation of national indicators that inform policy makers, these issues deserve more attention than they have received in the past.

A third form of validity is *convergent validity*. Convergent validity reflects the extent to which the answers that a researcher gets from one measure of well-being correspond to the answers he or she gets from a different measure, and therefore this criterion relies on the correlation between measures of well-being for validation. The essential proposition is that if measure A is a measure of well-being and measure B is another measure of well-being, then measures A and B should be highly correlated. Convergent validity is most useful if one measure has already been validated. In this case, the correlation between a new measure and an old measure can be used to validate the newer measure of well-being.

The first step of demonstrating convergent validity is to correlate several self-report measures of well-being with each other. A measure that does not correlate with other measures is likely to be problematic. For example, the measure might not correlate because the wording of the items could be unclear. Virtually all self-ratings of well-being pass this first test (Andrews & Whithey, 1976; Lucas, Diener, & Suh, 1996; Watson, 1988). Even measures with different content show convergent validity, in that global life satisfaction, average domain satisfaction, and affective measures are moderately to highly correlated with each other (Andrews & Whithey, 1976; Lucas et al., 1996; Schimmack, Diener, & Oishi, 2002).

However, evidence for convergent validity between measures that share the same method (self-ratings) can be inflated by shared method variance.

For this reason, it is important to establish convergent validity across measures that use different methods (Campbell & Fiske, 1959). The main difficulty in demonstrating convergent validity across methods is finding measures that use different methods to assess the same construct. For subjective constructs like well-being, the most frequently used alternative to self-ratings is informant ratings by knowledgeable informants. A knowledgeable informant has information about the life circumstances and events in the target's life. He or she also has information about the target's preferences. Thus, it is possible to measure subjective well-being using informant reports. The judgment remains subjective because the informant relies on the target's preferences rather than his or her own preferences.

The prediction of convergent validity between self-ratings and informant ratings of well-being is based on a set of assumptions. Violations of these assumptions would lower evidence for convergent validity and can reveal problems in self-ratings, informant ratings, or both. First, these tests assume that respondents have valid information about their own well-being. Second, they assume that when asked, respondents can and do accurately report this information. Third, they assume that informants also have valid information about the respondents' well-being. And finally, they assume that when asked, informants accurately report the relevant information.

The study of convergent validity using informant reports has a long history in the psychological research on well-being. A review by Wilson (1967) reported results from two studies with an average cross-method correlation of $r = .37$. A more recent meta-analysis yielded a slightly higher estimate of $r = .40$ (Schneider & Schimmack, in press). The meta-analysis uncovered several moderating factors. Not surprisingly, multiple-item measures with higher reliability produced higher self-informant agreement. Thus, to some extent low validity is simply a consequence of random error. Another noteworthy finding was that global life satisfaction judgments had higher convergent validity than affective measures. This finding may be due to the more private nature of emotional experiences, but it may also reflect problems in the assessment of affective experiences. The meta-analysis also revealed numerous gaps in the literature. For example, few studies have examined self-informant agreement for domain satisfaction judgments and few have compared the convergent validity of global evaluative judgments to the convergent validity of averaged domain satisfaction. Schimmack (2008) found that self-ratings of average domain satisfaction correlated nearly as highly with self-ratings of global life satisfaction as with global ratings of life satisfaction by informants. This finding provides some evidence of convergent validity of ratings of domain satisfaction.

Although convergent validation procedures are widely used when assessing the validity of well-being measures, they are not without problems. One problem is that if weak correlations emerge, it is unclear which measure is driving this effect. A correlation of .3 could reflect perfect validity in self-ratings and moderate validity in informant ratings, equal amounts of validity in both measures, or greater validity in informant ratings than self-ratings. This concern becomes particularly germane when examining convergence with measures of well-being that are quite different from the self-report methods that are typically used. For instance, many researchers would like to find a substitute for well-being measures that could completely eliminate the need for verbal reports (either by a target or by an informant). This is why the possibility of developing psychophysiological measures of well-being is so appealing. Presumably, if one could measure well-being by assessing psychophysiological processes in the brain, then concerns about deception and an inability to translate internal feelings to options on response scales could be eliminated.

Some progress has been made linking self-reports of well-being to psychophysiological and reaction time measures that are difficult to fake. However, the theories about the processes underlying these measures are still quite unsophisticated. Psychophysiological measures such as hemispheric asymmetry in prefrontal activation are sometimes only weakly related to self-ratings (Smit, Posthuma, Boomsma, & De Geus, 2007). Moreover, relatively more activity on the left side also increases in response to anger, an unpleasant emotion that is elicited in response to events that undermine well-being (Harmon-Jones & Sigelman, 2001). So it is quite difficult to draw strong conclusions about the validity of well-being measures from the moderate correlations that have been reported in other studies (Urry et al., 2004). Other studies have tried to use indirect measures or reaction time tasks to measure well-being (Walker & Schimmack, 2008). However, these tasks typically show very weak correlations with self and informant ratings, which undermines their validity as measures of well-being. Given that there is very little validity evidence for psychophysiological or other unobtrusive measures of well-being (much less than for self- and informant-report measures), and given that the theories of the processes that underlie these measures are still relatively undeveloped, we conclude that it will not yet be fruitful to attempt to validate existing measures using these relatively poorly understood criteria. That being said, this is certainly an area where future research and future theoretical development could lead to changes in our understanding that make such measures useful criteria for validation work, and may one day produce measures that can complement other measures of well-being.

A fourth form of validity is *discriminant validity*. In testing discriminant validity, researchers attempt to validate a measure by demonstrating that it does not actually measure a related, but different, construct. In other words, discriminant validation is used to rule out alternative hypotheses about what the measures might assess and why it might be related to criteria and outcomes of interest. It is important to note that to demonstrate discriminant validity, correlations between two constructs need not be zero. In fact, demonstrations of discriminant validity are most impressive when they are conducted with measures that should theoretically be related, but separable. It would not be surprising if a well-being measure were unrelated to a measure of how much a person likes the color green. Showing that this correlation was zero would be an unimpressive demonstration of discriminant validity, and this demonstration would convince very few that the well-being measure was a good one. However, there might be legitimate concerns about the extent to which well-being measures are separable from related, yet distinct, constructs such as self-esteem or optimism. Showing that well-being is related to but separable from these constructs would then be a more important demonstration of discriminant validity. This means that when testing discriminant validity, researchers must usually compare the correlations between two theoretically related, but distinct, constructs to the correlations between two different measures of the same construct.

Lucas et al. (1996) examined the discriminant validity of well-being measures from constructs like self-esteem and optimism. Theories of well-being would suggest that these constructs should be related. People who feel good about themselves and who expect positive things to happen in their future might be expected to have many things going well in their lives; and having many things going for oneself may instill optimism and self-esteem. On the other hand, people could have high opinions about themselves and their abilities, even if their lives were not going well at that moment due to external factors beyond their control. Similarly, they might also be optimistic about the future, even though their present and past circumstances were miserable. Given the conceptual distinction between well-being, self-esteem, and optimism, a measure of well-being should show discriminant validity from these other constructs. Lucas et al. (1996) found higher self-informant correlations for ratings of the same construct (e.g., $rs = .46$ to $.50$) than for ratings of different constructs (e.g., $rs = .34$ to $.41$). Unfortunately, few studies have examined the discriminant validity of well-being measures, and therefore a comprehensive examination of discriminant validity of different well-being measures is lacking. However, the evidence reviewed below on criterion validity often shows or implies that well-being measures behave differently than measures of related, yet distinct, constructs.

Face validity, content validity, convergent validity, and discriminant validity usually reflect preliminary steps that researchers must take to show that their measures could reasonably be expected to assess the underlying construct of interest. However, the main test of the validity of a measure is to demonstrate that a measure performs in accordance with theoretical predictions. A measure may not produce all expected findings because theoretical expectations can be wrong, but a good measure is likely to behave in accordance with theoretical predictions most of the time. The process of investigation of these theoretical predictions is the process of *construct validation*.

In the following section we address several ways that the construct validity of well-being measures can be tested. However, many tests of construct validity simultaneously test validity and an underlying theoretical proposition. For instance, we can ask whether people who have lost a spouse report lower scores on well-being measures than do people who have not lost a spouse. An empirical investigation that attempted to answer this question would really be doing two things simultaneously—testing whether the underlying construct changes when this important life circumstance changes and testing whether the measure that we used to assess the underlying construct was sensitive to changes in that underlying construct. If scores on the measure did not change over time, this might mean that well-being itself does not change following a change in life circumstances or it might mean that well-being does change but the measure that we use is not sensitive enough or valid enough to assess this change. For this reason, our review in this section of the chapter focuses on the most straightforward theoretical predictions that could be used to validate measures of well-being. Additional empirical evidence that is relevant to this question is also presented in Chapter 6. Specifically, we address questions about whether well-being can change and what factors are most likely to lead to such change. Furthermore, in Chapter 11, we address existing studies that have already used well-being measures to address policy-related questions, and the results from these studies also demonstrate the validity of the measures that were used. And of course, throughout this book we focus on empirical findings regarding the associations between well-being and various life circumstances. Each time such correlations are identified, the confidence in the measures grows.

Money and Well-Being

One of the most basic theoretical principles that guides research on subjective well-being is the idea that the conditions in people's lives should affect their well-being. When things are going well for people, then the conditions of their lives are likely to match their preferences and expectations, and this should lead to high well-being. When things are going poorly, then the conditions of their lives are less likely to match preferences and expectations, and this should lead to low well-being. Of course, people have different preferences, which means that some life circumstances will relate to well-being only for some people. But there are certain general features of a life that most would agree are beneficial. For instance, good health is better than bad health, having sufficient food and adequate shelter is better than the lack of such resources, and having enough financial resources that one can withstand economic shocks is better than being unable to cope with downturns in the economy or the loss of a job. Notably, many of these important characteristics that one would assume should correlate with well-being also correlate with income. And although money is not everything, and many other factors will likely contribute to well-being, it would be surprising if money and all of the things it can buy were unrelated to well-being. Thus, one important test of construct validity is to determine whether subjective well-being measures correlate with income. We will first discuss the links between income and well-being at the national level and then at the individual level.

Standard economic theories of well-being predict a strong correlation between nations' wealth and well-being. The reason is that there are large differences in wealth and consumptions across nations. In some nations, poverty prevents many people from the adequate fulfillment of basic needs. In addition, for most people fulfillment of basic needs is evaluated positively. Thus, a well-being measure should show positive correlations with national levels of wealth because wealth enables people to fulfill basic needs.

An influential article by Easterlin (1974) suggested that well-being measures are unrelated to national wealth. However, this finding was based on a small sample of nations. Moreover, the actual correlation in his two data sets was $r = .5$ (Veenhoven, 1991). Subsequent studies have all replicated the finding that nations' wealth is positively correlated with subjective ratings of well-being. Furthermore, once more data from more nations became available, even clearer evidence of a correlation between national wealth and subjective well-being measures emerged (Diener, Diener, & Diener, 1995; Diener & Oishi, 2000). Multiple studies have examined this association, and it is now clear that there is a relatively strong correlation between national levels of income and well-being (Deaton, 2008; Helliwell, 2008; Stevenson & Wolfers, 2008). The observed correlation between nations' income and average life satisfaction judgments stands somewhere between $r = .6$ and $r = .8$. The correlations that are found in such studies should be seen as a lower estimate of the true correlation because it is likely to be attenuated by measurement error. Thus, as predicted, income is consistently and relatively strongly linked with higher levels of subjective well-being. This finding validates the subjective ratings of well-being and at the same time provides some support for the common practice in standard economic theory to use per capita GDP as an indicator of nations' well-being.

Results from individual-level analyses are a bit more complicated. As with nation-level effects, there are strong theoretical reasons to believe that income will be associated with well-being, at least at lower levels of the income range. Results consistently show this to be the case (Easterlin, 1974). Most nationally representative studies, along with meta-analyses of existing studies, show that there are small to moderate correlations between income and well-being (i.e., rs around .20) (Diener & Oishi, 2000; Diener, Suh, Lucas, & Smith, 1999; Schimmack, 2008). Importantly, although the correlations do vary somewhat from study to study, and although many researchers (including the authors of this book) have described these effects as small, the correlations are almost never negative. One reason why we might obtain consistently positive yet small correlations is that the true correlation is higher than is typically found, but it is attenuated by random measurement error. As noted earlier, random error will reduce the magnitude of correlations, but it does not change the sign of a correlation. Thus, one reason why correlations at the individual level might be weaker than correlations at the national level is that random error attenuates correlations at the individual level more than at the national level.

It is also important to point out that correlation coefficients are somewhat difficult to interpret. It is not straightforward to come up with a point prediction for the size of a correlation that one would expect based on an underlying theory. How strong should the correlation between income and well-being be to match our expectation that income is important for well-being? What size correlation would reflect the intuition that rich people are substantially happier than the poor? Recently we showed that even a small correlation of just .18 between income and life satisfaction can translate into very large differences between the rich and the poor (Lucas & Schimmack, 2007). For instance, in analyses using data from the German Socio-Economic Panel Study, we found that those who made the equivalent of over 200,000 dollars a year were more than three-quarters of a standard deviation more satisfied with their lives than were people who made less than the equivalent of 10,000 dollars a year. Furthermore, those who made the equivalent of over 200,000 dollars a year were more than a half of a standard deviation more satisfied with their lives than were people who made an average income (of about 55,000 dollars a year). The consistently positive correlation, along with the substantial differences between the rich and the poor, means that well-being measures behave as we would expect—they are higher among those with higher levels of income. This supports the validity of the measures.

To fully support the theory, it would be helpful to be able to show that income actually causes differences in well-being, but evidence regarding this point is mixed. On the one hand, there is the famous study by Brickman, Coates, and Janoff-Bulman (1978) showing that lottery winners are not significantly happier than a sample of controls. However, this study involved an extremely small sample of participants. Without replication, very little weight should be placed on these results. At least two larger studies of lottery winners contradict the early Brickman et al. findings. For instance, Smith and Razzell (1975) found that lottery winners were about a half of a standard deviation happier than a sample of controls, and Gardner and Oswald (2007) used longitudinal data to show that lottery winners were happier after their win than they were before the win. Thus, some studies suggest that winning the lottery is associated with increases in well-being.

Other studies also do show an effect of income on well-being, although the effects may be only temporary (adaptation is a different issue, here we simply say income increases well-being). Using panel data, Di Tella, Haisken-DeNew, and MacCulloch (2005) found increases in income were associated with increases in life satisfaction, although these effects did not last. We will discuss the latter finding of adaptation in a different section. In the present context, the results do show that well-being measures change in response to changes in financial status, which validates these measures. Finally, it should be noted that the processes underlying these effects seem to make sense given our theories of how income should affect well-being. Specifically, Schimmack (2008a) showed that financial satisfaction mediates the relation between income and life satisfaction. Together, these results show that income is related to well-being measures in ways that are consistent with theories of well-being. This finding validates these measures.

Relationships and Well-Being

Like income, social relationships can be seen as a broad resource that could improve people's lives in many different ways (Lucas & Dyrenforth, 2006). For instance, most people rank social relationships as one of their highest preferences (Oishi, Schimmack, Diener, & Suh, 1998). Some have even argued that humans have a basic need for strong relationships. Regardless of whether this last point is true, it may be a part of normative development to enter into a lasting romantic relationship, and deviations from this pattern may have psychological effects. Many basic theories of well-being suggest that positive social relationships should be linked with well-being because of the broad set of resources these relationships can provide. And as with income, the evidence supports this idea (Myers, 2000).

For instance, married individuals consistently report higher levels of well-being than divorced or widowed individuals (the evidence for differences between married people and singles is much weaker) (Diener et al., 1999). It is also the case that marital transitions are linked with well-being. Although the beginning of a marriage appears to be associated with relatively small gains in well-being (at least on average; see Lucas, Clark, Georgellis, & Diener, 2003), the end of a relationship through either divorce or widowhood is associated with larger changes. For instance, Lucas et al. (2003) showed that the levels of life satisfaction of people who became widowed dropped substantially around the time that they lost their spouse. Life satisfaction levels rebounded over time, but the effects of the loss lasted eight years on average. Thus, well-being measures were sensitive to this major change in life circumstances for many years after the event.

Similarly, divorce is associated with drops in life satisfaction. More importantly, the time course of changes in life satisfaction that occur around the time of divorce makes theoretical sense, which supports the validity of the measures used to track well-being. For instance, divorce can occur for various reasons, but one reason is low marital satisfaction. Because marital satisfaction is an important part of well-being, it is reasonable to predict that well-being levels should be relatively low before a divorce. Empirical studies support this prediction not only for measures that assess domain satisfactions like marital satisfaction (Gottman & Levenson, 2000) and sexual satisfaction (Clements, Stanley, & Markman, 2004), but also for measures that assess broad life satisfaction judgments (Gardner & Oswald, 2006; Lucas, 2005). Using longitudinal panel data, Lucas (2005) showed that life satisfaction declined steadily as the year of divorce approached, reaching its lowest level in the year preceding the divorce.

Moreover, divorce can be seen as an active coping response to a problem. If this coping response is successful, then well-being should increase after the divorce occurs. Again, empirical evidence supports this prediction (Gardner & Oswald, 2006; Lucas, 2005). Lucas showed that there was a boost in life satisfaction during the year that the divorce occurred, and then further increases followed in the subsequent years. To be sure, the divorce may create its own set of new problems, and for this reason, people who go through a divorce may not always return to their initial levels of life satisfaction. But the trajectory of life satisfaction scores suggests that life satisfaction declines before the divorce and then rebounds after it occurs. Moreover, divorced people with a new partner have well-being levels that are similar to well-being levels of individuals who remained married (Lucas, 2005).

It is important to note that the example of divorce also provides some evidence that subjective measures provide novel information that economic indicators cannot reveal. Divorce usually has negative consequences for an individual's income, especially for women. Thus, the trajectory of economic well-being varies quite a bit from the trajectory of subjective well-being before and after divorce. Therefore, the actual behavior of choosing to get a divorce is only rational if we consider the effects of the divorce on the subjective measures. People who get divorced after a bad marriage act rationally in terms of this behavior's effect on their subjective well-being, even if the action has the consequence of lowering their economic well-being. The behavior only appears irrational when income is used as the sole indicator of an individuals' well-being.

Suicide

The above sections examined the links between well-being measures and two variables—relationships and income—that most theories predict should be related with the underlying construct of well-being. In addition to examining the predictors of well-being, it is also possible to identify known groups of individuals who would be expected to exhibit low levels of life satisfaction. One particularly salient group consists of those who attempt or commit suicide. Presumably, if individuals are willing to take their own life, there must be something that they perceive to be terrible about that life. Therefore, we expect that those who succeed at or even attempt suicide should report lower levels of well-being than those who do not. Again, this would not be a headline-making finding; rather it is a basic demonstration that the measures capture something that matches our theories about well-being.

It is undisputed that clinical depression is a strong predictor of suicide especially in males (Blair-West, Cantor, Mellsop, & Eyeson-Annon, 1999). In these studies, depression is typically assessed with a clinical interview. Although clinical interviews differ from self-report measures of well-being, they also require willingness and ability of individuals to report their subjective states accurately. Furthermore, clinically diagnosed depression is highly correlated with shorter self-report measures of depression, and depression is highly correlated with more common well-being measures such as life satisfaction judgments (Schimmack, Oishi, Furr, & Funder, 2004). In addition, direct evidence shows that well-being measures predict suicide. Koivumaa-Honkanen et al. (2001) examined suicide in a nationwide sample of 29,173 respondents. Participants completed a four-item well-being measure (interest in life, happiness, ease of living, and loneliness) at baseline, and then they were followed for 20 years. The well-being measure was a significant predictor of suicide risk; odds ratios were increased by a factor of 4. Specifically, 1 out of 100 men with average or high levels of well-being at baseline committed suicide, whereas 4 out of 100 men in the low satisfaction group committed suicide.

The increase in risk was higher in the short term (first 10 years) than in the long term (second 10 years). In other words, how happy a person is predicts whether he or she will commit suicide in the near future better than it predicts whether he or she will commit suicide in the distant future. This finding suggests that changes in well-being over time are associated with changes in suicide risks. If a person is extremely dissatisfied with life right now but survives past this risky period to a time when life gets better, the initial low well-being does not lead to much of an increase in suicide risk. This is important because it suggests that there is something beyond just a temperamental trait toward unhappiness and depression that is being assessed in these measures and whatever this additional component is predictive of the outcome of suicide. If suicide were entirely determined by the stable trait component of well-being, risks should be the same over short and long time intervals.

This study also showed clear evidence that the correlation between well-being and suicide was attenuated by measurement error. For a large subsample ($n = 21,329$), well-being was assessed twice, six years apart. The combining information of both measures increased the prediction of suicide risk.

The relation between well-being and suicide was nonlinear. There were relatively small differences between groups with high to moderate levels of well-being and large differences between groups with moderate to low levels of well-being. This finding also reveals that suicide rates are an inappropriate well-being indicator because they fail to discriminate between individuals who are merely not dissatisfied and those who are extremely satisfied. Furthermore, suicidal intent is such a low base rate activity that it cannot serve as a single well-being measure of the general population.

One limitation of this study as a validation study of well-being measures is that the four-item scale includes common well-being measures (happiness) as well as less common items (loneliness). This limitation was addressed by a subsequent study on the same sample that used only the happiness item to predict suicide (Koivumaa-Honkanen, Honkanen, Koskenvuo, & Kaprio, 2003). This study not only replicated the finding that well-being predicts suicide, it also showed a surprisingly linear relation between happiness and suicide risk, with risks increasing for each response category from 1.0 for the highest level (reference group) to 2.73, 4.64, 6.69, and 10.84 to the lowest category. The article also reports that happiness has the strongest predictive validity of the four items used in the well-being scale.

Regarding AWB, Weitoft and Rosen (2005) demonstrated the predictive validity of a single anxiety item ("Do you possibly have any of these: inconvenience with nervousness, uneasiness, and anxiety?") for suicide attempts in a large Swedish sample ($N = 34,511$). Together these studies provide strong evidence that those who appear to be very dissatisfied with the state of their lives actually do report lower well-being on standard well-being measures. The use of a behavioral outcome like suicide provides a strong test of the validity of these measures. The ability of subjective measures to predict suicide, which is an important objective indicator of nations' well-being before people commit suicide, suggests that national accounts of subjective measures are useful to plan policies aimed at preventing suicides. Pavot and Diener (1993) reviewed related mental health studies that examine life satisfaction. They found that people seeing a psychologist for problems reported low life satisfaction, and that people hospitalized for mental problems reported very low life satisfaction. It is noteworthy that outpatients' life satisfaction rose after their therapy was complete, although not to the levels typically seen in community samples.

Domain Satisfaction and the Links with Behavior Change

The same theory that links overall life satisfaction to suicide also suggests a link between satisfaction and behavior/choice in specific life domains. In the work domain, low satisfaction with work should predict higher turnover. A meta-analysis provides empirical support for this prediction (Tett & Meyer, 1993). The corrected average correlation between job satisfaction and turnover across 49 samples ($N = 13,722$) was $r = -.25$ (95% CI $= -.29$ to $-.21$) (uncorrected $r = -.15$). A newer meta-analysis obtained a slightly lower estimate, $r = -.19$ (Griffeth, Hom, & Gaertner, 2000). It is noteworthy that turnover is a heavily skewed dichotomous variable. As a result, a correlation coefficient underestimates the effect of low job satisfaction on turnover.

Furthermore, it is noteworthy that the availability of alternative jobs is another significant predictor of turnover (Griffeth et al., 2000). This finding suggests that subjective satisfaction measures might be better indicators of work-related well-being than an objective measure of turnover. That is because some workers will remain in unsatisfying jobs because they lack the freedom to choose a better alternative. The subjective domain or satisfaction measure would pick up on the differences in work-related well-being, regardless of the actual behavior.

It is also possible to examine the links between specific job characteristics and well-being, though the theoretical links are not quite as straightforward for these associations as they are for the links between well-being and turnover. For example, some workers may enjoy high autonomy, whereas others may prefer a job with clearly assigned roles. But one characteristic that is likely to be universally valued is high pay. Although work may be intrinsically enjoyable, few people are willing to do the same work for free because one of the main functions of work is to allow a person to make a living. Thus, it seems plausible that higher paying jobs produce more satisfaction because they fulfill a common goal more effectively. Perhaps surprisingly, we found few studies that tested this prediction. One study with a single-item job satisfaction measure supported the prediction (Weaver, 1977). In this study, job satisfaction for individuals with pay below 10,000 dollars in 1974 dollar terms was notably lower than job satisfaction for workers receiving more than 15,000 dollars. Although study of a national representative sample in Britain found no relation between income and job satisfaction (Clark & Oswald, 1996), an examination of this relation in the German Socio-Economic Panel shows a small but robust correlation ($N = 3,949$). Pay in 2006 and 2007 are highly positively related, $r = .91$. Job satisfaction ratings also show stability, $r = .55$. Correlations between pay and job satisfaction range from .09 to .12 both in the same year and across years (Schimmack, 2008).

Job level or job prestige provides another theoretical link between objective job characteristics and job satisfaction. Social scientists have developed elaborate classification systems of jobs that imply an evaluation of jobs from more positive (higher levels) to more negative (lower levels). If this objective classification of jobs is valid, workers with higher-level jobs should have higher job satisfaction than workers with lower-level jobs. This prediction is also consistent with the economic argument that people are willing to invest time and other resources to obtain more valued goods, and many students invest resources to increase their chances to get higher-level jobs. A meta-analysis of the relation between job level and job satisfaction supports this prediction (Robie, Ryan, Schmieder, Parra, & Smith, 1998).

The same theory that links job satisfaction and income predicts an even higher correlation between income and income satisfaction (also known as pay and pay satisfaction). A meta-analysis confirms this prediction with an average corrected correlation of $r = .29$ across 64 samples ($N = 29,754$) (Williams, McDaniel, & Nguyen, 2006).

Finally, the same processes that might motivate people who are satisfied with their job to change this job may also motivate change in other domains. Housing satisfaction is systematically related to moving. In the years before moving, housing satisfaction of individuals is lower than housing satisfaction of those who do not move. Housing satisfaction dramatically increases during the year of the move. It then decreases, but remains higher than in the years before people moved. Moreover, housing satisfaction is systematically related to the size and the quality of a home (Nakazato, Schimmack, & Oishi, 2008).

Summary

The procedures for assessing and evaluating the quality of measures are straightforward and uncontroversial. If a gold-standard measure already existed and researchers wanted to know whether a new measure is a good one, they could simply compare the responses they obtain from the new measure with the responses from the old measure. If these responses correlate highly, then the new measure would appear to be a good one. If no gold-standard measure exists—as is the case with subjective well-being—the process is a bit more complicated. We would compare the results that we get from the new measure to our expectations for how the measure should behave based on our theories of the underlying construct, as well as with other established measures.

It is clear that standard well-being measures pass the basic tests described above. The measures themselves are reliable and valid enough to provide information about individual's well-being. Any weaknesses that they have in this regard can be corrected with careful research design, appropriate analytic techniques, and informed interpretation of results. Furthermore, many well-being measures (particularly those that are designed to measure the same thing, whether that be life satisfaction, a particular domain satisfaction, or affective feelings) exhibit considerable convergence with one another. This means that they are tapping into some common underlying construct. More importantly, the standard self-report measures that will likely be used in national accounts of well-being often converge with measures that use techniques other than self-report. This is particularly impressive given the concerns about the subjective, internal nature of the well-being construct.

Well-being measures also behave as they would be expected to behave given widely accepted ideas about what well-being is. It would be unreasonable to expect those in abject poverty to report well-being levels that were as high as the richest individuals in the richest nations in the world. And research consistently shows that money matters for well-being. National levels of wealth correlate strongly with national average levels of subjective well-being; within-nation correlations are almost always positive, though small in size; and careful analyses show that even with small correlations, the rich are considerably happier than the poor. At the same time as we would expect, not every rich person has high life satisfaction. Diener, Horwitz, and Emmons (1985) found that several of the extremely wealthy people they studied had low life satisfaction. Although more theoretical questions about the links between money and well-being remain (e.g., "Are the rich happier than those who have basic needs met?"), this most basic theoretical principle seems to be supported by a vast amount of empirical research. The other research reviewed in this chapter shows that other variables and characteristics that would be expected to be linked with well-being are in fact associated with it.

It is important to note that our review of the evidence in support of the validity of well-being measures in this chapter is not complete. In the rest of this book, we refer to additional evidence regarding these standard principles for validating measures in the context of more substantive questions about well-being. For instance, in Chapter 6, we present considerable evidence that additional life circumstances like health and disability status are linked with well-being in predictable ways. Again, some of these empirical findings go beyond basic validation work, but, in general, they support the quality of the measures while testing additional hypotheses.

It is also clear from our review that additional work needs to be conducted. One of the unfortunate consequences of the economists' early assumption that well-being measures could not be valid is that many opportunities for testing validity were missed. Many large-scale studies that currently exist could easily have included well-being measures, but they did not. Only recently has the inclusion of such measures become more common (see Chapter 12). As more and more large-scale studies are conducted, the evidence is building that well-being measures have sufficient validity to use them to make new empirical discoveries about the determinants of well-being that can be useful for innovations in public policy.

Chapter 6

Issues Regarding the Use of Well-Being Measures for Policy

Even if well-being measures are reliable and valid, concerns may be raised about the extent to which these measures will be useful in policy settings. For instance, assume that well-being measures could perfectly capture an individual's subjective sense that his or her life is going well. We might find that subjective reports correspond perfectly both to observer reports and to some underlying physiological state, which would support the belief that participants were not lying when they reported their well-being. Furthermore, we might find that people who are satisfied with their life do the things we would expect them to do—they might have high levels of energy, which would allow them to function well at work; they might feel positive toward others, which could lead to strong social relationships; and they might be less likely to experience depression, commit suicide, or suffer from stress-related symptoms and diseases. If such conditions were true, we could be quite confident that subjective reports of well-being tap a meaningful underlying construct that has real implications for the conditions in a person's life. Yet even under these ideal conditions, objections could still be raised about the utility of well-being measures for policy decisions.

One major objection is that even if well-being measures are reliable and valid, the construct itself—the well-being of an individual—is something that policy decisions are unlikely to change. For instance, if well-being is strongly determined by inborn genetic factors, then the individual differences that exist would not result from external conditions, but from personality influences. If so, then changing the conditions in a person's life would lead to very little change in well-being. Similarly, it is possible that well-being judgments are responsive to external circumstances, but they are inherently comparative. In other words, well-being may result not from a direct evaluation of the objective conditions in a person's life, but from the comparison an individual makes between those conditions and various other standards including a person's past experiences, his or her future expectations, or comparisons with relevant others. Again, if well-being resulted from such comparison processes, then broad changes at the societal level would have little hope of affecting average levels of well-being. Objective conditions could change, but comparison processes could prevent well-being measures—and the actual state of well-being that individuals experience—from following suit.

If subjective responses to the environment inevitably return to some baseline level (through personality or comparison processes), it is possible that even those individuals in the worst imaginable conditions may actually be found to be as happy as those in the best possible circumstances. If true, then at best, using survey research to examine the predictors of well-being would not be fruitful. At worst, these surveys could be used to justify keeping people in undesirable circumstances. For instance, one could argue that if our best scientific methods show that the destitute are satisfied in what would appear to be less than ideal circumstances, policy makers should not be concerned with improving their standard of living. Alternatively, if low aspiration levels keep well-being high, governments could quickly and cheaply increase well-being simply by lowering expectations. This possibility has provided the motivation for some to adopt a functioning or capabilities approach as an alternative to subjective well-being. Such approaches develop lists of objective conditions that must be met for a life to be considered good.

These and other concerns are understandable, but the extent to which they affect the use of well-being measures in policy discussions depends on the empirical evidence demonstrating these effects. We believe that many of the concerns about the power of these processes result from a misreading of the psychological literature on these topics. In the current chapter, we discuss the expectations one should have for well-being measures based on both theories and intuitions about the links between well-being and external circumstances. We then review the psychological and economic literature on adaptation and comparison effects.

What Should Our Well-Being Measures Do?

Before judging whether the existing empirical evidence supports the idea that adaptation and comparison effects are so strong as to make well-being a poor guide for policy, we must ask what we should expect from these measures. Specifically, when considering expectations for the associations between well-being measures and external circumstances, there is some amount of tension between the belief that these associations should match intuition and the belief that well-being measures should tell us something novel. For instance, Diener and Seligman (2004) argued that one important reason for moving beyond income and other economic indicators as the criteria against which policy decisions should be based is that income and well-being are moderately correlated. In other words, well-being measures tell us something new about a person's life that objective information about his or her economic situation cannot, and that is why they have value. On the other hand, the relatively low correlation between income and well-being measures has also been used as evidence for the fact that these indicators have limited utility. For instance, Schwarz and Strack (1999) argued that the consistently weak correlations between well-being and intuitively appealing predictors means that the measures themselves are probably wrong. Schwarz and Strack were essentially arguing that if well-being measures really do assess what laypeople mean by happiness, life satisfaction, or well-being, then these measures should be responsive to external circumstances. In other words, the associations that are found should match our intuitions about the factors that affect well-being. If someone who is destitute says that he or she is happy, then this violates our intuition about what is required for a good life, and thus we may want to reject the answer that these subjective measures provide, even when the measures themselves appear to be reliable and valid.

What one really wants out of a well-being measure is some middle ground between these two extremes. It would be disconcerting if those who were living in conditions that were widely agreed upon as being negative reported well-being levels that were equivalent to those living in more privileged states, even if we could show that these reports were reliable and valid. Any measure that consistently contradicted intuitions about the effects of life circumstances would likely be of little use in influencing public policy. Conversely, the value of these measures would be quite limited if they only confirmed what we already knew. Therefore, well-being measures will be most valuable when they behave in ways that often match our intuition, but also provide novel insights about the relative importance of distinct life circumstances.

In raising this issue, we alert readers to a major point about existing accounts of the state of literature. As noted above, there is a tension between the belief that well-being judgments are constructed in a relatively intuitive manner and the idea that counterintuitive processes guide these judgments. Those interested in developing theories of well-being often focus on and emphasize the latter, because counterintuitive findings often provide stronger tests of underlying theories than do relatively intuitive commonsense findings. But this may bias theoretical researchers in the direction of accepting relatively rare but intriguing counterintuitive findings, even when more mundane commonsense findings are more common and robust. We believe that this has occurred in the well-being literature, and this bias has resulted in a skewed picture of the factors that influence well-being.

Adaptation and the Hedonic Treadmill

One of the strongest objections to the use of well-being measures concerns the possibility that people adapt to life circumstances (Haybron, 2008). The theory of adaptation is based on an analogy to human's sensory perception. Imagine walking into a darkened house after being outside around noon on a bright, sunny day. At first, you might have a hard time seeing. After a few minutes, the eyes adapt to the darkened room and you begin to see again. Similarly, if you step out of a darkened room into the bright sunlight, visual perception is first impaired. After some time, the sensory system adjusts to the new conditions, and it functions as well outside on a bright sunny day as it does inside the darkened room. Adaptation theories assume that similar processes influence individuals' evaluations of their lives. If life gets objectively better, evaluation standards increase as well, thus neutralizing any well-being gains. If life gets objectively worse, evaluation standards decrease, again neutralizing well-being losses. As a result, an individual with an objectively good life has the same subjective well-being as an individual with an objectively bad life. Moreover, both individuals have high well-being because their standards adapt to their actual lives, leading to favorable evaluations independent of any variation in objective life circumstances.

There is no doubt that some amount of adaptation does occur as adaptation processes are evident in a wide variety of psychological phenomena. As Frederick and Loewenstein (1999) pointed out, adaptation protects people from potentially dangerous psychological and physiological consequences of prolonged emotional states. In other words, emotional reactions are functional in the short term, but they have a cost in the long run (Sapolsky, 1994). Adaptation allows for the short-term benefits of these emotional reactions, while preventing the long-term damage. In addition, adaptation processes allow unchanging stimuli to fade into the attentional background. This ensures that changing stimuli (which are most likely to be important) receive more attention than constant stimuli. Rayo and Becker (2007) offered an evolutionary explanation of why adaptation processes are likely to occur. They argued that physiological limitations require that organisms make relative judgments rather than absolute judgments. Thus, relative judgments are always made in the context of some standard, and this facilitates adaptation.

Four robust findings have been used to support the idea that adaptation exists (Diener, Suh, Lucas, & Smith, 1999). First, although intuition would suggest that life circumstances such as income, health, age, and a variety of other demographic characteristics should influence well-being, the associations between these variables and well-being tend to be relatively small. Second, in comparison to these small associations with external circumstances, correlations with stable personality characteristics can be large. Third, well-being itself is stable over time, even in the face of changing life circumstances. And finally, well-being—particularly the stable component of well-being—is partially heritable. These robust findings, combined with some particularly salient studies that purport to show adaptation to even the most extreme life circumstances, have been used to argue that individuals are stuck on a *hedonic treadmill* (e.g., Brickman & Campbell, 1971). According to this perspective, we can strive toward greater well-being by accomplishing goals and acquiring desired outcomes, but we inevitably adapt to these changes and end up no happier than we initially were.

There is little doubt that well-being is influenced by stable internal factors such as the personality that one was born with, and that some amount of adaptation occurs. This fact should temper expectations about the size of the effects that one can reasonably expect from an intervention or policy decision. However, the question that policy makers must ask is whether these effects are so strong as to rule out the possibility of meaningful change. In other words, even if well-being is stable, can noticeable improvements be made? Recent research examining these issues shows that change is in fact possible. Thus, the robust research findings that are often used as evidence that well-being cannot change must be reconsidered in a new light.

Take the example of the heritability of well-being. The most common way to assess the influence of genes is to conduct twin studies, where the similarity of well-being across pairs of identical twins is compared to the similarity of well-being across pairs of fraternal twins. Identical twins share 100% of their genes, whereas fraternal twins share 50% of their genes. Therefore, if identical twins were more similar than fraternal twins, this would imply genetic effects. In the best of these studies, some of the twins in the sample are reared in separate households so the effect of shared environment can also be isolated.

Twin studies consistently show that a substantial amount of the variance in well-being can be explained by genes. Furthermore, studies that examine twins raised apart rarely find evidence for shared environment effects. In perhaps the most striking study examining the heritability of well-being, Lykken and Tellegen (1996) examined twins on two occasions separated by 10 years. They showed that when only the variance that was stable across that 10-year period was examined, the heritability rose to 80%. Findings like this have led some to conclude that attempts to change well-being may not be successful.

However, there are a number of facts to remember when interpreting heritability estimates. First, it is often assumed that because we cannot change our genes, heritability coefficients provide an estimate of the proportion of well-being that cannot be changed. But this is not the case. Genes code for proteins, and these proteins guide the development of the structures of the body. Specific differences in these structures have wide-ranging effects on the behavior of the organism. But the effects of genes on well-being must flow through some mediating process, and these mediating processes may vary in the extent to which they are amenable to change. For instance, some genes may directly affect the physiological systems that govern emotional reactivity. Individuals who have highly reactive negative emotional systems may respond more negatively to unpleasant life circumstances. Such effects may be relatively stable. Other genes, however, may affect well-being indirectly. For instance, the tendency to marry or divorce has been shown to be heritable, and the genetic effects on well-being may flow through these life decisions. Presumably, if marital status were the causal mechanism, and policy changes affected decisions to marry or divorce (we know, for instance, that marriage rates vary considerably across cultures), the causal chain flowing from genes to well-being could be interrupted. Thus, until the precise mechanisms that underlie genetic effects are known, it is possible that interventions could affect the mediating processes by which genes affect well-being. One should certainly avoid the temptation to say that if well-being is 50% heritable, there is only 50% left that can be changed (Diener, 2008).

Heritability estimates alone tell us little about the possibility for change in a population. As noted behavior geneticist Michael Rutter has stated, estimates of heritability "provide no unambiguous implications for theory, policy, or practice" (1997; p. 391). To be sure, this research reveals that something that individuals are born with affects their later well-being. In addition, behavioral genetic studies can help clarify the processes that lead to increased well-being. But even very high heritability does not mean that change is impossible or that policy will not be effective. The best case for this position comes from research on intelligence. IQ scores appear to be approximately 75% heritable among adults (Neisser et al., 1996). Yet in spite of this remarkably high heritability, there have been dramatic increases in IQ over the past 100 years (Dickens & Flynn, 2001). Mean levels of IQ have increased with more and better education (along with other changes in modern living), even if individual differences in IQ at any one time are strongly heritable. Well-being, even if substantially heritable, may be similarly amenable to change. Differences in well-being across nations suggest that societal changes could result in substantial changes in average levels of happiness.

With reference to inherited characteristics, it is useful to consider the impact of environmental factors in various areas to see the influence that policies can have even on highly heritable attributes. The following characteristics are all heritable to some degree: longevity, weight, height, and divorce—yet, the circumstances in a society heavily affect each of these. For example, height is extremely heritable, and yet nutritional factors such as protein intake and calorie availability can have a large effect on height, and average height can increase dramatically when there is an increase in protein in peoples' diets. In part, this is a reflection of the fact that heritability estimates are usually established within societies and therefore do not reflect the influence of broad societal factors that influence virtually everyone in the society where the study is conducted, but which could vary substantially between societies. Thus, heritabilities tell us little about the potential impact of societal changes on well-being.

It is important to keep in mind that heritability studies are often interpreted to be important because they tell us something about stability. However, as discussed above, the links between heritability and stability are not direct, and a clearer way to address questions about stability is to examine this issue directly. For instance, Lykken and Tellegen concluded that 80% of the stable component of happiness is heritable, which meant that "trying to be happier [may be] as futile as trying to be taller" (1996; p. 189). However, the important issue for policy decisions is not the extent to which the stable part is heritable, but the extent to which well-being is stable in the first place. If the stable component makes up only a small proportion of the total amount of variance, then it does not matter how heritable that component is because a considerable amount of change is occurring. In contrast, if the stability of well-being measures is perfect, then it does not matter whether this stability is due to early environment or to genetic factors. If well-being cannot change, it cannot change, regardless of whether the stability is based in biology or early childhood upbringing. Ultimately, questions about the extent to which well-being can change should be resolved not by reference to twin studies or other methods that shed light on heritability, but by studies that directly address the issue of stability over time.

Fortunately, numerous studies have examined this question, and these studies consistently show that well-being measures show a moderate amount of stability, but it is far from perfect. For instance, a number of researchers have used large-scale panel studies to assess the stability of well-being measures over very long periods of time. Fujita and Diener (2005) examined 17 years of data from the German Socio-Economic Panel (GSOEP) Study. Year-to-year stabilities were moderately high—around .50 or .60—but these coefficients dropped off with increasing lengths of time. Over the 17 years of the study, stability coefficients were approximately .30.

Others have used these data to model the stable component more explicitly. For instance, Lucas and Donnellan (2007; also see Ehrhardt, Saris, & Veenhoven, 2000) used structural equation modeling techniques to isolate the component of each person's well-being scores that was stable over the 21-year period they examined. They found that approximately 34% of the variance in any one occasion could be accounted for by a stable trait that did not change over the course of the study (Ehrhardt et al. estimated that about 29% of the variance was stable). Lucas and Donnellan also replicated this finding in a second panel study (the British Household Panel Study), where they found that about 38% of the variance was stable over the course of the nine-year study. Together, these results suggest that about one-third of the variance in a single administration of a life satisfaction measure is stable variance that does not change, even over very long periods of times. This means that long-term stabilities will likely bottom out around .30. To be sure, these correlations are depressed somewhat by measurement error, but given that year-to-year correlations are much higher (around .60), this indicates that real change is occurring over the years.

Moderate stability over long periods of time is theoretically important and impressive. It suggests that individuals do carry something with them that remains constant even with changing life circumstances (for a more direct examination of this issue see Costa, McCrae, & Zonderman, 1987). However, it is not the case that the stabilities are perfect and that deviations from perfect stability result solely from measurement error. Furthermore, when compared to the stability coefficients for personality traits, it becomes clear that well-being is less stable than these other characteristics. For instance, Fujita and Diener (2005) compared the stability of life satisfaction in the GSOEP to the stability of personality as estimated in a meta-analysis by Roberts and DelVecchio (2000). Stability coefficients were similar in the short term (e.g., one-year stabilities), but they diverged over the long term. Stability dropped off more quickly in the life satisfaction measure than in the personality traits. Thus, although there is some degree of stability in well-being, well-being is more malleable than personality, which itself is not perfectly stable over time.

Although issues regarding the heritability and stability of well-being are somewhat relevant when considering the use of these measures in policy decisions, some of the most salient concerns arise from studies examining the effects of major life events on well-being. It has often been said that people's capacity for adaptation is so strong that even extreme events have little effect on well-being. For instance, in one of the most famous studies in the well-being literature, Brickman, Coates, and Janoff-Bulman (1978) examined happiness ratings among a group of lottery winners, a group of patients with spinal-cord injuries, and a control group. Although one common interpretation of this study is that the three groups did not differ from one another (demonstrating the power of adaptation processes), this is a mistake. It is true that the small group of lottery winners ($N = 22$) was only slightly and nonsignificantly happier than the small group of controls ($N = 22$), but this was not true for the comparison of patients and controls. As Brickman et al. noted, those in the spinal-cord-injured group were significantly less happy than controls and lottery winners. Furthermore, these significant differences were actually quite large in size. However, many have interpreted the differences to be small because Brickman et al. concluded that the participants from the spinal-cord-injured group were not as unhappy as one might expect. Our point is worth repeating—although many have interpreted the Brickman et al. study as evidence for adaptation, it actually shows that those who have experienced an extreme negative event are substantially less happy than groups who have not experienced such an event. Furthermore, the findings from the Brickman et al. study have been replicated in just about every study that has examined similar groups (Lucas, 2007).

This conclusion raises an issue that both researchers and policy makers must wrestle with when interpreting the literature on well-being—how big must an effect be for it to be meaningful? In the Brickman et al. (1978) study, the average happiness score among those with spinal-cord injuries was 2.96 on a scale that ranged from 0 to 5. The controls reported an average score of 3.82, and the lottery winners reported an average score of 4.00. It is probably unreasonable to expect the average score for any group of people to be much higher than a 4 on a scale that ranges from 0 to 5 (for at least some of these people may also have health problems, relationship difficulties, or other negative circumstances that would prevent them from being perfectly happy), and therefore the scores of the lottery winners are probably not that surprising. However, the fact that those with spinal-cord injuries are not at the extreme end of the scale has been surprising to some. Unfortunately, raw scale score differences are difficult to interpret, and therefore an alternative metric is needed to interpret these effects.

It is often useful to translate raw scores into standardized scores, so differences can be interpreted relative to the amount of variance that exists in the sample. Specifically, researchers often use d-metric effect sizes, where differences are reported in standard deviation units. In normally distributed variables, 68% of people fall within one standard deviation above and below the mean of that distribution. Thus, if someone moves from the mean score to a score that is one standard deviation above the mean, we know that she has moved from the 50th percentile to the 84th percentile. In other words, this person has moved from being average in well-being to one of the happiest people in the sample. Alternatively, if we consider two groups, one of which has a mean well-being score that is one standard deviation above the mean of the other, then we know that the average person from the happier group reports well-being scores that are higher than those of 84% of the members of the lower group. Thus, standard deviation units and the d-metric effect size are useful because they have a relatively intuitive interpretation. Of course, some judgment is still required when interpreting whether a particular d-metric effect is large and important or not, as even very small effects can be important in many instances. But social scientists often cite the rules of thumb that effect sizes of 0.2, 0.5, and 0.8 be considered to be small, medium, and large, respectively (Cohen, 1988).

When examined in the context of standardized mean differences, we see that the effects reported in the Brickman et al. (1978) study are in fact quite large. Individuals in the spinal-cord-injured group reported happiness scores that were approximately eight-tenths of a standard deviation lower than the mean of the control group. This means that the average control participant was happier than approximately 79% of the participants in the spinal-cord-injured group, and the difference between the injured group and the lottery winners was even larger. It is possible to debate whether these effects are as large as one might expect, but the main point is that relative to the amount of variance that exists in well-being measures, the effect of the injury was quite large.

Importantly, this finding has been replicated quite often. For instance, in 1997, Dijkers compiled a review of existing studies in which participants with spinal-cord injuries reported subjective well-being. The nine effect sizes that could be calculated from the Dijkers' data were 0.18, 0.40, 0.56, 0.61, 0.76, 0.76, 0.99, 1.02, and 1.26. Consistent with our reinterpretation of Brickman et al.'s (1978) study, most studies show medium to large effects when comparing spinal-cord-injured patients to control groups or population norms. Furthermore, even within a single study, there is variance in the reactions that people have. Patients who are classified as having spinal-cord injuries may vary considerably in the symptoms they show, and those with relatively minor symptoms may reduce the overall effect. In support of this idea, Dijkers (1999) found that among those with spinal-cord injuries, those who had 100% mobility reported life satisfaction scores that were only slightly lower than population norms (ds around 0.25). However, once mobility is restricted, effects become much larger. Those with high but limited mobility, moderate mobility, and low mobility reported scores that were approximately 0.85, 1.10, and 1.58 standard deviations below population norms, respectively.

Of course, correlational studies cannot determine whether these conditions actually cause the differences in well-being that are found. Those who experience disabling conditions may have some characteristics that predisposed them to experience both low well-being and the disabling circumstance. And because experimental designs are impossible with this type of life event, the best evidence for the causal effect of disability on well-being comes from prospective longitudinal studies (though even these cannot establish causality definitively). Lucas (2007) used two nationally representative panel studies to examine the association between the onset of a disability and changes in life satisfaction. Individuals who began the study without a disability, acquired a disability at some point in the study, and then retained that disability until the most recent wave of data collection was examined. Before the onset of their disability, these individuals reported levels of life satisfaction that were no different than population norms. But consistent with the results from cross-sectional studies, those who experienced a lasting disability reported declines in life satisfaction that were on average 0.60 standard deviations from their initial baseline level. Importantly, in one of the two studies, information about the severity of the disability was available, and those with the most severe disabilities reported declines of 1.20 standard deviations from their initial baseline level. Thus, research consistently shows that spinal-cord injuries and other disabilities are associated with medium to large differences in subjective well-being. And although we can never say for sure that the disabilities themselves caused these differences, the prospective longitudinal studies show that at the very least, the differences between those with disabilities and those without disabilities are not due to preexisting differences in well-being.

Health problems are not the only domain in which life events and life circumstances matter for subjective well-being. For instance, our research examining within-person change in life satisfaction following major life events shows that people experience lasting changes from early baselines following a single bout of unemployment (Lucas, Clark, Georgellis, & Diener, 2004). This effect (which is consistent with a large body of cross-sectional research) was evident even though the participants in our sample had become reemployed. Similarly, individuals who experience divorce do bounce back from the low point of satisfaction that they experienced at the end of their failed marriage, but they do not come back quickly or fully to their premarriage levels (Lucas, 2005). Other events, like widowhood, do result in eventual adaptation. However, this adaptation process can take quite a long time—on average eight years. So even in cases where adaptation does occur, the effects of the life event are seen for quite a long time in the reports of well-being.

Recently, we proposed an updated model that added several revisions to the basic set-point idea that people adapt to most life events (Diener, Lucas, & Scollon, 2006). First, based on research like that reviewed above, we suggested that there is no single answer to the question of whether adaptation occurs. Instead, it appears that adaptation processes vary considerably across life events. At least in the German sample that we investigated, people adapted to marriage relatively quickly, whereas adaptation to widowhood took much longer. Adaptation to divorce, disability, and unemployment in this large sample was never complete. In addition, the changes from baseline that occurred for the events that were associated with lasting changes differed, suggesting that well-being measures are responsive to differences among life events.

In addition, a pattern that emerged in all the analyses we conducted was that adaptation effects varied considerably among the individuals that we examined. For instance, in the case of marriage, the average effect was adaptation back to the original baseline—on average, participants ended up no more satisfied after their marriage than they were before the marriage. However, there was considerable variability in this effect. Some people appeared to have large and lasting positive effects after they became married. However, these gains were balanced by people who declined in life satisfaction following their marriage and remained at that lowered level over time. Thus, the lack of an association between marriage and lasting changes in well-being may not result from adaptation. This null result may simply reflect the fact that most life events vary in the implications that they have for individuals. Especially for positive events like marriage, the objective changes that occur in the person's life may include a mix of positive, neutral, and negative circumstances. Thus, an examination of the individual variability in these events may provide a better technique for examining the potential effects that life events may have on measures of subjective well-being.

Research on life events and subjective well-being shows that people are surprisingly resilient. Well-being scores tend to fall above the theoretical neutral point of the scales that are used, even among people who have experienced traumatic life events. Furthermore, we know that people are bad at affective forecasting. If you ask laypeople to predict how happy they would be if they experienced a variety of unfortunate life circumstances, in most cases they overpredict the impact of these events and assume that they will be miserable. The research findings that contradict these predictions are important and impressive and demonstrate the remarkable resilience that people have. However, it is important not to interpret evidence regarding resilience and misprediction as evidence that adaptation has occurred. In many cases, evidence for either of the former phenomena does not bear on the question of adaptation. Furthermore, although it might be an interesting exercise to compare people's predictions regarding the effect of life circumstances to the actual data, the fact that people mispredict does not mean that the effects themselves are small. For 30 years, psychologists have been mistakenly repeating the idea that adaptation to spinal-cord injury and other disabilities is almost complete when there is almost no evidence that that is true. Research consistently shows that well-being is affected by life circumstances—particularly extreme life circumstances. Thus, although some amount of adaptation surely occurs, these effects are not so strong as to eliminate the benefits of well-being measures in a policy context.

An analogy to consider is that of adaptation to temperature. Well-being researchers often liken the process of adaptation to life events to the process of adaptation that occurs when we place our cold hand in warm water, or when we step inside a warm room from the cold outdoors. In these circumstances, some adaptation occurs. Water that once felt hot may eventually be experienced as only warm; a room that felt stifling may gradually become comfortable. Yet it is clear that complete adaptation to temperature occurs only within a relatively small range of the temperature continuum. For many people, indoor temperatures below 60 degrees Fahrenheit will be experienced as noticeably (and enduringly) too cold; whereas indoor temperatures above 80 degrees Fahrenheit will be experienced as noticeably too hot. We believe that the existing evidence suggests that adaptation to life events and life circumstances is similar.

Within a restricted range of events and circumstances, complete adaptation does occur. Furthermore, some relatively extreme events may become less extreme with increased experience. But the fact that these adaptation processes exist does not mean that the events and circumstances cannot change well-being in a lasting way. Existing evidence suggests that many life events and life circumstances are in fact linked to substantial differences in well-being scores.

A final concern that emerges when reviewing the literature on adaptation to life events concerns the extent to which positive life events matter. After hearing our research findings, many ask whether we have found any positive life events that have been shown to affect well-being. Of course, this is an important concern given that policy decisions are often designed to improve people's lives. It is true that the life events that have been shown to be associated with lasting changes in well-being in large-scale prospective studies tend to be negative, but there are two things to keep in mind when considering this concern. First, even if it were true that only negative circumstances show lasting effects on well-being, it should be possible to raise well-being by eliminating or undoing the negative events that led to these circumstances. Second, only a relatively small number of events thus far have been studied using rigorous methods, so it is possible that additional positive events that do affect well-being will eventually be found.

Furthermore, it is difficult to find major life events that are universally positive. As noted above, for example, we believe that one of the reasons why marriage is not associated with lasting positive changes is that marriages vary considerably in their quality. So it is not that marriages cannot produce lasting changes in well-being, it is just that marriage is not universally positive and many people actually experience declines following this life event. It is difficult to think of many positive life events for which this is not true. Negative events, on the other hand, are often universally negative. Although positive outcomes may result from negative events (e.g., people who experience a disability may meet a romantic partner in a support group), the event itself is usually universally experienced as negative. Thus, the lack of research findings in which positive events are shown to be associated with lasting changes should not be cause for pessimism when considering the use of well-being for policy purposes.

It is also important to distinguish between hedonic adaptation and adaptation of preferences. Many of the concerns about adaptation are based on studies of hedonic adaptation. For example, after receiving a transplant organ, patients report extremely high levels of positive affect. Over time, their affect levels reduce to normal levels. However, this process of hedonic adaptation does not imply that they evaluate the reception of a transplant any less positively than on the day they received the transplant. Hedonic adaptation is only problematic for objective definitions of well-being that make positive feelings the ultimate criterion to evaluate lives. In contrast, our subjective definition, as well as standard economic theories, suggests that people's well-being could increase after receiving a transplant organ, even if perfect hedonic adaptation occurred. Our definition is challenged only if patients who are waiting for a transplant organ and fail to get one would no longer want a transplant organ and their life satisfaction remained high. Thus, the findings we review on life satisfaction and adaptation are most central to our core definition of well-being, and do indicate that people often do not completely adapt to conditions.

Subjective Well-Being Is Susceptible to the Aspiration Spiral

A concern related to adaptation is what has been called the *aspiration spiral*. Some researchers have been concerned by the fact that objective indicators of well-being like income or a nation's gross domestic product suggest that well-being has increased considerably, whereas subjective measures have shown relatively little or no increases in well-being (Easterlin, 1974; Hagerty & Veenhoven, 2003), although this conclusion has recently been called into question (Inglehart, 2008; Stevenson & Wolfers, 2008). One interpretation of this finding is that objective life circumstances and aspirations rise in tandem, but well-being fails to increase because it is defined as the match between life circumstances and aspirations. Thus, objective measure of life circumstances would be better indicators of well-being.

The first problem with this interpretation is its implicit assumption that an objective standard can be used to determine whether lives have improved. An alternative explanation is that improvements in some aspects have been accompanied by negative changes in other aspects of people's lives. For example, the invention of air conditioning and TV has increased comfort and entertainment, but has decreased social relationships because fewer people are spending hot summer nights outside with their neighbors.

A more serious problem of this argument against a subjective definition of well-being is that it confuses aspirations with the evaluation standards of lives. Aspirations are directed at the future. Thus, they cannot be used to evaluate one's current or past life. It makes no sense to say that I am dissatisfied with the million dollars I made last year, because I want to make two million dollar next year. I am dissatisfied if I made one million dollars last year and would have liked to have made two million dollars last year. Similarly, it is possible to have high well-being in the presence of unfulfilled aspirations for the future. Currently having a million dollars and being satisfied with this amount does not mean that the person does not want to have more in the future. Thus, constantly increasing aspirations can coexist with high well-being.

The aspiration spiral is also limited to a few aspects of people's lives. Other aspects of people's lives that influence their well-being do not follow the pattern of an aspiration spiral. For example, once optimal levels of comfort and safety have been reached, people do not form higher aspirations.

Finally, it is possible that aspiration effects may reflect problems of subjective indicators rather than a subjective definition of well-being. For example, we pointed out that income is only an objective indicator that is based on a subjective definition of well-being. Thus, increased income suggests that well-being has actually increased. If subjective indicators do not show these increases, it is possible that the indicators are flawed. For example, if circumstances and evaluation standards rose, the distant past should be evaluated more positively than the present or recent past.

Social Comparison

In addition to concerns about adaptation, many have suggested that social comparison processes limit the role that well-being can play in policy decisions. Social comparison occurs when individuals refer to proximal or salient others as a standard of comparison when making well-being judgments. Social comparison effects could potentially be problematic for the use of well-being measures in policy decisions because policies that increased the standing of every member of a community would also raise the comparison standard. This would result in no overall change for the individuals within that community. Social comparison processes are one component of broader set of comparison processes that could be used to evaluate current circumstances. For instance, Michalos (1985) suggested that people have multiple discrepancies that they use to evaluate their lives, including discrepancies between current circumstances and (1) past circumstances, (2) expectations for future circumstances, and (3) ideal levels that might be affected by other goals and needs.

Discrepancy theories make sense because certain judgments are inherently comparative. For instance, if a person is interested in achieving status, this judgment is based on comparisons with others—a person only has high status relative to the other members of his or her community. Thus, satisfaction with this domain will necessarily be strongly influenced by social comparison processes. But there are questions about the extent to which factors such as income and health are inherently comparative. To be sure, one's expectations about his or her level of health may change with age, but there are still certain objective characteristics of poor health that could potentially affect well-being, even if they are normatively appropriate.

Thus, as with adaptation, questions remain about the strength of comparison processes relative to absolute effects. One must ask whether some absolute, noncomparative effects of a life circumstance exist. Then, the absolute and relative effects must be compared. For instance, a person with chronic pain may get a boost in life satisfaction if a new treatment reduces his or her level of pain in comparison to an earlier state, even if the pain is not cured entirely. But if the person still experiences pain in day-to-day life (even if at a reduced level), that daily unpleasant experience could still lower life satisfaction in an absolute sense. Thus, when evaluating social comparison effects, it is important to consider the domain in which they occur and to compare the relative to the absolute effects. As we will see, there is evidence that social comparison effects exist, but these effects are often quite complicated. Furthermore, there is no evidence that social comparison effects swamp absolute judgments when evaluating well-being.

Social comparison effects in well-being research constitute one line of work in a broader literature on comparison processes in social psychology (Festinger, 1954). Early models emphasized contrast effects, positing that people who were exposed to higher comparison standards would experience low well-being. People who were exposed to lower comparison standards would experience high well-being. Furthermore, early models posited that people would inevitably compare themselves to proximal and relevant others. A considerable amount of empirical work has been dedicated to testing these ideas. However, after decades of research, the early, relatively simple formulation of social comparison processes has been rejected. Modern comparison researchers believe that the process is more complicated than these original formulations suggested (Diener & Fujita, 1997).

For instance, it is now clear that the choice of comparison standard is somewhat flexible. Personality and goals may determine who a person chooses as a comparison standard, and sometimes this choice can even be made strategically as part of a coping process (Diener & Fujita, 1997). Gibbons, Benbow, and Gerrard (1994), for example, found that after failure, students reduced the amount of social comparison in which they engaged. This suggests that people can selectively attend to comparison standards depending on how these standards affect their well-being (also see Dutton & Brown, 1997). In support of this, Lyubomirsky and Ross (1997) found that temperamentally happy people tended to make downward comparisons (which serve to maintain their happiness), whereas temperamentally unhappy people tended to use both types of comparisons.

In addition to the specific choice of comparison target, the way that information is used varies across individuals depending on their personalities and goals. Consistent with early formulations of social comparison effects, an upward comparison might result in lowered satisfaction because the person who is making that comparison would see himself or herself as worse off than would be true if the comparison standard did not exist. Or alternatively, the upward comparison might result in elevated satisfaction because the comparer may see that standard as a realistic goal that he or she could achieve. In support of this idea, Buunk, Collins, Taylor, Van Yperen, and Dakof (1990) found that the direction of social comparisons does not always affect well-being in a consistent manner (also see Barrington-Leigh & Helliwell, 2008; Kingdon & Knight, 2007).

The social comparison research that is most relevant for discussions of policy decisions is research that relies on real-world comparison using representative data. Numerous studies have been conducted, and they seem to converge on the idea that some amount of social comparison occurs. Of course, there are caveats and unanswered questions, but social comparisons do seem to matter. For instance, Luttmer (2005) used a large sample of respondents from the United States to assess the effect of absolute and relative income on life satisfaction judgments. Specifically, he tested whether the income of one's neighbors (defined as a relatively large group of individuals living in the same geographic area) was negatively associated with life satisfaction after controlling for a person's absolute income. Luttmer was able to rule out a number of alternative explanations of the effect. For instance, if wealthier neighborhoods are associated with a higher cost of living, this factor may reduce the well-being of those living there. But Luttmer showed that even after controlling for such effects, neighborhood income negatively predicted well-being, meaning that a person's well-being suffered when his or her neighbors had greater incomes (also see Barrington-Leigh & Helliwell, 2008; Ferrer-i-Carbonell, 2005; Helliwell & Huang, 2009; Stutzer, 2004).

Importantly, the size of the absolute income effect in Luttmer's study (in terms of unstandardized regression coefficients) was no larger than the size of the neighborhood income effect. This means that increasing an entire neighborhood's income by the same amount would lead to no overall gain in well-being. However, one must be careful in interpreting these coefficients. The income standard deviations for aggregated units (like neighborhoods, cities, and states) are much smaller than the income standard deviations for individuals. For instance, in Luttmer's studies, the income standard deviation was three to four times as large for the individual data as for the neighborhood units. This means that the standardized effects of absolute income are much larger than the standardized effects of neighbors' incomes, which in turn means that absolute income likely accounts for more variance than relative income, even though the unstandardized coefficients are the same. Another related reason for exercising care when interpreting these comparison effects is that the underlying comparison people make is between their own permanent or expected income and that of their neighbors'. But their own current income is a noisy measure of their permanent income. This will tend to lower the coefficient on one's own income relative to that on comparison income, since the latter has been averaged enough to substantially reduce the amount of noise.

Importantly, we must consider the social comparison coefficients in the context of realistic scenarios of change. If a person received a pay raise that moved him or her from the mean household income to an income that was one standard deviation above the mean (say about a 45,000 dollar raise), the person would probably not move to a neighborhood that had a median income that was 45,000 dollars more than his or her previous neighborhood. Instead, the person would probably move to a neighborhood that reflected his or her new relative position. Thus, we might expect him or her to move to a neighborhood that was one standard deviation above the mean neighborhood income, which might only be 15,000 dollars more than the person's current neighborhood. This would mean that the overall net gain in terms of satisfaction would still be relatively large even with these comparison effects. Of course, this would not be true if the income of all individuals was raised, but our point is that the real-world implications of such social comparison studies are not as clear as the coefficients from studies like Luttmer's might initially suggest.

Additional studies have shown similar effects (e.g., Barrington-Leigh & Helliwell, 2008; Helliwell & Huang, 2009), but again, the implications for policy decisions are not always clear. For instance, Barrington-Leigh and Helliwell examined the effects of comparisons with groups of neighbors of various sizes in a large Canadian data set. Specifically, they compared the effect of a person's absolute income to the effects of the average income within his or her Dissemination Area (median population = 540), Census Tract (median population = 4,300), Census Subdivisions (which reflect city boundaries), Metropolitan Areas, and Provinces. Notably, social comparison effects varied across these different reference groups. For instance, although the effect of average Metropolitan Area income was consistently negative, the effect of Dissemination Area income (the smallest and most local reference group) was frequently (though not always) positive. These results are limited by the relatively small number of Metropolitan Areas, which makes it difficult to separate the effects of income from those of other factors that affect the quality of life in the richer cities. Using a larger set of controls tends to move the location of maximum negative comparison closer to home, to the level of the Census Tract.

Together, these studies show that social comparison processes are complex and not always straightforward. Laboratory studies show that simple contrast effects do not always emerge. Instead, people are quite flexible in terms of whom they choose as comparison standards and how they use that information. Naturalistic studies confirm this; both Barrington-Leigh and Helliwell (2008) and Kingdon and Knight (2007) showed that comparisons with different groups often result in different types of effects on well-being. Furthermore, although unstandardized effects of comparison standards have been found to be similar in size to the effects of absolute income, this may not be the only relevant comparison. Because income standard deviations for aggregated levels tend to be quite small relative to the standard deviations for absolute income of individuals, comparison standards may explain less variance than absolute income. Thus, although comparison effects surely exist, it is far from clear that these effects can outweigh those of absolute income or other objective circumstances.

More importantly, comparison effects are likely to be different for different aspects of life. Although the so-called *externalities* of material consumption may be negative, as indicated by positive life satisfaction effects from one's own income, and negative ones from neighborhood (or contextual) income, there is some evidence of positive externalities elsewhere. For example, Putnam (2001, p. 134) presents evidence suggesting that community levels of human and social capital tend to increase well-being, while level of community income reduces it, in all cases after allowing for the positive well-being effects of one's own human capital, social capital, and income, all of which have positive effects. Even though social comparisons might influence how much we eat or how frequently we have sex, these effects are likely to be small compared to our personal desires in these areas and the inherent pleasantness of the activities involved. In other words, social comparison might be small when it comes to many factors that influence subjective well-being.

Do Life Circumstances Matter?

Ultimately, questions about adaptation and social comparison boil down to questions about whether life circumstances matter, as these are the things that policy can affect. We have argued above that neither adaptation nor comparison effects are so strong as to swamp the effects of absolute circumstances. But this leaves us in the position of demonstrating effects of circumstances, and some maintain that these effects are small. Again, however, the evidence for this must be evaluated carefully.

In general, researchers examining the effect of circumstances point to a few important findings. First, studies that have examined circumstances and demographic characteristics show that these circumstances explain only a small percentage of the variance in well-being outcomes (Diener et al., 1999). For instance, most reviews suggest that approximately 15% of the variance in well-being measures can be explained by the demographic variables and life circumstances that are typically assessed (e.g., income, age, sex, education). In addition, specific predictors that should theoretically be linked with well-being tend to correlate only weakly with it. These findings have led some to dismiss the importance of external circumstances in relation to well-being outcomes (and we have been guilty of this, too, in our past writings).

However, there are a number of reasons to remain optimistic in spite of these small effects. First, well-being is a complex phenomenon that should theoretically be influenced by a wide variety of factors. However, with each additional factor that could play a role, the influence of any one factor diminishes. For instance, in demonstrating the limits in prediction of specific behaviors from personality traits, Ahadi and Diener (1989) used a Monte Carlo simulation to show that the maximum association between any one factor and an outcome diminishes quickly as the number of actual predictors increases. For instance, the average correlation for outcomes with three and four predictors were .50 and .45, respectively, even though these traits completely determined the outcome in this simulation. Subjective well-being is thought to be an overarching judgment that results from the evaluation of many different areas in a person's life. Thus, with many factors at play, each factor can predict only a small amount of the variance in well-being outcomes. Although one might be surprised by the small correlation between income and life satisfaction when that factor is considered on its own, the size of the correlation makes sense when we consider that a person's health, his or her social relationships, the quality of leisure time, and many other factors all influence the same outcome.

Second, the effect size indexes that social scientists typically use to investigate the effects of life circumstances are notoriously difficult to interpret. As we noted above, because of this difficulty, social scientists often use crude rules of thumb to interpret the size of various effects. But these rules of thumb often hide the fact that effects that are typically described as being small can often be quite important. Furthermore, one can get different pictures from different effect size metrics. For instance, Lucas and Schimmack (in press) noted that whether a person is employed or unemployed accounts for a very small amount of variance in life satisfaction ratings (around 4%). This translates to a relatively small correlation of .20. However, when standardized mean differences are compared, this very small effect translates into a large mean difference: The employed are 0.80 standard deviations happier than the unemployed. This means that the average employed person is happier than 83% of those who are unemployed. Thus, effects that look small and account for very small amounts of variance can reflect large differences. In the case of unemployment and well-being, the discrepancy in effect size interpretations results from the fact that correlations are base-rate-sensitive whereas d-metric effect sizes are not (McGrath & Meyer, 2006). Thus, relatively large effects may look small when the base rates for the predictor variable are very high or very low.

Lucas and Schimmack (in press) also showed that difficulties in interpreting effect sizes apply in the case of income. They noted that the correlation between income and well-being tends to fall around .20. This correlation is often interpreted as being quite small. However, if even moderately extreme income groups are compared, this small correlation can translate into moderate or even large effects. For instance, in their study, those who made over 200,000 dollars per year reported life satisfaction scores that were over eight-tenths of a standard deviation above those who made less than 10,000 dollars a year and over one-half of one standard deviation above those who made an average income. Thus, the rich are considerably more satisfied than the poor or even those with average incomes. In this case, the weak correlation (and the discrepancy between this correlation and intuitions about the effects of income) results from the fact that the standard deviation of income is small relative to the range of incomes that people think about. For instance, based on the correlation of .20, a one standard deviation increase in income should be associated with a small 0.20 standard deviation increase in life satisfaction. However, income standard deviations tend to be small relative to the range of incomes that exist. Thus, small correlations that do not explain substantial amounts of variance might result from the fact that only a relatively small percentage of people in a sample are wealthy or live in dire poverty, and do not suggest anything about the possible impact that income and other explanatory variables might have.

To be sure, these explanations of the discrepancies between intuitions and actual data are speculative. Our point, however, is that effect sizes that have been interpreted to be small can often have important implications for well-being. Even though the correlation between unemployment status and life satisfaction is quite small, moving all unemployed people to the life satisfaction level of employed people would make a large difference in their subjective well-being. In medical and epidemiological studies, factors that can explain several percent of variance often are thought to have important practical implications. Thus, consistent with our reexamination of adaptation and social comparison effects, a reevaluation of the literature on effect sizes associated with external circumstances shows that these circumstances often do have an effect, which provides suggestive evidence that well-being measures can be used fruitfully in guiding policy decisions.

Subjective Well-Being Fails to Show the Benefits of Technological/Scientific Advances

A related concern about subjective well-being is that technological advances increase individuals' dreams or ideals about their lives. Even a few years ago, few people were bothered by the lack of opportunities to travel into space. Now space travel is around the corner, and some people will desire such an experience, even though many will not be able to afford it. Thus, the invention of space travel may actually reduce subjective well-being because it creates new preferences that become increasingly difficult for the average person to fulfill. The same argument may be applied to any technological advance that is only available to a small minority of the population. Based on this argument, the world would be a better place without technological advances that constantly increase the number and the range of preferences.

The main problem with this argument is that preferences can exist independent of the technological possibilities at a certain time. Take air travel as an example. The preference is not to sit for 24 hours in a narrow seat in a noisy plane. The preference may be to attend the wedding of one's only daughter who happens to live 4,000 miles away. Planes were only invented and commercialized in response to ideals that existed before technological advances made it possible to make one's actual life closer to these ideals.

We are not proposing that every new invention has positive effects on subjective well-being. For example, air travel has increased mobility, which has created a world in which close family members live thousands of miles apart. This dispersion of close relatives might have negative effects on well-being. A national system for tracking subjective well-being can reveal the effects of technological advances on well-being.

The alternatives are not very appealing to us. We can assume that technological advances always increase well-being because they are driven by economic goals, which always maximize well-being based on the standard economic model of utility. Or we can assume that technological advances have negative effects on well-being because they remove human beings more and more from the world that shaped human nature. Or we can assume that technological advances are merely a part of an aspiration spiral. Just when previous inventions start improving people's lives, people aspire to a life that takes advantage of today's inventions. Because it is not clear how technological progress influences subjective well-being, it is important to examine the impact of modern technology on well-being.

Summary

Concerns about the use of well-being measures for public policy decisions extend beyond concerns about the quality of the measures. Specific theories of emotions and well-being that have been advanced over the years raise numerous issues that must be addressed before these programs can be implemented. In this chapter, we have presented the concerns that have come up most frequently in response to the suggestion that well-being measures be used to guide policy. The most important of these concerns reflect the possibility that people adapt to all life circumstances or that well-being judgments are inherently comparative (which would mean that policies designed to increase well-being would be doomed to fail). But our review shows that although these concerns are based on some empirical research, the impact of these processes is not so large as to rule out the utility of well-being-based policy. Adaptation does occur, and this is functional—but the processes are not so strong that the effects of life circumstances cannot be detected, and many life circumstances have relatively strong effects on well-being. Similarly, social comparison effects occur, but they have not been shown to overwhelm absolute standing.

Chapter 7

The Desirability of Well-Being as a Guide for Policy

In the previous chapter we addressed the issue of whether well-being can serve as a criterion for evaluating specific policy decisions. Although critics have suggested that adaptation and comparison processes are so strong that well-being cannot change, most research shows otherwise. Well-being measures are sensitive to differences in important life circumstances, especially those circumstances that are thought to be particularly strong. Yet additional concerns remain about the desirability of using well-being measures to guide policy. Specifically, the fact that well-being *could* be used for such purposes does not necessarily mean that it *should* be used in this way. It is possible that by focusing attention on well-being, and by shaping policies in such a way that well-being is maximized, negative consequences for society and organizations could result. In this chapter, we address additional concerns that could potentially limit the value of well-being measures as a guide for policy decisions.

Subjectively Defined Well-Being Captures Irrelevant Information

Early on in this book, we made a distinction between objective definitions and subjective definitions of well-being. We favor subjective definitions because they collect evidence directly from those whose well-being is being assessed. This is preferable to objective list definitions, in which lists of characteristics must be generated either through consensus or on the basis of theory. It is often difficult to justify why one person's list is better than another's, and thus disagreements about the definition of well-being will inevitably arise with objective definitions.

However, a common objection to subjective definitions of well-being is that people can evaluate their lives on an infinite number of aspects, and most of these would be irrelevant to their true well-being. We believe that this is not a major problem for subjective definitions of well-being because people clearly value some aspects of their lives more than others. More importantly, most trivial aspects of a life have no notable impact on well-being because they fail to enter people's evaluations. Empirical studies of well-being judgments show that people weigh life aspects in accordance with the subjective importance attached to these attributes (Andrews & Withey, 1976; Schimmack & Oishi, 2005). For example, most people say that they have preferences about the type of weather that they would like to experience (e.g., they prefer dry, warm, sunny days over hot and muggy or cold and rainy days). However, respondents typically rate weather as a relatively unimportant attribute of their lives. Consistent with this rating, self-reports of satisfaction with weather are often unrelated to satisfaction with life in general. Thus, empirical evidence suggests that trivial concerns do not have a large influence on well-being measures, and thus the measures likely reflect the important circumstances in people's lives.

Subjective Well-Being Can Be Manipulated

A second concern about subjective definitions of well-being is that because they are based on people's own values and ideals, it may be possible to influence well-being by manipulating people's preferences (Sen, 1987, cited in Sumner, 1996). For example, the traditional Indian caste system may prevent people from forming preferences about jobs that only members of other castes may do. If the preferences do not exist, well-being will remain high even when the underprivileged caste members experience objectively undesirable conditions. Thus, the caste system could be used by privileged castes to enjoy objectively better life conditions, even though there might be no differences in subjective well-being between castes.

This is a potential concern for a subjective definition of well-being. However, there are several reasons why this concern is not a fatal blow to a subjective definition of well-being or the use of well-being measures to inform policy decisions. First, the concern requires that there is ultimately some objective criterion by which one can evaluate lives. We have to assume that the life of those in higher castes is better than the life of those in lower castes by some objective standard. Second, we have to assume that preferences can be easily manipulated, and that lower castes do not form a preference to have access to the same jobs and opportunities as higher castes. Very little research evidence has addressed this issue. And furthermore, history suggests otherwise, whether we use the French Revolution or the fall of the Berlin Wall as an example.

There are also several remedies that can be used to address distortions of this kind when using subjective measures of well-being. First, we are not proposing that well-being is the only criterion for social policy. For example, men and women report equal levels of well-being even though evidence exists that they do not have equal employment opportunities. This fact does not imply that society should abolish the goal of equal employment opportunities for men and women in the workplace. Other concerns and additional values may necessitate improvements in this area, even if it has no long-term effect on the well-being of women or men. Second, Sumner (1996) proposed that preferences can be examined in terms of their origin. Only preferences that are formed under free conditions should be used to assess well-being. Thus, it can be useful to examine whether the subjective well-being of minority groups is based on imposed cultural norms or whether they freely chose their ideals. At least some women do choose a part-time job over a career. We find no reason to infer that these women's well-being is objectively lower than the well-being of successful business women.

The best approach is to consider the information from both objective and subjective indicators of well-being when making policy decisions. Without subjective information, a main concern is that the objective indicators fail to reflect individual's own evaluations of their lives. Without evidence that preferences are ill-conceived, subjective indicators are likely to provide a more accurate picture of well-being. An analogy can be found in the example of voting in democratic societies. Unless it can be shown that votes were bought or manipulated in some other way, we accept people's votes as a valid reflection of their political preferences. Similarly, "a person's own view of her life satisfaction carries an initial presumption of authenticity, and thus of authority. It can be mistaken, even deeply distorted. But it must be shown to be so before we can have any grounds for discounting it" (Sumner, 1996, p. 171).

An additional concern is that if policy makers rely on well-being surveys to guide policy decisions, people may respond strategically to well-being surveys. In other words, if people knew that their self-reports of life satisfaction were being used to guide policy, they might change their responses to influence those policies. For instance, members of groups who thought that they were being treated unfairly might intentionally report lowered well-being to attract government resources and attention. Thus, well-being measures might have value in the early stages of their use, but once people realized that these measures were in place, they could manipulate their scores to get what they wanted.

Such concerns are commonplace in behavioral science research—the participants in the research often know that they are being studied, and they can change their behavior and responses to influence the results of the study. But one must consider how plausible it is that responses could be manipulated in such a way as to have a large effect on the responses that emerge. For instance, carefully conducted surveys can hide the purpose of the survey, which would make it difficult for participants to determine whether their group was of interest to the survey organizers. One reasonable strategy is to ask general well-being questions early on in the survey to prevent group-relevant questions from priming group status and influencing responses. In addition, most people can identify with many different groups (e.g., groups based on their ethnicity, gender, city, region, and occupation). It would be difficult for any individual respondent to determine how they should respond to get the governmental response that they desired for all the groups to which they belonged.

Furthermore, if people were acting in this self-interested way, it is unlikely that there would be cross-group differences in the tendency to artificially lower their scores. In other words, most groups would likely have similar self-interested motivations, and it would only be those who were generally the least satisfied who would feel the need to report dissatisfaction to attract resources and attention to change their situation. Of course, it is possible that there might be organized efforts to get large groups of people to shift their answers below what they would normally report. But again, the plausibility of such scenarios is questionable. It is not clear how such efforts would be organized and whether they could ever be successful.

Finally, policy makers use public polling data already, and they appear to work as intended even though concerns about survey respondents manipulating data could be raised. For instance, the University of Michigan tracks monthly consumer confidence in its Consumer Sentiment Index, and this index appears to predict and perhaps even affect other economic indicators including stock performance. If the opinions voiced by respondents have the power to affect the economy itself, then one might expect respondents to overestimate their confidence in the economy with the hopes that such optimism would result in a self-fulfilling prophecy. But the Consumer Sentiment Index does vary over time and appears to be sensitive to real-world economic conditions. Thus, existing survey data suggest that such data can be used even when there is motivation for respondents to influence the results.

Is Subjective Well-Being a Good Thing?

Each of the above concerns reflects practical considerations regarding the use of well-being measures to guide policy decisions. But more philosophical concerns about the value of high levels of well-being can also be raised. For instance, some might suggest that well-being itself is not a desirable goal for policy makers—or society—to have. These critics might argue that it would be dangerous for society to focus on well-being because high levels of well-being make people lazy and stupid. According to critics who raise this concern, to attain states of high well-being, people might sacrifice hard work, benevolence, and other desirable behaviors to achieve ever-increasing levels of positive states. For example, people might abandon empathy for the poor in a world where poverty is a serious problem because they will be happier if they avoid thinking about this problem. At the extreme, one might expect people to give up work altogether and focus entirely on taking drugs, watching television, and pursuing other sensory pleasures that have little societal value. Well-being, then, could be seen as something that is good only in moderation. This broad issue actually comprises two related concerns: The first is the concern that well-being would encourage hedonistic pursuits. The second is the potential problem that too much well-being can be bad for people and can make them lazy. We address these two issues in turn.

The first concern about well-being and hedonism results from a misunderstanding of both the construct of well-being and the processes that lead to it. First, as we have described earlier, subjective well-being is a broad construct that incorporates one's emotional reactions and one's cognitive judgment that life is going well. These various components of well-being are related to one another, but far from identical (Lucas, Diener, & Suh, 1996). A person could experience pleasant affect much of the time, yet find that he or she is not satisfied with life. Cognitive judgments have the potential of incorporating many different types of experiences, including the feeling of meaning or finding pleasure in helping others. Thus, those who experience high well-being are not necessarily those who feel happy and joyful at every moment of their lives.

Furthermore, it is not clear that pursuing pleasure is the royal road to high levels of well-being. For instance, certain types of enjoyable experiences, namely *flow* experiences, seem to come mostly from challenging activities. Specifically, these flow experiences come from activities where the challenge of the activity matches the skills and abilities of the person pursuing that activity (Csikszentmihalyi, 1990). Furthermore, Steger, Kashdan, and Oishi (2007) examined the extent to which activities that were designed to further hedonic pursuits actually led to increased well-being. They found that activities that were designed to further hedonic pursuits were less strongly linked with well-being than were activities that were designed to further eudemonic (or inherently meaningful) goals. It would not be surprising if many of the activities that are pleasant in small doses would actually be counterproductive in the long run. Thus, even if people pursued hedonic goals, it is possible that these attempts would backfire, and our well-being measures could show the negative consequences of these decisions.

It is also important to note that we can separate the extent to which *individuals* pursue well-being and the extent to which *policy makers* track well-being and use this information to guide policies. Eleanor Roosevelt once said that "happiness is not a goal; it is a by-product." It is entirely possible that living one's life with the goal of making oneself happier will be counterproductive, and that true well-being is an outcome that can only be achieved by pursuing other goals. However, that fact does not prevent policy makers from shaping decisions and environments in such a way as to let that by-product emerge. There is little reason to believe that if implemented correctly, using well-being measures to guide policy would shift individual goals toward hedonistic pleasures.

The pursuit of well-being as a policy goal is therefore not the pursuit of hedonism. There is no evidence to suggest that creating conditions that allow people to thrive in a subjective sense will lead to a nation of television watchers and drug addicts. But what will it achieve for us? The second concern about using well-being measures is that well-being itself (regardless of what causes it) is bad for us. This belief arises from commonsense notions regarding the functions of positive emotions, along with some carefully conducted research on the cognitive consequences of these emotions. Common sense suggests that pleasant feelings result from a successful attempt to attain a goal. If all goes well, happiness and a cognitive sense of satisfaction ensue. Thus, these positive emotions could be seen as a signal that little to no further energy is required for the task at hand (see Carver & Scheier, 1990, for a more detailed discussion of this idea). Although Carver (2003) believes that this positive affect will signal a person that they can move on to a different goal or task, it is easy to see why one might believe that a person who experiences positive emotions may stop and relax.

Similarly, in the literature on cognition and affect, there is considerable evidence that happiness and positive emotions can in some situations lead to less than ideal outcomes. As with the commonsense idea described above, theories about affect and cognition suggest that positive emotions, in a sense, make people lazy. One prominent theory suggests that people rely on their feelings to determine a course of action. For instance, positive emotions might signal that things are going well and that one can proceed, or that there is no danger and that he or she does not have to consider actions carefully. Negative emotions, on the other hand, signal that one should stop and consider his or her actions, as the wrong choice could lead to something bad happening. Consistent with this idea, numerous studies have found that positive emotions can lead to less careful processing, greater reliance on stereotypes, and other effects that can be grouped together as examples of *lazy* thinking (see Oishi, Diener, & Lucas, 2007, for a review).

Yet interpretations of this effect vary. Although positive moods may appear to make people lazy, it also helps them deal quickly and efficiently with complex stimuli in the environment. In a sense, positive moods may signal people to shift their attention from easy tasks that can be handled somewhat automatically to more difficult tasks that require more effort (Carver, 2003). In the long run, this flexible process can be efficient. Furthermore, some research shows that the effects of positive mood vary depending on the context. Although happy people may think less carefully in circumstances that are not personally important, this effect can disappear when important tasks are considered (e.g., Aspinwall, 1998; Bodenhausen, Kramer, & Süsser, 1994). Thus, these potentially detrimental effects of positive mood can be *turned off* when the situation demands it.

But more importantly for those interested in increasing well-being, positive mood may have more direct beneficial effects. Fredrickson (2003) proposed a theory of positive emotions in which these pleasant states are not simply an outcome of things going well. Instead, positive emotions—like negative emotions—have important functions without which humans would not be able to thrive. Specifically, Fredrickson suggested that the function of positive emotions is to broaden and build people's resources. When individuals experience positive emotions and moods, they are more likely to explore, to think creatively, to try new things, and to approach new people. In short, by exploring new things and new relationships, individuals with high positive affect can learn new skills, build supportive relationships, and acquire resources that can aid them and others when times are not so good.

To test this idea, Lyubomirsky, King, and Diener (2005) meta-analytically combined cross-sectional, longitudinal, and experimental studies linking well-being with a variety of outcomes. In support of the broaden-and-build model, they found that in three different domains—work, love, and health—happier people experienced more positive outcomes. Thus, it seems as though the idea that well-being is bad for people is not true. In general, people with higher levels of well-being have more good things happen to them, and there is some of causal linkages running from well-being to these desirable life circumstances, as well as in the reverse direction (see Lyubomirsky et al., for a review).

We must caution, however, that more well-being is not always a good thing. Oishi et al. (2007) used cross-sectional and longitudinal data to address the links between well-being and certain outcomes, while attending to the optimal level of well-being for these domains. In some domains— social relationships and volunteer work—increased levels of well-being were associated with linearly increasing levels of the desirable outcome. But for other domains—specifically, income and work domains—the association between well-being and outcomes was curvilinear. There appeared to be an optimal level of well-being that was below the maximum of the scale. For instance, in two nationally representative longitudinal data sets, initial levels of life satisfaction were positively associated with later income (even after controlling for initial income), but the maximum incomes were seen at satisfaction scores that were a couple of points below the maximum (on 7- and 11-point scales). Thus, for these domains, there does seem to be evidence that the highest levels of well-being are associated with less successful outcomes. But it is questionable whether the interventions that policy makers can implement would move people to these extremes. Furthermore, there may be something about individuals who are particularly satisfied that leads to these negative outcomes (e.g., manic people may not consider risks), and these effects would not generalize to people in the normal range of well-being who were made very satisfied by desirable life circumstances. Thus, we believe that concerns about people being too high in well-being are unfounded.

Subjective Definitions of Well-Being Condone Immoral Behavior

Although we believe that well-being is a desirable goal and that well-being itself does not lead to undesirable outcomes, questions can be raised about the means that can be used to increase well-being. Specifically, it is possible that well-being could be increased through immoral means. The relation between well-being and morality is an ancient philosophical question (Sumner, 1996). A common philosophical solution to this problem is to define well-being in such a way as to exclude immoral pursuits from the construct. We believe that this approach is both unsatisfactory and unnecessary. It is unsatisfactory because the morality constraint contradicts common intuitions about well-being. Many criminal acts are committed out of a desire to improve one's own well-being at the expense of others' well-being. For example, a man who steals is acting immorally with the intention of increasing his well-being. This solution is unnecessary because the concern about immoral actions that could increase well-being is an objection to utilitarianism rather than subjective definitions of well-being (Sumner, 1996).

There are good reasons to enforce moral norms even if this leads to lower average levels of well-being. Furthermore, if people are socialized in the values and norms of their cultures, it is likely that acting morally will usually make them happy, whereas acting immorally will usually make them unhappy. In addition, even if attempts to maximize well-being would give way to moral concerns, it would still be desirable to maintain national measures of well-being. First, many moral concerns exist with the well-being of citizens in mind. Petty acts of crime like vandalism are often criminalized precisely because they are believed to affect the well-being of those who are exposed to the vandalism itself. National accounts of well-being can reveal which moral norms actually reflect the impact of actions on well-being and which do not. Second, people can often choose among a variety of moral behaviors, and national measures of well-being can reveal which moral pursuits are particularly likely to increase well-being. Finally, it is comforting that morality and well-being are often aligned. For example, cross-national comparisons show that the highest levels of well-being occur in countries that have the lowest levels of corruption.

Which Well-Being Measure Should Be Used?

A final concern that could be raised about using well-being measures to guide policy is that at least at this point, there is no single index that reflects overall subjective well-being. As we have noted throughout this book, there are multiple components of well-being, with some focused more on affective feelings and others focused more on cognitive judgments. It is important to measure these distinct components because they are not all the same thing, and each may react differently to different life circumstances. However, this means that when one investigates the effect of a policy decision or a specific life event on subjective well-being, researchers might come up with different answers depending on the type of well-being indicator that is assessed.

Our response to this concern is that the situation is no different than it is with any other set of indicators that one might want to use. There is no single economic indicator that provides an overall evaluation of how a nation is doing. Gross domestic product is important, but it is not identical to and cannot provide the same information as inflation rates, unemployment rates, or average household disposable income. Furthermore, some policies might affect the various indicators in different ways, and some policies can move economic indicators in different directions. Economists and policy makers track many different types of economic indicators because the economic health of a nation is complicated. Similarly, well-being is a multifaceted concept, and multiple indicators are required to capture its breadth.

We should also note that future research can help resolve questions about the different answers that different well-being measures provide. For instance, it is possible that global life satisfaction judgments reflect an overarching judgment that incorporates affective responses, domain satisfactions, and all other components that one might want to include. Future research that examines the processes that underlie well-being judgments may show that if we want the broadest level of assessment, such judgments may provide the best conclusions. We are not yet ready to make the argument that life satisfaction is this highest-level assessment; we are simply noting that future research can clarify how the various components interrelate, and this research can aid decisions about which components to assess and how to interpret their differences.

Summary

The issues discussed in this chapter focus on the desirability of using well-being measures to guide policy decisions. Specifically, questions can be raised about the subjective definition of well-being that guides the recommendations that we present in this book—Can the measures be too sensitive to irrelevant concerns? Is well-being too diffuse a construct to be useful as a guide for policy decisions? In addition, questions can be raised about the goal of improving well-being itself. Are high levels of well-being a good thing? Should governments pursue and promote well-being if it can be obtained through immoral means? These concerns certainly must be addressed, but they are not unique to well-being measures. Most policy decisions involve conflicting goals and uncertain criteria by which to evaluate success. Furthermore, there are often both moral and immoral paths toward increases in the outcomes that already guide policy decisions (e.g., increases in wealth).

It is also important to note that many of the concerns are based on assumptions about the effects of well-being that are not correct. For instance, psychological research shows that positive emotions in particular, but also general well-being ratings, are associated with cognitive styles that reflect carelessness and lazy thinking. However, these cognitive effects may actually be part of a functional strategy to increase efficiency, and positive emotions also have many beneficial effects. Happy people do good things and have good things happen to them. Thus, research on the positive and negative effects of well-being must be evaluated carefully when considered in the context of using well-being measures to guide policy decisions.

Ultimately, the concerns discussed in this chapter are not unique to systems that attend to and emphasize well-being. We do not wish to downplay their importance, we simply want to make the point that they are reflect challenges that any system for guiding policy decisions must face. Each system or set of criteria will have flaws, which is part of the reason why well-being measures can be used as a supplement to existing strategies. By included measures with distinct strengths and weaknesses, existing debates can be resolved and better decisions can be made.

Section III

Examples of Policy Uses of Well-Being Measures

Chapter 8

Health and Well-Being: Policy Examples

In the following sections we present examples of instances where measures of well-being could be helpful to policy makers. In most of these instances, researchers have already examined questions that are relevant to the potential effects of government policies on subjective well-being. Although in these cases the existing data are far from definitive, the examples are meant to provide ideas about specific ways that well-being measures could prove useful. In addition, we do not provide an exhaustive examination of the extant data within each area. Instead, we focus on specific but limited examples to show how such data could inform policy. Stronger evidence will come from future investigations, and the data that result will ultimately yield a more solid basis for policy formation. For the time being, we simply hope to show that well-being measures can provide useful information for a broad range of very diverse policy decisions.

Health Spending

In industrialized nations, health and longevity have increased at an unprecedented rate. One consequence of this improvement is that the focus of health organizations has, to a large extent, shifted away from simply extending life and toward improving life over the course of a longer lifespan (Kurth, 2005). For instance, the KIGGS report written for the World Health Organization (WHO) recommends "placing emphasis on physical, mental and social welfare as the future task of its policy rather than a mere increase in life expectancy" (p. 1). Consequently, WHO's slogan has changed from "Add years to life" to "Add life to years." The policy mandate is now to enhance people's physical and mental health—including feelings of well-being—rather than simply to prevent mortal diseases.

Modern nations spend vast amounts of money on disease treatment and prevention. Yet there are rarely, if ever, enough resources to meet all research, treatment, and public health needs. Therefore, in all nations, medical care is necessarily *rationed*, either through prohibitive costs, waiting lists, or through some other mechanisms (Dolan, 2007). Even the wealthiest nations do not spend enough money to address all existing health care needs. When governments spend money on health care, they face the question of how best to allocate funds. In addition, when wealthy nations allocate money for health research, they must also decide which diseases and conditions should become the focus of research attention.

In an ideal world, these decisions would be guided by two fundamental concerns: Which diseases cause the most misery and which are most amenable to intervention. Unfortunately, it is often difficult to answer these questions definitively, and thus other considerations come into play. For instance, at least some health-related policy decisions are influenced by special interest groups who lobby government officials to fund research and treatment for a specific illness. Part of these lobbying efforts entail convincing officials that the disease causes much suffering and that a cure (or at least a treatment for the symptoms) is right around the corner. Similarly, public perceptions about the seriousness and prevalence of health conditions (perceptions that are inevitably influenced by media reports) play a role in influencing health care and research spending. Of course, more systematic decision strategies that are based on the input of physicians and scientists also occur. For example, illnesses that actually do affect more people, such as coronary diseases, are likely to receive more research money than diseases that affect few people, such as Crohn's disease. But in many cases, relevant information about where investments will lead to the greatest payoff is not available.

Decision makers take several factors into account when allocating funding for health-related treatment and research. These factors usually fall under one of the two decision criteria described above; they relate to either the seriousness of the disease or the likelihood that treatment of the disease can reduce suffering. For instance, policy makers might consider the age at which a disease tends to occur, because diseases that emerge early in life can potentially affect well-being for a much longer time than can diseases that emerge toward the end of life. In other words, early-onset diseases place a larger burden on individuals and societies than do late-onset diseases. Thus, finding a cure for a disease that emerged early in life would have a greater impact on the well-being of society than would finding a cure for a disease that emerged later in life. Although these decisions are not always explicitly linked to concerns about well-being, this principle often underlies these decisions.

A number of methods exist for evaluating the quality of life associated with different health states (see Dolan, 2007, for a review). Because many of these were developed by health economists, the methods often mirror the economic approaches to assessing the value of nonmarket goods (which we discussed in Chapter 2). For instance, one approach is to evaluate people's revealed preferences as observed in health-related market behavior. This would be most clearly revealed by the amount that a person actually spends to correct the state that he or she is in. However, this method does not work as well in some health-related areas, especially where health insurance or nationalized insurance covers expenses. Furthermore, because market behavior cannot be easily observed for the avoidance of many health states, economists have instead turned to willingness-to-pay methods, in which participants are asked how much of their income they would spend to avoid contracting certain health conditions.

Additional techniques that ask people to make hypothetical trade-offs can also be used. For instance, health economists often ask respondents about their willingness to exchange extra years of life with a specific malady for a life that had fewer years in excellent health. If respondents typically say that they would be willing to trade many years of life in poor health for just one year of good health, then theoretically this means that they consider life with the disease to be almost as bad as being dead. The extra years of life with the condition are worth very little to them. In contrast, if respondents indicate that they would not be willing to sacrifice any years of life with the condition to obtain fewer years of perfect health, then that would mean that life with the condition is still very valuable. Through such techniques, precise estimates of the value of life with a specific condition can be obtained.

Similarly, in the standard gamble approach, respondents are asked to choose between two options regarding their health condition. If participants chose the first option, they would have a chance at full health, but also a chance of death. If participants chose the second option, they would continue to experience the specific health condition for the rest of their life. For instance, participants might be asked, "Would you prefer a 30% likelihood of full health and a 70% likelihood of death, versus the certainty of having paraplegia for the remainder of your natural life?" If the disease causes little suffering, people will probably not risk death for the chance to cure it. If, however, quality of life is quite miserable with the disease, then people might choose a moderate chance of death if it also meant that they had a high likelihood of being cured. If people perceived the condition to be little better than death itself, then they would be willing to risk even a very large chance of death for the opportunity to receive a cure. The probabilities presented to respondents can be manipulated until people are equally likely to choose either of the two options. This equilibrium point provides a value to the quality of life that respondents perceive for people with the problem.

One issue that comes up with methods that are based on hypothetical decisions concerns who the appropriate respondents are for such surveys. When studying a particular disease or condition, should the general public, medical practitioners who have specialized knowledge about the disease, or people who are actually affected by the condition participate in the studies designed to evaluate the quality of life of the specific health state? If respondents who do not actually have the condition are recruited, then they might base their responses on general stereotypes or other forms of misinformation. Who can imagine what it is like to be blind, for example, unless they actually are or have been blind? On the other hand, people who actually have the condition may not have an accurate perception of what it would like to be in full health. There is no clear answer as to who should provide ratings.

Another serious issue with methods that are based on hypotheticals is that when answering questions about these states, the respondent's attention is necessarily focused on the health state. However, individuals who actually live with the condition will have many other things attracting their attention and determining their quality of life. The majority of their time is likely to be focused on other factors such as relationships and work. As Dolan (2008) has pointed out, these other factors could be unaffected or even enhanced by quite negative health states. Because of these problems, Dolan suggested that the best way to evaluate the quality of life with various conditions is to examine reports of subjective well-being of people who actually have the condition. These reports can then be used to calculate Happiness Adjusted Life Years (HALYs, a measure that is similar to the more commonly used Quality Adjusted Life Years, or QALYs) that can inform decisions regarding the specific health state. Unlike disease symptoms that vary across illnesses, these measures could be used as a common metric across conditions.

An example of the HALY approach is a study by Groot and van den Brink (2007) in which the researchers calculated how much income would be needed to bring the life satisfaction of people with heart disease up to the levels of life satisfaction of people in excellent health. Thus, if heart disease can be treated for less than the estimated amount, the authors suggest that it would be a good trade-off for society. This type of calculation can also be used when comparing treatments for a single disease that differ substantially in cost. By focusing on the improvements to well-being that results from each (and translating them into metrics like the HALY), health economists might be able to identify where money might best be spent to most enhance well-being.

In a direct comparison of the standard gamble and life satisfaction approaches to valuing health states, Dolan (2007) found that conditions that interfere with physical functioning or produce severe pain are seen as more negative when the standard gamble approach is compared to the subjective well-being method. In contrast, the well-being approach suggests that mental health problems are worse than the standard gamble approach. Thus, the subjective well-being approach indicates that more dollars should be spent on mental health conditions than the standard gamble approach dictates. However, in both approaches we still need to know additional information, such as the effectiveness of treatments and the likely longevity of people with each condition. The subjective well-being approach can be used to evaluate the quality of life of people with a disease compared to fully healthy individuals who have the same demographic characteristics. It can also be used to compare the quality of life of those who have had particular treatments with those who have not. Thus, subjective well-being represents a useful metric to help evaluate health spending and by which to allocate research funding.

One possible problem with using the subjective well-being approach to value health states is that if respondents know the purpose of the study, their responses might be influenced because of what they think might happen when the numbers are used by policy makers. However, if national accounts of well-being were standardized and ongoing, the health state of the respondent need not stand out when the survey is administered.

Caregiving Burden

During our lives most of us will take care of someone who is unable to do so himself or herself. The difficulties of caring for someone who is infirm are substantial, especially because this duty often occurs in addition to one's other ongoing responsibilities. In recent years the burden of caregivers has received increased research attention, perhaps because as the population ages, more caregiving is needed for people with Alzheimer's disease and other afflictions of aging. However, caregiving can occur for people with many conditions, ranging from those with mental illness to those receiving organ transplants, and from those with chronic diseases to those with terminal cancer. Thus, although we might conceive of the prototypical caregiver as an elderly spouse, parents caring for a child and middle-aged adults caring for an elderly parent also frequently fill this role.

Caregivers face a number of challenges. They must assume responsibilities that were formerly taken care of by the person for whom they are caring, and they must provide emotional support to that person as well. The patient usually requires physical care and medical treatments. Furthermore, the shift to caregiving is often accompanied by decreased income and increased expenses. Thus, there are substantial difficulties in the typical caregiving situation. How does caregiving influence people's subjective well-being, and is this a concern for policy makers?

Caregiver burden, as it is called in the research literature, is of concern to policy makers for several reasons. First, the responsibilities that are involved in caring for others often reduce the well-being of those who provide the care. For example, Hooley, Butler, and Howlett (2005) examined the well-being of those who were caring for family members with congestive heart failure. They found that 20% of caregivers scored in the depressed range on the Beck Depression Inventory. Similarly, those who care for stroke victims tend to report low levels of life satisfaction and are often found to be at substantial risk for depression (Han & Haley, 1999; Visser-Meily, Post, Schepers, & Lindeman, 2005). Pakenham, Chiu, Bursnall, Cannon, and Okochi (2006) studied young caregivers, aged 10 to 25, who were responsible for a sick or disabled parent. Compared to a group of similar young people, the caregiving youths had lower life satisfaction and higher levels of physical complaints. Part of the explanation for the lowered life satisfaction that the caregiving youth reported was the isolation that resulted from their caregiving duties. Thus, the lowered well-being that caregivers experience is in itself a problem that health researchers will need to address.

However, there are additional reasons why the well-being of caregivers is an important health-policy concern. First, if caregivers feel particularly burdened and their well-being is affected then they will be more likely to make the choice to move the family member into an institution. This shifts the burden of caregiving to society. Although this may often be necessary to get the expert care that a person needs, there may be some cases where care could be provided more efficiently and effectively at home. In these cases, simple interventions to increase the well-being of caregivers could benefit all involved. For instance, one method of helping caregivers is to provide free or reduced-cost adult day care so the caregiver can get a break from his or her caregiving responsibilities. These programs are popular because they give the caregiver time to themselves and provide socializing opportunities for the patient (Warren, Kerr, Smith, Godkin, & Schalm, 2003).

If improving the well-being of care providers leads to better care, then well-being measures can be used as a tool for evaluating the effectiveness of caregiver-focused interventions. For instance, Gremier and Gorey (1998) found that many types of social work interventions were effective in reducing caregiver burden. Cummings et al. (2004) concluded after reviewing the literature that the most consistent support for efficacious interventions was for treatments that used cognitive-behavioral, problem-solving, and reminiscence techniques. Knight, Lutzky, and Macofsky-Urban (1993) concluded that respite care and individual psychosocial interventions are moderately effective in reducing caregiver distress, whereas group interventions are less effective. Gallagher-Thompson et al. (2000) found that relatively low-cost interventions focused on teaching specific coping skills reduced subjective caregiver burden, and Toseland and McCallion (1997) showed in a literature review that many interventions have a positive, but moderate, impact on reducing caregiver depression.

In some cases, interventions do not seem to affect the outcomes that are assessed. For instance, Han and Haley (1999) concluded that many interventions are ineffective in reducing depression in caregivers. However, including a broader range of well-being measures into intervention studies might help identify which types of programs are more or less sensitive. Interventions like those discussed above might show greater effects when these additional measures are used because constructs like life satisfaction might be more sensitive to the effects of caregiver burden even among those who are not necessarily depressed. Policy makers will need to know which treatments work and which do not before spending resources on these interventions. Whatever the most effective interventions turn out to be, the measures of well-being will certainly be essential in identifying them.

Few of the intervention studies discussed above analyzed the costs involved in the programs and used these estimates to conduct cost–benefit analyses; but such techniques could easily be incorporated. For instance, Mittelman et al. (1993) conducted an intervention study for caregivers of patients with Alzheimer's disease. Caregivers were provided with counseling and support groups (relatively inexpensive treatments), and then nursing home admissions among the patients themselves were tracked. In the year after the intervention, half as many patients whose caregivers participated in the intervention were placed in a nursing home as were patients whose caregivers participated in a control treatment. Mittelman et al. discuss the savings that accrue from such interventions, but the precise costs could be calculated explicitly. The cost of the intervention could be multiplied by the number of caregivers who need received it, and this could be compared to the cost savings that result from the precise reduction in the number of institutionalizations that resulted (also see Peak, Toseland,

& Banks, 1995). Thus, well-being data have much promise in helping to evaluate interventions, and provide a common metric on which they can be compared. However, the research to date has not been sufficient to thoroughly evaluate and compare the interventions. National systems for measuring well-being could therefore be quite helpful in this area.

Checkups for School Children

National and regional governments are beginning to seriously consider the need to monitor the mental health of children. A few highly publicized incidents of in-school violence are perhaps partly responsible for the attention that this issue has received. However, a much broader impetus is the recognition that a significant number of children and adolescents suffer from mental health problems including depression and anxiety. Monitoring the well-being of students serves the function of helping to protect their health, but it also yields information on where societal problems lie and how resources can be used most effectively.

In the United States, the President's New Freedom Commission on Mental Health (2003) called for the early detection of mental health problems in both children and adults. The report stated,

> a child whose serious emotional disturbance is identified early will receive care, preventing the potential onset of a co-occurring substance use disorder and breaking a cycle that otherwise can lead to school failure and subsequent problems. Quality screening and early intervention will occur in both readily accessible, low stigma settings, such as primary health care facilities and schools (p. 11).

As well as in traditional mental health and welfare settings. "For consumers of all ages, early detection, assessment, and links with treatment and supports will help prevent mental health problems from worsening" (p. 11). The report calls for expansion and improvement of current school mental health programs. Assessing subjective well-being is an inherent aspect of such monitoring programs.

There are important reasons to monitor the mental health of students. On the one hand, mental health problems have direct consequences for the overall well-being of children. For instance, suicide is the third leading cause of death among youth in the United States (Spencer, 2006). But in addition, these mental health problems also predict a variety of outcomes that will have negative consequences for young people throughout the rest of their lives. For example, anxiety disorders in children and adolescents predict both proximal outcomes like dropping out of school (Kessler, Foster, Saunders, & Stang, 1995) and more distal outcomes including problems that occur later on in life (Kessler, 2003; Woodward & Fergusson, 2001). Social phobias (which are related to lower life satisfaction) predict the likelihood of failing a grade or dropping out of school (Stein & Kean, 2000). Asarnow et al. (2005) found that depression was predictive of decrements in school performance and educational achievement, and Marmorstein and Iacono (2001) found that depression in adolescent girls was predictive of outcomes such as failing grades and suspension from school. Chen, Rubin, and Li (1995) found that Chinese youngsters who scored highest on an inventory of depression scored lower in academic achievement. Katja, Päivi, Marja-Terttu, and Pekka (2002) found that low subjective well-being predicted dissatisfaction with school, low body satisfaction, and high-intensity drinking among teenage girls in secondary school in Finland. To be sure, the processes that link these variables are complex, and it is surely not the case that well-being is responsible for all of these negative outcomes. However, well-being measures can be used as an effective screening tool to identify which children are in trouble.

Children's well-being can be monitored along with their physical health in periodic school checkups. Initial forays into assessing the subjective well-being of children have occurred as part of mental health screenings for children and adolescents. Large and representative studies on the well-being of children are becoming widespread. For example, the Child and Adolescent Component of the National Survey of Mental Health and Well-being assesses well-being-related variables in a nationally representative sample of Australian children (Sawyer et al., 2000). Similarly, Bradshaw, Hoelscher, and Richardson (2006) reported on the subjective well-being of children in the European Union. The life satisfaction of children was assessed, and the scores varied from a low in the Baltic nations to a high in Netherlands, Greece, and Finland. The life satisfaction scores were highly inversely correlated with feelings of loneliness. More specific forms of subjective well-being were also assessed. For example, children were asked about their feelings about themselves. Children's perceptions of themselves are important in that they can be associated with feelings of depression, as well as the likelihood of being a target of bullying (Salmivalli & Isaacs, 2005). Children were also asked about their perceptions of their own health. In Spain and Greece 10% of children felt they experienced poor health, whereas in Lithuania this number was 32%. Other subjective measures included feeling like an *outsider*, relationships with family and friends, feeling pressured by schoolwork, and liking for school. The

European Union study provides an initial prototype for national monitoring of student well-being.

Spencer (2006) reports that in early tests of a voluntary program called TeenScreen, a large number of adolescents who had not previously been identified by school personnel were identified to have considered or attempted suicide. A large percentage of the cases of depression found in the TeenScreen program had previously gone undetected. Gall, Pagano, Desmond, Perrin, and Murphy (2000) found that those who received mental health services after referral based on screenings by the school health center showed reduced tardiness and absenteeism. Thus, tracking well-being of children might help solve practical education problems.

Objections have been raised about screening school children for well-being and mental illness (Spencer, 2006). One concern is that children might be unfairly labeled as mentally ill, or inappropriately given psychotropic medications. Another objection is that mental health problems ought to be handled in the family, not by the schools. Yet another issue that has been raised is that the measures of mental illness and well-being are inherently subjective and flawed, and therefore many children who are temporarily upset by a current event might be unnecessarily channeled into mental health treatment. Even the voluntary TeenScreen program, which involved written informed consent by guardians, met strong resistance among some parents (Spencer, 2006).

Of course, such objections must be seriously considered and analyzed, and the costs of school well-being assessments must be weighed against their benefits. Some of the objections revolve around the validity of measurement, and others are concerned with the appropriate role of schools versus family in the well-being of children. One concern is that children and adolescents who are screened for depression and suicide might make them more likely to attempt suicide, but research has not supported this concern (Spencer, 2006). Vision, hearing, immunizations, and language development are all regularly monitored in schools, and many societies might decide that the same should be done for mental health and subjective well-being if valid tools and interventions are available.

In the other examples of the policy uses of well-being, we focused on the implications for policies of well-being scores. In the proposal for national well-being checkups for children we are suggesting that the well-being measures are themselves the target of policy, to be implemented as a means of improving the well-being of children. Of course other policies might follow from the findings of school well-being checkups, but the programs' main purpose is to identify children with low well-being, and offer help to them.

Subjective Health

The WHO (1948) defines health as "a state of complete physical, mental, and social well-being—not merely the absence of disease or infirmity" (Official Records No. 2, p. 100). Researchers and policy makers who study the ways that health (and perceptions of health) affects people's lives work in the area of *health-related quality of life*. The concept of health-related quality of life was developed at the U.S. Center for Disease Control and Prevention (CDC) to encompass people's self-perceptions of health as well as the physical, mental, and social functioning that results from their health status (Moriarty, Zack, & Kobau, 2003). Existing work in this area demonstrates the value that subjective measures of the conditions in people's lives can have for guiding policy decisions.

As societies move from a state where infectious diseases and acute illnesses are the major causes of death to a state where chronic and degenerative diseases are more widespread, the monitoring of the secondary effects of health states becomes increasingly important. Subjective feelings, including feelings about health and well-being, will play an increasingly central role in guiding policies that relate to these effects. First of all, subjective measures, including global evaluations of health status, often provide valid information about a person's true health status. Because these measures can be collected very quickly and easily, they often provide a more efficient method for studying the causes and effects of poor health.

Various measures of subjective health exist. Sometimes these measures simply ask people to categorize their health using descriptors such as *poor, fair, good*, or *excellent*. Other measures focus on people's satisfaction with their health. Still others inquire about specific outcomes that might result from poor health, including the number of working days that were missed for mental or physical health reasons. Each measures likely taps into different aspects of health, but all can be valuable for understanding people's perception of their health and its effects on their lives. For instance, questions that ask people to categorize their health as bad or good might result in a rating that can provide a valid indicator of objective health. Health satisfaction, on the other hand, might be more heavily influenced by people's expectancies and comparison standards. Octogenarians might report *fair* health, but say they are extremely satisfied with their health because they believe that most people of their age have terrible health. Ruggeri, Warner, Bisoffi, & Fontecedro (2001) claim that subjective measures provide independent information from objective measures of health, and thus they can help to provide a more complete picture of the quality of life of patients.

In support of these claims, research shows that health-related quality-of-life measures can validly assess objective health status (Beatty,

Schechter, & Whitaker, 1996; BRFSS, 2006). Simple self-rated health measures predict subsequent mortality (Hennessy, Moriarty, Zack, Scherr, & Brackbill, 1994). In fact, Edler and Benyamini (1997) found that in 23 of 27 studies they reviewed, self-rated health predicted survival or longevity. Furthermore, a number of studies have shown that subjective reports of health can predict outcomes such as longevity, even after controlling for objective reports of health (Ganz, Lee, & Siau, 1991; McClellan, Anson, Birkeli, & Tuttle, 1991; Mossey & Shapiro, 1982; Rumsfeld et al., 1999). This supports the idea that subjective measures include additional valid information that is not included in the objective reports that might typically be used.

Additional research shows similar findings in other domains. Brzenchek et al. (2001) found that the health-related quality-of-life-measures could predict whether older people were likely to experience Alzheimer's disease in the future. Härter, Conway, & Merikangas (2003) found that items related to depression and anxiety predicted subsequent hospitalization for cardiac problems. In light of the fact that the subjective measures can be obtained on large populations much more cheaply than assessments based on medical checkups, they can have a high benefit-to-cost ratio in epidemiological studies even if they were less valid than physician ratings based on a thorough medical examination.

In cases where subjective measures do not correspond well to overall objective health (e.g., Deaton, 2008), research into the causes of these discrepancies can provide insight into expectancies, problem areas, and people's likely behavior. For instance, the fact that citizens of the United States have lower confidence in their health care system than do those in much poorer nations such as India, Iran, or Sierra Leone (Deaton, 2008) does not mean that the medical treatment per se is inferior, but that there are issues such as affordability or accessibility that trouble people. We should not ignore low ratings such as those in the United States just because they might not at first make sense in relation to objective conditions that exist in these nations. Instead, we can ask what we might learn from the low satisfaction ratings. For instance, Crow et al. (2002) found that satisfaction with health care depends on the patient–practitioner relationship, and one hypothesis is that Americans feel that this aspect of their health care could be improved. Crow et al. also compared the satisfaction with care produced by different systems such as fee-for-service, prepaid schemes, and gate-keeping arrangements. Thus, satisfaction with treatment can reveal information beyond just treatment effectiveness.

It is certainly important that subjective measures of health and well-being correspond to objective circumstances. However, a broader goal for these measures is to guide decisions in the policy arena. Moriarty et al.

(2003) suggested that self-reports of health can be "particularly useful for finding unmet health needs, identifying disparities among demographic and socioeconomic subpopulations, characterizing the symptom burden of disabilities and chronic diseases, and tracking population patterns and trends" (p. 1). Thus, societies that systematically track subjective health can identify health conditions that are receiving too little attention. Furthermore, these measures enable policy makers to locate segments of the population that experience above-average problems with their health. Because the links between specific health conditions and the problems that result may not be intuitive, such studies can provide information that even detailed knowledge about symptoms could not. For example, Lackner et al. (2006) found that those with irritable bowel syndrome reported greater numbers of sick days than did those with arthritis, diabetes, heart disease, or cancer. Subjective measures might reveal how and why such conditions affect economic outcomes including loss of work. As an example from a different domain, people who are low in social integration report twice the number of sick days as do people high in social integration (Ôunpuu, Chambers, Patterson, Chan, & Yusuf, 2001). This suggests that monitoring people's social lives in addition to their health might help researchers and practitioners understand the links between health status and work-related outcomes.

Another aspect of subjective health is people's satisfaction with their medical treatment. Sans-Corrales et al. (2006) reviewed 356 articles and found that several factors were associated with consumers' satisfaction with their family health care: accessibility, consultation time, relationships with their doctor, and continuity of care. Several of these factors also predicted improvement in patients' health. Accessibility was based on receiving an appointment soon, and a short time spent in the waiting room. Patients were more satisfied with a doctor who was confident, warm, and friendly. Although patient satisfaction with health care does not invariably mean better health care, it is one element in medical treatment that should not be ignored. After all, a medical system that wastes patients' time with long waits, frustrates them with inaccessibility, and treats them with disrespect is not the most desirable system.

Summary

Doctors and medical researchers have developed powerful diagnostic tools for recognizing disease states and the conditions that lead to them. Subjective measures of well-being, health satisfaction, and treatment satisfaction can be added to this armamentarium of assessment tools. These measures can help predict health and illness, and help assist in identifying people who would most benefit from interventions. The subjective well-being measures can also serve to help indicate where health dollars can best be spent, and to measure the improvements in quality of life that are produced by interventions. Thus, policy leaders will find subjective measures to be a valuable adjunct in formulating health and prevention policies.

Chapter 9

The Environment and Well-Being: Policy Examples

The policy examples presented in the previous chapter involve the use of subjective measures to assess something about the person who is doing the reporting—his or her health state and the effects that this health state have on daily functioning. But people's judgments of their own well-being can also reveal something about the features of the environment in which people live. In this chapter, we present four examples of policy questions regarding the environment that can be informed by well-being measures.

Airport Noise

A recent example of using well-being measures to supplement economic indicators comes from a study of airport noise around Schipol airport in Amsterdam (Van Praag and Ferrer-i-Carbonell 2004, Van Praag & Baarsma 2005). In earlier studies, the impact of airport noise was estimated by comparing the price of houses located in areas with different amounts of aircraft noise. The presumption, borne out by the evidence, was that airport noise is a nuisance that leads to lower housing prices for homes that are most affected by the noise. Presumably, this difference in price reflects something about the quality of life that could be maintained while living in the house, rather than something objectively different about the houses in the different areas.

Unfortunately, there are limitations to using either assessed values or market values of differentially affected houses to set a value on aircraft noise. First of all, prices must adjust rapidly for there to be a fluid market that reveals preferences. However, housing markets might turn over very slowly. There may be market restrictions including price controls, and there are often high costs associated with moving, which may keep people in the same residence even if they wished to move. Second, prices might not reflect the impact of airport noise because buyers might not fully realize how airport noise will affect them. They might underestimate the number of planes that fly past the house, or they may assume that they will rapidly adapt to the noise that exists. Until someone buys a home and lives in the noisy location for some time, it is impossible for that person to understand the long-term effects. A problem with purchasing decisions is that they are based on the perceived impact of the goods in question, rather than on the actual objective impact. Thus, although such methods might be able to reveal people's beliefs about the effects of noise, they may have more difficulty in assessing how long-term noise is actually experienced.

Measures of subjective well-being provide an alternate way to assess the value of the nuisance caused by aircraft noise. Van Praag and Ferrer-i-Carbonell (see also Van Praag & Baarsma, 2005) compared reported life satisfaction of respondents who lived in the Amsterdam area, but who experienced different levels of aircraft noise. Previous studies had found a statistically significant negative impact of noise on housing prices, though the size of this effect differed greatly across the 20 studies that Van Praag and Ferrer-i-Carbonell reviewed. Consistent with these results, the new study found that aircraft noise produced a significant negative effect on life satisfaction, even after controlling for other relevant factors. Furthermore, Van Praag and Ferrer-i-Carbonell found a number of variables that affected the degree to which airport noise was related to lowered life satisfaction. Specifically, those living with larger families, in more expensive housing, and in residences with outdoor space like a garden all had more negative responses to aircraft noise. Whereas the revealed preference approach and the contingent valuation method each produces estimates of the harmful effects of noise, the life satisfaction approach produced an estimate of noise effects based on experienced utility. The estimate of value was provided by those who were actually living with the nuisance over a period of time.

Importantly, these life satisfaction-based indexes not only reveal where problems exist, they can also provide critical information about the utility of possible solutions to these problems. After conducting their initial analyses Van Praag and Ferrer-i-Carbonell (2004) went on to examine potential interventions that could ameliorate the noise problems. For instance, one option would be to calculate the effects of aircraft noise on life satisfaction and then use the known association between income and life satisfaction to come up with a reasonable amount by which homeowners in affected areas could be compensated. Van Praag and Ferrer-i-Carbonell calculated the amount of compensation that would be required, and it was substantial.

Alternatively, researchers could investigate whether there are any other factors that moderate the impact of noise on well-being and determine whether those factors could be changed to affect well-being. Specifically, Van Praag and Ferrer-i-Carbonell investigated the effect of insulation on residents' response to noise. They discovered that noise insulation substantially reduced the negative effects of noise. In fact, insulation cuts the effect of aircraft noise on life satisfaction by more than half. Such results allow policy makers to compute the monetary value for the insulation that would be required to return affected residents' subjective well-being to what it would be without the aircraft noise. This might be a reasonable form of compensation given that aircraft noise is a nuisance created by a public benefit that has negative effects only for some households. Policy makers can use the revealed preference method, contingent valuation figures, or a well-being analysis to guide the calculation of the correct amount of compensation. Each of the methods has its own strengths and limitations, but Van Praag and Ferrer-i-Carbonell argue that the well-being approach has distinct advantages over the others.

More studies need to be conducted on the well-being effects of airport noise and the moderators of these effects. A replication study conducted by Schreckenberg and Meis (2007) around an airport in Frankfurt, Germany, examined the associations between noise and different domain satisfaction scores. They found that different outcome variables were differentially associated with aircraft noise. As expected, those who lived in areas with the highest levels of noise reported the lowest residential satisfaction. But those who lived with moderate levels of noise had the lowest health satisfaction, and those in the highest noise areas had the highest levels of satisfaction with family and friends. Although respondents were annoyed by aircraft noise, especially during outdoor activities, their life satisfaction did not seem to be seriously harmed by it. It could be that there are differences in the outcomes depending on the degree of noise, what time of day it occurs, whether there are other significant sources of noise, the amount of time people spend outdoors, the turnover of the local housing market, the knowledge buyers have of the effects of airport noise, and so forth. In order to calculate the amount of compensation due to homeowners or renters, or the amount that should be spent on noise insulation, the effects of important moderators will be useful information for policy makers.

When policy makers consider paying for noise insulation for new homes or for retrofitting older homes, the effect of noise on life satisfaction is just one consideration, and other factors must also come into play. Airports might have other detrimental effects for those who live near them, and not all of these effects will emerge in life satisfaction-based analyses. For example, Bechtel and Churchman (2002) reviewed the effects of noise on physical health and children's language development. They concluded that noise negatively affects people's physical health through sleep disturbance, hearing loss, and increased stress. Similarly, Hygge, Evans, and Bullinger (2002) found that cognitive performance of schoolchildren was affected by airport noise. These effects are likely to heighten the concerns of policy makers about noise beyond the effects on subjective well-being. Thus, life satisfaction is an important consideration when evaluating policies aimed at noise remediation and compensation, but not the only one. Nevertheless, life satisfaction provides one method for setting the amount of compensation that should be made available to people affected by a public nuisance like airport noise. Although much more research is needed on the effects of airport noise, the Schipol study and others like it provide vivid case studies on how life satisfaction data could be used by policy makers.

Commuting

The world is becoming increasingly urbanized, and this urbanization has brought concerns about transportation and commuting. As cities grow, a greater percentage of people in urban areas must commute to work (e.g., Pisarski, 1987). It is now estimated that 100 million Americans commute to work each day (Evans & Wener, 2006). An overwhelming majority of the U.S. labor force commutes by private automobile (Novaco, Stokols, & Milanesi, 1990), and the majority of these commuters travel alone (Collier & Christiansen, 1992; Liss, 1991). In many cities the number of cars has increased much faster than the number of people (Novaco & Collier, 1994) and most streets and freeways have much greater congestion than they did several decades ago (e.g., Novaco et al., 1990). As a result, commuting times in the United States continue to increase (Reschovsky, 2004). It is not surprising then, that policy makers are concerned about the impact of cars and other forms of transportation on the quality of life within their cities. In order to address commuting problems, urban planners have suggested more freeways, more public transportation, renewal of downtown living areas, and greater "Internet commuting" to work.

There is no question that commuting has an effect on many areas of a person's life. It costs money, it uses natural resources, and when traffic or construction slows down a commute, it can lower productivity by reducing the amount of time people have available for work. But are there also effects that can be picked up by subjective measures? Does commuting lower people's subjective feelings of quality of life? Intuition alone cannot answer this question, as the reasons for commuting are often quite complicated. People might choose to commute because moving away from their workplace allows them to buy a bigger house in a nicer neighborhood with a better school district for their children. Thus, although the commute itself might be unpleasant, on balance, positive life circumstances that long commutes can provide might enhance their overall well-being. In contrast, even though people think that a bigger house in a nicer neighborhood will compensate for the misery of a long commute, they might underestimate the toll that this daily routine will take. Research has shown that people tend to overestimate the life satisfaction they will derive from material possessions (such as a larger house) and to underestimate the life satisfaction from more time spent with family and friends. If so, the positive effects of long commutes might not outweigh the negative, resulting in an overall loss of subjective well-being.

Furthermore, the average well-being of a society might be lower when there is a great deal of commuting even if each individual makes the correct individual decision about the length of commute that provides the best balance for his or her life. Because commuting has many potential externalities, even ideal individual decisions might have negative consequences for society as a whole. Each additional person who commutes adds to the total amount of commuting within an area, and this could increase the overall costs to each person. Specifically, with each additional commuter, travel times increase, infrastructure costs rise, and the frustration that results from dense traffic is more likely to occur.

There have been a number of studies that have examined the well-being consequences of commuting. Hagihara, Tarumi, Babazono, Nobutomo, and Morimoto (1998) found that professional men in Japan who commute more than 90 minutes per day reported lower job satisfaction than do those who commute less, even after controlling for many work and nonwork factors. Ahn (2005) found similar results in Spain, with women showing the most negative effects on life satisfaction from commuting. Stokols and Novaco (1981) reviewed many of the factors that moderate the quality of commuting time. Commuting in crowded conditions and long commutes were both associated with lower levels of frustration tolerance, job stability, health, and work absences. In addition, these factors were associated with lowered mood and life satisfaction (Novaco, 1992; Novaco, Kliewer, & Broquet, 1991; Novaco et al., 1990;). Novaco and Collier (1994) found that commuting stress was higher in those with longer commutes. In addition, they found that the stress was worse for women than for men. Importantly, they found that ride sharing helped mitigate some of the commuting-generated stress.

Kahneman and Krueger (2006) used the Day Reconstruction Method (DRM) to assess moods during various activities of the day in a large sample of women. They found that the lowest mood of the day occurred while commuting to work (commuting home from work also was low compared to most other activities). In contrast, they found that time spent with family and friends, having sex, praying, talking on the phone, exercising, and watching TV were all much more pleasurable. Similarly, Schwarz, Kahneman, and Xu (2008) found that negative emotions were relatively high and positive emotions were very low during commuting, resulting in the lowest *affect balance* score (preponderance of positive over negative feelings) of all activities that were studied (see also Kahneman, Krueger, Schkade, Schwarz, & Stone, 2004; Prizmic & Kaliterna-Lipovcan, 2008). Thus, commuting not only lowers subjective well-being by causing increased stress, it also reduces the time spent on more enjoyable activities.

Consistent with this evidence, Frey and Stutzer (2004) and Stutzer and Frey (2008) found that people with long commutes reported lower life satisfaction than people with short commutes. Importantly, some of the moderators of this effect give insight into potential processes that underlie this effect. Frey and Stutzer examined the links between external orientation and the effects of commuting on satisfaction. People with high external orientation are more motivated by factors such as money and prestige, whereas those with low external orientation might be motivated more by internal factors including job satisfaction or the desire to build skills. Frey and Stutzer found that those with high external orientation suffered more from longer commutes. This finding suggests that the misprediction of the utility that will be derived from the commute choice might lead to lower life satisfaction. Externally oriented individuals might be likely to focus on income and housing when making choices regarding which job to take and where to live. In turn, they might neglect the importance of the subjective experiences such as commuting and spending time with family and friends.

Consistent with this idea, Peasgood (2007) reported that respondents in the United Kingdom who commuted an hour or more per day had much higher incomes and consumption than the average of their sample. But this increased economic well-being was not reflected in their subjective well-being; this relatively wealthy group reported life satisfaction levels that were just average. Stutzer and Frey (2007a) examined commuting effects in the German Socio-Economic Panel Study, and they estimated that it would take a 19% increase in income to raise a commuter's life satisfaction to the life satisfaction of those who have no commuting time whatsoever. They also reported that life satisfaction is lower for respondents whose partners commute longer, suggesting that commuting might have negative externalities for other family members.

A question that is relevant for policy development is whether commuting on public transportation has the same negative effects on well-being as does commuting in a car. Just as studies of car commuting have shown deleterious cardiovascular outcomes (e.g., Robinson, 1991), so too have studies of rail passengers (Singer, Lundberg, & Frankenhaeuser, 1978; White & Rotton, 1998). A study of New York commuters by Evans and Wener (2006) showed that those with longer commutes reported higher stress. Furthermore, they showed higher cortisol on commuting days than on noncommuting days, and this was related in a dose–response linear pattern to the length of the commute. Commuters in this study also showed poorer proofreading performance, a measure of accuracy and motivation, and this performance was related to the length of their commute. Finally, studies of commuters show that they have worse task persistence after commuting (Koslowsky, Kluger, & Reich, 1995; White & Rotton, 1998).

A quasi-experimental study by Wener, Evans, Phillips, and Nadler (2003) found that improving rail service by reducing the number of transfers that were required, along with overall commuting time, led to decreases in stress. Some commuters from New Jersey began taking a new connection in their commute to New York City, whereas others continued the old route that was longer and had an additional connection. The new, shorter route produced improvements in self-report measures of stress, cortisol levels, and a proofreading attention measure. In a second experimental study in which role-playing commuters were randomly assigned to the old or new commutes, the shorter commute showed beneficial effects for stress, cortisol levels, and proofreading performance.

Data indicating that commuting leads to lower well-being are now extensive. And although additional research is needed (particularly research using longitudinal or experimental techniques), the existing body of research is quite strong. In the studies discussed above, relevant control variables were often assessed and statistically removed, yet the negative effects of commuting still emerged. Furthermore, methods like the DRM allow researchers to sample the same person's moods across many different activities. This means that many of the comparisons discussed above are within-person comparisons. Thus, preexisting differences in income, job satisfaction, or some other individual-level characteristic cannot explain these effects.

With the accumulation of evidence, policy implications are beginning to emerge. First, the data indicate that commuting has a negative effect on both health and subjective well-being. Furthermore, commuting is linked with relatively low levels of mood compared to most alternative activities.

Because commuting time is increasing, many people are spending more time in a less pleasurable activity and less time in more pleasurable ones such as time with family and friends. This research also shows that reducing the length of commutes and ride sharing help reduce stress and improve the quality of commuting time. This means that policy decisions that help reduce the length of commutes or those that encourage carpooling could potentially increase well-being. Importantly, the effects of commuting are not limited to automobile travel, which means that simply replacing automobile commuting with public transportation commuting may not be able to solve all problems. Interestingly, advances in technology might change this part of the equation. New technologies for portable entertainment, communication, and productivity (which are difficult to use while driving but easy to use on public transportation) might increase the difference in well-being effects of public versus solo commuting. Social interactions might be improved by either car-pooling or appropriate design for public transportation. Future research is needed to address these possibilities.

Of course, the specific course of action that community leaders take will depend on a variety of other factors. Reductions in the length of time spent commuting could come from policies designed to increase carpooling or to facilitate telecommuting, or they could come from the revitalization of urban residential areas and better urban planning with increased integration of work and residential areas. Furthermore, policies could encourage different choices by households by changing the incentives that are linked with different commuting decisions. Finally, the well-being data point to an increasing role of education. Policy makers and commuters alike need to realize that the costs of commuting affect the well-being of many others, in both current and future generations. If people were better informed about the consequences of their choices for themselves and others, they might make better choices.

Parks and Green Spaces

Contact with nature has a positive influence on many aspects of life (see Bird, 2007, for a review). It is associated with higher concentration levels, lower levels of aggression, lower levels of stress, and higher levels of well-being. For instance, experimental studies have found that subjects perform better on tasks such as proofreading when they are exposed to a natural environment as compared to performance while exposed to an urban environment (Hartig, Mang, & Evans, 1991). Other studies show that university students scored higher on a test when they had views of nature (Tennessen & Cimprich, 1995). In addition, exposure to nature has been linked with a variety of health outcomes including faster recovery times among hospital patients, decreased mortality among senior citizens, and fewer sick call visits for prisoners (Lavin, Higgins, Metcalfe, & Jordan, 2006; Maller, Townsend, Pryor, Brown, & St. Leger, 2006; Moore, 1981). Even just exposing patients to nature scenes can lead to reduction in the use of painkillers (Ulrich, 1984).

Bird (2007) described three major theories that might explain why contact with nature has such beneficial effects. First, the biophilia hypothesis suggests that humans have hardwired positive feelings for nature. When people are given a choice about the landscapes they prefer, they select those with water and variety, and those which resemble a *savanna* (Bird, 2007; Kaplan, 2001). Some have suggested that this desire is the result of selection processes in which people that pursued such environments were more likely to survive. If so, then the *need* for such contact might function like any other basic need—when satisfied, positive outcomes result. Second, the *restoration hypothesis* suggests that the brain is restored and recharged by exposure to nature. According to this theory, direct attention involves concentration, which causes mental fatigue. Exposure to nature does not require focused attention and permits faster restoration of energy levels. The third hypothesis is that natural environments allow people to overcome the physiological stress response.

It is also possible that at least in some circumstances, exposure to nature might foster social contact and build social capital because it encourages people to go outside and interact with one another. Kweon, Sullivan, and Wiley (1998) reported that green space fosters both individual social ties and a broader sense of community in neighborhoods. This may, in turn, lead to positive outcomes within neighborhoods and communities. Kuo and Sullivan (2001a, 2001b), for instance, found that vegetation reduced crime in inner-city housing. In the sample they studied, there were 52% fewer crimes in the housing units with the most vegetation as compared to housing units with the least vegetation. There were also 56% fewer violent crimes.

Given these benefits, does exposure to nature increase subjective well-being? Vemuri and Costanza (2006) attempted to answer this question by examining the differences in *natural capital* across 171 nations of the world. Natural capital was assessed by calculating the amount of specific types of landcover that each nation had, and then weighting these values by the ecosystem value of the landcover. This measure of natural environment resources correlated significantly with life satisfaction of countries, even after controlling for other factors including education and income.

Other studies that have examined the association at the individual level have also found an effect. Talbot and Kaplan (1991) found that seniors who had close access to a place where they could enjoy nature had higher life satisfaction and residential satisfaction. Workplace views of nature have been related to lower stress, lesser likelihood of quitting, and higher job satisfaction (Kaplan & Kaplan, 1989; Leather, Pygras, Beale, & Lawrence, 1998). Wells and Evans (2003) found that children who have stressful lives report less subjective stress responses and have higher self-esteem if they are exposed to nature. A survey in the United Kingdom showed that over 90% of respondents reported that it is important to have green space near where they live.

Experimental studies also support the idea that exposure to nature is a causal factor in reducing stress and increasing well-being. In these studies, people are exposed to a stressor and then presented with nature scenes or a control stimulus. For example, in one study, participants were first asked to watch a terrifying horror film. After this anxiety-provoking experience, they would were exposed to either nature scenes or urban scenes. Physiological reactions were monitored throughout. Those who viewed nature scenes returned to baseline on the physiological measures more quickly than did those who were exposed to the urban scenes (Ulrich et al., 1991). In another study, participants were exposed to a stressor and then asked to watch a movie simulating either a drive through a natural landscape or a drive through an urban area. Again, those who viewed the natural scenes showed faster recovery from the stressful event (Parsons, Tassinary, Ulrich, Hebl, & Grossman-Alexander, 1998). In addition, viewing the nature scenes had a protective effect when participants encountered a subsequent additional stressor. These effects appear to generalize when more realistic natural stimuli are used. For instance, in one study, young adults were asked to walk through either a natural or urban setting. Anger decreased and positive emotions increased during the nature walk, whereas the reverse was true during the urban walk (Hartig, Evans, Jamner, David, & Garling, 2003).

Similar effects also emerge when research is conducted among those who are not necessarily undergoing a stressful event. For instance, participants who are exposed to views of nature show more positive moods than those who are exposed to urban views (Rohde & Kendle, 1994; Ulrich, 1979), and in a health care setting, patients showed less stress on days when the waiting room contained a mural of nature rather than a blank wall. This effect was reflected in both self-ratings of stress and heart rate measurements (Heerwagen 1990; White & Heerwagen, 1998). Kaplan (2001) found that apartment dwellers had higher satisfaction with their neighborhood, and a higher sense of well-being, when they had views of nature from their residences; simply having a window was not sufficient. The view required the existence of a natural scene to enhance well-being. A broad range of correlational and experimental research suggests that green space has a causal role in well-being, and that the association is not simply due to some third variable such as wealth (see Morris, 2003; Ulrich, 2002, for a review).

The implications for policy makers are clear. Hard concrete and asphalt urban landscapes do not generate feelings of well-being as well as views of greenery and nature do. This points to the desirability not only of urban parks but also of trees planted around buildings, plants within buildings, and views of nature from building windows. Zoning and building permits could be designed to include green space in urban designs. Not only can this have a salutary effect on health and behavior, but it can also increase people's subjective well-being. As the world becomes increasingly urbanized, people's well-being can be heightened by including frequent contact with nature in our cities, and measures of well-being should reveal the benefits in urban areas varying in greenery.

Air Pollution

Air pollution due to human sources is a threat to health and the environment, as well as to people's subjective well-being. Although some gains have been made in combating air pollution in economically developed nations, the threat remains and is particularly pronounced in developing nations. What does air quality cost society, and how much should we spend on its remediation? Economic analyses of this question might consider the cost to health and medical care, along with the costs to fix the environmental damage that has been done. However, an alternative method that is based on well-being measures would be to evaluate whether regions with high air pollution have lower well-being scores. These effects could be compared to the effects that could be obtained through other policies that governments might consider enacting. Resource allocation could then be determined by which policy will result in the largest well-being benefit. Initial research suggests that well-being is sensitive to differences in air pollution. For instance, Welsch (2006) found that over time air pollution levels were related to life satisfaction in 10 European nations, and Jacobs, Evans, Catalano, and Dooley (1984) found that symptoms of depression were related to air quality in Los Angeles. Thus, such approaches for guiding policy could be fruitful.

The life satisfaction approach to valuing air quality is exemplified in an informative study by Luechinger (2007). The study is exemplary in that it involved not only an examination of areas in several nations that varied in air pollution due to sulfur dioxide, but also because it included longitudinal data across a period where air pollution was brought under control. Specifically, the authors studied the impact that the installation of industrial scrubbers had on reports of life satisfaction. Importantly, the authors of the study were able to use a quasi-experimental design. Specific areas were divided into treatment and control groups based on the time of introduction of scrubbers, as well as on the prevailing wind directions from the plants (communities that were downwind from the new equipment should see more of an environmental benefit than communities that were upwind).

The central finding was that sulfur dioxide emissions negatively affected the life satisfaction of areas. Furthermore, Luechinger (2007) compared the estimated effect based on life satisfaction data to that which would be obtained from housing price differentials using the revealed preference approach. Housing prices were sensitive to the influence of air pollution, but the effect was much smaller than for the life satisfaction-based analyses. As noted in our discussion of the limitations of economic measures, housing prices and rent may not reflect the true cost of pollution because there are additional costs associated with moving that serve to balance the negative effects of the pollution. Whatever the reason, it appears that an analysis of the housing market yields a smaller estimate for the negative effects of air pollution than does the life satisfaction method. Luechinger's analysis also suggests that the costs of power plant desulfurization were small compared to the willingness-to-pay estimates derived from the life satisfaction or housing data.

Thus, not only is air pollution bad for health and the environment, it appears that it is also bad for subjective well-being. We do not yet know the threshold levels of air pollution that influence well-being or the types of pollution that matter most. Indeed, we do not yet know the underlying processes that connect air pollution to lower well-being. However, the fact that air pollution lowers feelings of well-being and increases feelings of depression is clearly a matter of immense importance for policy makers. The prevalence of this problem will be apparent when accounts of well-being are widespread. Furthermore, additional data like that described by Luechinger (2007) can help policy makers identify cost-effective strategies for reducing pollution's effects.

Conclusions

Aircraft noise, commuting, air pollution, and safe and accessible public spaces all have important externalities, because decisions by individuals affect the consequences for others. This provides a classic requirement for public policies designed to increase positive externalities and decrease negative ones. Appropriate collection and use of life satisfaction data offer many opportunities for measuring the extent of these externalities. In addition, they allow researchers and decision makers to evaluate various ways of removing the negative effects and adding to the positive ones. The well-being data allow decision makers to evaluate the costs of various policies and to balance these against the outcomes that will result. Furthermore, if multiple solutions exist, policy makers can compare the impact of various interventions with one another.

Chapter 10

Work, the Economy, and Well-Being: Policy Examples

Economic theories suggest that income and wealth should provide relatively strong indicators of a person's overall well-being. Because money allows people to satisfy preferences, those who have lots of money should be closer to their ideal states, all other things being equal. Yet, as we noted earlier, this link between money and well-being requires a few assumptions, not all of which are always reasonable (at least in their strongest forms). Because many economic theories—and the policies on which they are based—assume that money provides a reasonable proxy for general well-being, research that explicitly tests this assumption has the potential to provide much new policy-relevant information. Thus, policy-focused well-being research within the economic domain has the potential to be a particularly fruitful area.

Unemployment

Unemployment provides a particularly important test of the links between income and well-being. On the one hand, for the individuals involved, unemployment has clear financial implications. Those who experience unemployment lose their income, at least temporarily. Therefore, if income and wealth are proxies for well-being, then unemployment should affect subjective reports to the extent that income is affected. Furthermore, the amount of wealth that a person has amassed should moderate these effects, and any societal policies that are in place to protect the wealth of individuals who experience temporary bouts of unemployment (e.g., unemployment benefits that replace the lost income) should counteract any negative effects of job loss. Thus, the impact of unemployment on subjective measures of well-being might vary across nations or regions that have different policies in place.

Yet unemployment also has psychological effects on the individuals who lose their jobs. Depending on the cause of job loss, unemployment may signal to an individual that he or she is not as valuable as might have been thought by them, and this may impact a variety of psychological outcomes including self-esteem and optimism. If unemployment has additional negative effects that go beyond the economic impact of job loss, then policies that focus more on these psychological aspects (including job retraining and perhaps even psychological counseling) may be more successful at undoing the negative effects of unemployment than are purely economic measures. In the current section, we review the links between unemployment and well-being, focusing on the impact that these issues have for policy decisions.

Unemployment is a particularly vexing problem for economists. Although job loss and the inability to find work should, in most cases, be experienced as negative for the individuals who are affected, economists and policy makers have competing goals when addressing the problems that unemployment creates. For instance, there are often trade-offs between unemployment and inflation, and policies designed to improve one may have unintended negative consequences on the other. Furthermore, many economic models suggest that some degree of unemployment is necessary for efficient free market systems to work. And of course, some unemployment is voluntary, as people balance the cost of working with the benefits they receive from the specific type of work that is available too them.

In recent years, a number of studies have added to the economic debates about unemployment by examining effects of job loss and inability to find work on subjective well-being. Importantly, this work can not only determine whether unemployment is experienced as unpleasant, but it can help clarify the reasons why people become unemployed, it can isolate the factors that moderate reactions to unemployment, and it can determine the extent to which specific policies help people recover from unemployment, both psychologically and economically.

Most research shows that unemployment is associated with lower levels of subjective well-being. For example, Clark, Diener, Georgellis, and Lucas (2006) used panel data from the German Socio-Economic Panel Study (GSOEP), and they found that life satisfaction dropped after people became unemployed. Men were more negatively affected by layoffs than women, and men also showed less adjustment to the condition.

Furthermore, being high in satisfaction before the job loss seemed to provide no protection against the negative effects. Winkelmann and Winkelmann (1998) used a smaller subset of the GSOEP data, and they also found that unemployment was followed by a drop in life satisfaction, and Marks and Fleming (1999) found a similar pattern in Australian panel data. Stutzer and Frey (2007b) found that well-being falls when people lose their jobs and rises when they regain employment. These studies confirm that unemployment is experienced as being unpleasant and that well-being takes a hit when people lose their jobs.

However, the well-being studies also go beyond this simple conclusion. For instance, some economic models assume that being unemployed is a voluntary state that should not have a long-term impact on well-being. Although an initial job loss may be quite devastating, jobs are almost always available. An unemployed person must decide whether the pay that he or she would receive is sufficient to justify doing the work that is available. If not, then the rational decision would be to stay unemployed doing alternative nonpaid activities and waiting for a better opportunity to come along. The fact that those who stay unemployed for longer periods of time do not report higher levels of life satisfaction argues against this idea (Lucas, Clark, Georgellis, & Diener, 2004). Lucas et al. also found that people who had previously been unemployed did not react less negatively to a new bout of unemployment, suggesting that people do not quickly become accustomed to being unemployed.

Importantly, research that uses panel studies to assess the impact of unemployment on well-being allows researchers to determine whether the effect of unemployment is mostly on economic effects, or whether there are additional psychological consequences. For instance, most of the research examining the unemployment controls for income, meaning that the effects of unemployment are substantial even after accounting for the changes in income that occur. And perhaps more importantly, research shows that the effects of unemployment remain, even after people become reemployed. For instance, Clark, Georgellis, and Sanfey (2001) found that currently employed people with past unemployment episodes were more likely to report low life satisfaction than currently employed people with no past episodes. This *scarring* effect suggests that simply regaining employment does not undo the negative effects of the unemployment experience.

One plausible alternative explanation of this scarring effect is selection. It is very possible that people with repeated bouts of unemployment might have mental health problems that affect both their ability to hold a job and their subjective well-being. But Lucas et al. (2004) used additional waves from the GSOEP to show that even after becoming reemployed, those who experienced a bout of unemployment reported lower levels of life satisfaction than they did before the job loss occurred. The fact that these were within-person comparisons rules out selection effects.

The conclusions from these panel studies (which mainly use life satisfaction as an outcome) were confirmed in a meta-analysis of the associations between unemployment and various mental health outcomes, including reports of depression and subjective well-being. Paul (2005) found that unemployment was negatively associated with most aspects of mental health, and effect sizes were substantial. Consistent with the results reported above, the meta-analysis revealed that these negative effects emerged in both cross-sectional and panel-design studies. In addition, the data confirmed that psychological losses among the unemployed cannot be explained by their lost incomes. Thus, these effects are too large to be compensated by any feasible income transfer (Frey & Stutzer, 2002).

Also consistent with the panel studies described above, Paul's (2005) meta-analysis showed that selection effects (in which individuals with mental health problems or low subjective well-being are less likely to obtain and keep a full-time job) were smaller than the overall effects of unemployment. This suggests that the majority of the association between unemployment and mental health results from the unemployment experience itself rather than from the selection of unhappy people into unemployment. Therefore, the lasting psychological effects of unemployment appear to be real.

Importantly, meta-analyses can be used to examine the moderators of the unemployment effect, which can help determine the processes that underlie the differences that are found. For instance, Paul (2005) showed that the detrimental effects of unemployment were larger for working-class employees than for white-collar employees. In addition, the negative effects of unemployment were smaller in countries with higher income equality and in societies with a high level of unemployment protection. This suggests that various economic factors might offer some protection for those who lose their jobs. For instance, white-collar workers might fare better than blue-collar workers because they might have greater amassed wealth, which can protect them during temporary bouts of unemployment. Similarly, generous unemployment benefits reduce the economic consequences of unemployment, which might help maintain well-being. Thus, an important remaining question is whether any psychological effects remain for those who experience unemployment, but who have high wealth and good benefits to protect their economic standing while they look for more work.

Recently, Ahn, Garcia, and Jimeno (2004) used a cross-national study (the European Community Household Panel survey) to examine the factors that influence the impact of unemployment on well-being. Replicating the findings described above, they found that unemployment had a long-term effect on individual well-being. Consistent with Paul's meta-analysis, they also found that the effects of unemployment were smaller in nations where unemployment spells were shorter, where unemployment benefits were greater, where the unemployment rate was lower, and where job prospects were seen as better. Thus, both a healthy economy and benefits that maintain income helped buffer the negative effects of losing one's job. Ahn et al. found that Denmark and the Netherlands were exceptional in this respect. Similarly, Becchetti, Castriota, and Giuntella (2006) found that the costs of unemployment were much higher in countries with low job protection, as well as in middle-aged persons.

Some studies have shown that the effects of unemployment may extend beyond affected individuals and families and into the communities where these unemployed individuals live. For example, Catalano, Dooley, Novaco, Hough, and Wilson (1993) found that being laid off greatly increased the likelihood of violence in a community. However, Clark, Diener, Georgellis, Lucas (2006) found that the individual life satisfaction losses from unemployment are smaller in communities where average rates of unemployment are higher. Other studies using subjective well-being data suggest that unemployment spells end sooner for those who show large drops in happiness and who have not been repeatedly unemployed (Clark, Georgellis, & Sanfey, 2001).

The effects of specific employment policies on well-being can be studied using subjective well-being as an outcome. For example, Salvatori (2007) found that both temporary and permanent workers had higher life satisfaction when restrictions on temporary employment were eased. These effects were clearest for women and young workers. Using subjective well-being data in 12 European nations from 1995 to 2001, the researchers found clear evidence that private sector employees were negatively influenced by restrictions on temporary hiring. The findings ran counter to the idea that temporary workers are harmed by restrictions on firing permanent employees. Salvatori also found lower job satisfaction among temporary workers when the use of temporary labor was restricted. This finding suggests that permanent workers feel more secure in their jobs and like them more when employers are free to hire some workers on a temporary basis. Surprisingly, protection for permanent workers increased job satisfaction for temporary workers.

These examples show that an analysis of unemployment using well-being measures has the potential to increase knowledge beyond that which can be obtained by economic measures alone. Various assumptions can be made about the reasons why people become unemployed or remain unemployed even when jobs are available, but most of these explanations make reference to the feelings that people have and the judgments that people make about their lives. With well-being measures, these underlying processes can be examined. Although skepticism about the quality of the measures has prevented economists and psychologists from opening this black box, the research reviewed in this section shows that well-being measures are very sensitive to changes in employment status and provide important insight into the effects that these changes have. Importantly, these analyses have clear policy implications regarding the best ways to protect workers from the negative consequences of unemployment. In turn, these individual-level effects can have important effects on the broader community and the economy as a whole.

Well-Being in the Workplace

In many of the examples discussed in this section, we have focused on using well-being measures to supplement economic analyses and to clarify underlying processes, or because these measures provide a more direct measure of the outcome that policy makers are trying to achieve (well-being itself). However, sometimes policy makers might be interested in well-being measures because of what they predict. In other words, people who say that they are satisfied with their life may behave differently than people who do not. By studying who says they are satisfied and the processes by which satisfaction ratings lead to outcomes, policy makers can promote the positive outcomes that they wish to achieve. Using well-being measures to understand workplace performance is one area where such an approach could be used.

Organizational and industrial psychologists have a long history of analyzing how subjective well-being at work predicts work outcomes such as productivity. For example, Petty, McGee, and Cavender (1984) meta-analyzed 16 studies that examined the association between job satisfaction and job productivity. They found that the correlation between these two variables (after correcting for the unreliability of the measures) was .31. Similarly, in a much larger meta-analysis (with 74 studies), Iaffaldano and Muchinksy (1985) found a correlation of .29 between overall job satisfaction and job performance. And more recently, Judge, Thoreson, Bono, and Patton (2001) replicated these effects, finding an overall mean correlation of .30 between job satisfaction and performance.

Importantly, Judge et al.'s (2001) review showed that the link between job satisfaction and job performance varied across different types of jobs. Specifically, the effect was significantly stronger for jobs high in complexity compared to jobs of moderate or low complexity. This suggests that for some jobs, the average correlation that is typically found in meta-analyses likely underestimates the true effect (though, of course, this means that for other jobs, the two are likely to be unrelated). The authors concluded that if job satisfaction has a causal effect on performance, then these effects are not likely to be simple and direct. Instead, they are more likely to interact with other variables such as the character of the job, the self-esteem of the employee, and the contingency between pay and performance.

In support of these interactive effects, Wright and Bonett (2007) found that job satisfaction best predicted worker turnover for individuals who were also low in general well-being. Similarly, Colbert, Mount, Harter, Witt, and Barrick (2004) found that workplace deviance (which includes behaviors such as treating other workers in a negative way) was predicted by an interaction between feelings about the job and employees' personality. Specifically, positive perceptions of the workplace predicted low levels of deviant behaviors at work, but this association was strongest for employees low in conscientiousness. Either high conscientiousness or high well-being at work tended to reduce deviant behaviors.

Of course, simple correlations between job satisfaction and job performance tell us little about the direction of causality. Judge et al. (2001) also reviewed studies that might shed light on whether job satisfaction causes or follows from high work performance. As might be expected, their review suggested that there does appear to be a causal path from performance to satisfaction. A majority of the studies they reviewed provided at least suggestive evidence that job performance affects satisfaction. More importantly for the purposes of this book, some studies also suggested a causal effect of satisfaction on performance. For example, Schneider, Hanges, Smith, and Salvaggio (2003) used lagged analyses over time to analyze the causal relation between earnings and employee attitudes toward work. They found a strong relation running from organizational earnings and return on investment to job satisfaction, suggesting that successful workplaces tend to be happy ones. But Schneider et al. also found evidence for the reverse causal paths, suggesting a reciprocal relation between worker satisfaction and earnings. To be sure, without true experiments, there are always alternative explanations of these effects; but longitudinal studies like this provide suggestive evidence that workplace satisfaction might be able to influence job performance.

It is also clear that the relation between well-being and job performance depends on the precise constructs that are assessed. Both well-being and job performance are multifaceted constructs, and not all components exhibit the same associations. For instance, organizational and industrial psychologists have studied the links between work outcomes and job satisfaction, positive mood at work (George & Brief, 1992), trait levels of positive and negative affectivity (Cropanzano, James, & Konovsky, 1993), along with positive affect (Isen & Baron, 1991) and positive emotions (Staw & Barsade, 1993). Furthermore, any specific associations that exist between these narrow constructs and additional work outcomes might vary across occupations. For example, in an analysis involving multiple occupations, Shore and Martin (1989) found that job commitment was related to turnover intentions among hospital professionals, whereas job satisfaction was related to job performance for both bank tellers and hospital professionals. Consistent with this idea, Wright and Staw (1999) suggest that positive moods and emotions (particularly those experienced while on the job) might have different effects than job satisfaction.

It has also been suggested that more indirect forms of work behavior might be more closely linked to well-being than overall job performance. For instance, one aspect of work behavior that is only indirectly related to job performance is called organizational citizenship. Organizational citizenship reflects the degree to which workers perform positive activities that are not part of their formal job description, such as helping fellow workers and avoiding unnecessary sick days. Because organizational citizenship does not refer to the tasks that a person is required to do for his or her job, it might be assumed to be a relatively unimportant work outcome. However, if employees engage in considerable amounts of organizational citizenship, it can make coworkers more effective and create an environment with greater trust, lower turnover, and decreased absences. Because the types of behaviors that are associated with organizational citizenship (including prosocial behavior) have been associated with high levels of well-being in basic social psychological research, it has been suggested that organizational citizenship should show a particularly strong association with well-being (Murphy, Athanasou, & King, 2002; Organ, 1988). However, much more research is needed in this area before we know whether this suggestion is borne out in the data.

Most of the research described above focused on individual-level analyses. In other words, these studies test whether individual workers who are satisfied with their job exhibit above average individual job performance. But additional questions can be raised about the extent to which the average satisfaction within a work unit is linked to the average performance of that unit. Even if personal well-being does not predict personal performance, it is possible that work environments with high levels of satisfaction promote increased productivity for all who work there. Evidence suggests that this is in fact the case.

For instance, Harter and Creglow (1998) found that the average satisfaction of specific work units predicted factors such as profitability, productivity, and customer satisfaction. In addition, Harter, Schmidt, and

Hayes (2002) studied approximately 2,00,000 workers in 7,939 work units from 36 companies. Again, they found that unit-level satisfaction and work engagement predicted productivity, profitability, and customer satisfaction. Harter, Schmidt, and Keyes (2007) found that positive perceptions of work in organizational units, and positive feelings in these units, predicted customer loyalty, productivity, and lower turnover. Therefore, it appears that at the unit level, satisfaction predicts important criteria of success.

Of course, it is quite possible that satisfaction itself does not cause these work outcomes. Instead, well-being might be a useful proxy variable or measuring stick by which other desirable work characteristics are assessed. But even if this is true, then identifying the work characteristics that improve well-being should lead to better productivity, even if satisfaction has no causal effect.

In summary, research shows clear links between subjective well-being and worker productivity. These effects have emerged at the individual and work-unit level, and compared with effect sizes that are typically found in the social science literature, the effects are relatively large. The causal direction has not been determined, though there is evidence that well-being can lead to productivity. But more importantly, even if well-being is just an indicator of the quality of the job, it can be used to guide business decisions to improve performance, productivity, and profitability. Fortunately, researchers already know many of the job characteristics that lead to high subjective well-being (Warr, 2007), and these can be increased through workplace policies and training. For instance, optimal levels of personal control, supportive supervision, environmental clarity, and social support are all associated with happiness at work. Many of these are also associated with productivity. Thus, job attitudes and feelings are one source of information that can be used by managers and supervisors to improve workplace practices.

Although research on workplace well-being has focused primarily on satisfaction within specific organizations, broader measures of well-being will allow for broader conclusions. These conclusions will be relevant to decision makers beyond individual organizations, and they will inform community-level policies that have implications for work. For examples, cities, regions, and nations might increase productivity by instituting policies that will raise the well-being of workers across organizations. A region with happy workers might attract businesses and talented workers as well. Furthermore, an area where workers are more engaged and happier could be more efficient, productive, and creative, leading to an upward spiral of productivity and economic growth.

Natural Disasters and Risk Sharing

Many policies are designed to provide optimal societal functioning when things are going well, but societies also need to prepare for unpredictable events that have the potential to disrupt normal functioning. As with any policy decisions, various alternatives exist, and each has consequences for a community's reaction to the event, and for community functioning before and after the event. Sometimes, the goals for policy are clear, and policy makers must simply decide on how many resources to spend to accomplish these goals. For instance, nations may have standing armies in case of an unexpected war; policy debates often focus on the percentage of a government's budget that should be spent preparing for such an event. Regardless of whether the policy decision reflects a comparison among two or more alternatives or whether it involves decisions regarding the appropriate amount of resources to allocate, various criteria could be used. We argue that at least some consideration must be given to the well-being effects that these policies have. We demonstrate these ideas by focusing on one particularly salient unexpected effect—the occurrence of natural disasters.

Natural disasters are a fact of life, and how well a society copes with the consequences of these events often demonstrates the quality of communities and their governments. Preparation and response can take different forms. On the one hand, governments might make efforts to blunt the impact of disasters. Flood walls and levees are often built to protect residents who live in flood-prone areas, evacuation routes are planned and marked, and strategies for delivering aid are put in place in case disaster does, in fact, strike. However, even with such planning, damage from natural disasters is inevitable, and therefore policy makers and community leaders must address the issue of who will bear the cost of these events. Oftentimes, mechanisms such as disaster insurance are put in place to help spread the costs. Inevitably, issues arise as to what degree risk-transfer mechanisms is best for mitigating the effects of natural disasters.

In one relevant investigation, Luechinger and Raschky (2007) studied the impact of floods and flood exposure in 17 Organization of Economic Cooperation and Development (OECD) nations between 1973 and 2004. They conducted these analyses using both longitudinal and cross-sectional data. Actual flooding and flood exposure had a negative impact on life satisfaction, but only the former was robust to controls for gross domestic product (GDP) growth and unemployment in the region. An important question, then, is whether risk-transfer mechanisms such as mandatory flood insurance mitigate these effects in flood-prone areas.

Mandatory flood insurance has clear costs for those who live in affected areas. This insurance is often expensive and the fact that it is mandatory may create resentment about the lack of choice regarding these risks. Of course, these programs also have benefits (the payout should disaster strike), and policy makers often believe that the benefits outweigh the costs. This is why mandatory insurance programs exist. The exact cost–benefit ratio of such programs can be calculated quite accurately (particularly with data from many years and many regions), but it is an open question as to whether the financial cost–benefit ratio matches the well-being cost–benefit ratio. Studies that use well-being to assess the impact of risk-transfer mechanisms can help address this question.

Importantly, Luechinger and Raschky (2007) found large differences in the impact that floods had on life satisfaction depending on whether risk-transfer mechanisms, such as mandatory flood insurance, were in place in the region. For instance, the negative effects on life satisfaction in regions with mandatory insurance were only 11% of the impact in areas without such insurance. These results suggest that although people may object to the burden of extra insurance when buying property in an affected area, in the long run their well-being will benefit from this added expense.

As we have noted throughout this section on specific policy applications, the well-being approach is not the only option to assess the value of programs like mandatory flood insurance. The revealed preference method could also yield an estimate of the value that people place on flood danger, resources for reducing the impact of floods, and risk-sharing programs like flood insurance. However, the example of natural disasters raises an additional concern about this technique—some costs occur very rarely, so people have very little experience with them. Many people who experience a severe flood have never done so in the past, so there is no way they could evaluate the experience before they moved to the area. Well-being research that incorporates survey responses from thousands of people who have experienced such an event likely provides better data than the guesses of people who have never experienced such an event in the past.

Flood insurance is clearly not the only policy that could be evaluated using well-being data. For instance, the effects of more tangible resources including early warning systems and effective emergency relief could also be computed using life satisfaction as an outcome variable. Thus, measures of subjective well-being can help develop policies that are most efficient at ameliorating the misery caused by natural disasters. Again, there are often considerations policy makers must weigh besides subjective well-being. For example, they must examine whether risk-transfer mechanisms make people more likely to take risks by building their houses in dangerous places. In addition, some societies might decide that mandatory insurance programs are too paternalistic, even if research evidence shows that they would ultimately be good for citizens. Nevertheless, subjective well-being is one of the outcomes they should consider in evaluating policy alternatives.

Income Distribution and the Structure of Income Taxes

One role that governments have is to provide some degree of infrastructure so that economic activity can take place. However, to achieve this goal, governments require resources. And because in most cases, governments do not create products that produce income, the resources for infrastructure must come from taxing citizens. Once taxation is needed, debates inevitably emerge about the ideal tax structure. Progressive tax structures charge higher average rates for those with higher incomes. This can be contrasted with regressive tax structures, in which average rates are lower for those with higher incomes. Proportional tax structures have the same average rates at all income levels. Many decisions about the tax structures are based on theories and empirical evidence regarding the maximum income that can be raised by a government with the least burden to citizens. However, given that concepts like *tax burden* assume that the tax itself has some psychological effect on the people who must pay it, many of these make assumptions about the impact of taxation on well-being. Therefore, it might be useful to rely on well-being itself as a guide for policy decisions regarding the ideal tax structures.

For instance, Richard Layard (2005) argued that well-being research tends to strengthen the argument for the progressive structures that most national income tax schedules currently have. There are three main arguments that can be made. First, as we have discussed earlier, well-being research consistently shows that life satisfaction is correlated with income. However, the association is not strictly linear. Instead, life satisfaction rises with each proportionate increase in income (Deaton, 2008; Helliwell, 2008; Helliwell & Huang, 2005; Stevenson & Wolfers, 2008). This log-linear form implies that larger absolute amounts of income are required to create the same increases in life satisfaction for those at higher income levels as compared to the amount that is required to increase life satisfaction for those at lower income levels. If so, then the same taxation will be less of a burden (i.e., will have less of an impact on well-being) on those with higher incomes than on those with lower incomes.

It is not clear exactly what processes are responsible for this log-linear association between income and well-being. It may be that comparison processes drive this effect—an increase of 10,000 dollars seems like quite a large increase when compared to a base salary of 20,000 dollars, whereas it seems very small when compared to a base salary of a million dollars. Alternatively, the log-linear form might result from real differences in how the rich and the poor spend their money. Those with very little money spend it on essential goods that allow them to survive, and therefore each additional dollar can contribute to some very important resources. Those with lots of money, on the other hand, are not buying things that satisfy basic needs. So although the goods and services that they do purchase are nice and do serve to satisfy preferences, with each additional dollar of income, it gets less and less likely that the money is being spent on something critically important. This idea is supported by results from the Gallup World Poll, where not having enough money for food is associated with significantly lower life satisfaction, even after controlling for the effects of income. As would be expected, the estimated effect of income on life satisfaction is lower when food adequacy is controlled.

A second argument for progressive tax structures (along with luxury taxes) relates to the potentially negative effects that high levels of income— or at least the pursuit of high levels of income—might have on well-being. To be clear, there is no evidence that high incomes are associated with lower well-being. We are aware of no large-scale studies that show drop-offs in happiness at the highest income levels. However, it is possible that a focus on attaining income may take away from other pursuits that are more amenable to preserving and increasing levels of well-being. One problem is that increasing income may lead to increasing standards. A number of studies have now shown that after controlling for a person's own personal income, his or her well-being is actually negatively associated with the average income of the neighborhood in which the person lives (Helliwell & Huang, 2009; Luttmer, 2005). It may be that such comparison processes prevent ever-increasing income from leading to ever-increasing well-being, which would again suggest that taxation has less of an impact at higher levels of well-being.

In addition, some research suggests that high materialism is associated with low life satisfaction (e.g., Kasser & Ryan, 1993; Nickerson, Schwarz, Diener, & Kahneman, 2003). If people value money too highly, especially relative to the value that they place on family and friends, then their life satisfaction might suffer. However, not all research finds a negative relation between materialism and life satisfaction, in part because the higher incomes earned by people who emphasize materialistic goals tends to mitigate the negative association found when income is controlled (Nickerson, Schwarz, & Diener, 2007). Thus, the effects of material aspirations on happiness are not yet fully understood. However, evidence drawn from student housing lotteries has shown that people tend to overestimate the life satisfaction they derive from their consumption and physical surroundings, and they underestimate the importance of friends (Dunn, Wilson, & Gilbert, 2003). If such effects play out in real-world scenarios, then the pursuit of high levels of income may shift people's attention from pursuits which might be more likely to affect well-being in a positive manner.

Because of the clear links between well-being and the goals that policy makers have when setting tax structures, some researchers have begun to use well-being data to identify ideal tax structures. For instance, van Praag and Ferrer-i-Carbonell (2004) proposed that subjective well-being data can be used to help find tax structures that can raise the necessary revenues while maximizing the total utility of a society. Income taxes would be graduated, as they usually are now, so that those earning more pay at higher average rates. More specifically, however, levels of subjective well-being within specific income groups could be used to set the precise level of taxation so as to maximize utility (within the constraints of the overall tax revenues required by the society). Importantly, the justification for this procedure would not result from philosophical arguments related to fairness and equality of sacrifice. Instead, it could be based on empirical data regarding the precise way that the association between income and well-being changes as income rises. Thus, the justification for a graduated income tax is that taking away a greater percentage of income from the rich will affect their happiness little, whereas taxes can substantially lower the happiness of the poor.

These analyses can then be extended to other tax-related questions. For instance, governments often impose *sin taxes* for such activities as smoking and drinking, partly to discourage the behavior and partly because they want those who partake in these activities to have to compensate for the externalities that affect others. It then becomes an empirical question as to whether these goals are really accomplished. For instance, it is possible that the overall subjective well-being of smokers will increase if the government raised taxes on cigarettes to the point where few could afford them. Although the initial economic impact would be unpleasant, and any effects that resulted from quitting might be quite painful in the short term, the long-term effects might be positive if the effects of smoking tend to be negative (Gruber & Mullainathan, 2002, 2005). Again, some societies might decide that this response is too paternalistic; but the empirical data that such a study would provide would be useful to policy makers regardless of whether they decided to base their decisions on this knowledge.

National tax policies are usually designed to achieve many different goals. They are designed, first and foremost, to raise revenue to take care of the responsibilities that citizens have assigned to their governments. In addition, tax policies will ideally collect money in an efficient manner and in a way that supports economic growth and achieves an equitable distribution of income. Measures of subjective well-being, by providing a direct measure of utility, can help to estimate the overall effects of taxation, and hence aid in the design of tax systems.

Chapter 11

The Social Context of Well-Being: Policy Examples

The Importance of the Social Context

Ever since Aristotle, those who study well-being have recognized the importance of family, friends, and other forms of social contact. Despite this long intellectual history, economists and psychologists have tended over the past century to concentrate on individual needs and aspirations. Well-being has often been treated as an individual outcome that is based on the pursuit and achievement of individual goals. Both survey and experimental data on well-being, however, show the importance of the social context. Some of the most important factors that influence well-being revolve around the social features of people's lives.

One important reason for the renewed emphasis on the social context of well-being is the widespread interest in *social capital*. When Robert Putnam and his colleagues compared civic and political life in different regions of Italy (Putnam, 1993), they discovered that many aspects of life (ranging from the quality of local services to economic growth; Helliwell & Putnam, 1995) were better in those regions that were marked by horizontal structures and dense social ties. Borrowing a term used by Coleman (1990), Putnam suggested that these social factors were a form of *social capital* that benefited societies. He provided further development of this idea in an analysis of trends in the United States. Putnam showed that there was a long upward trend in social capital over the first 70 years of the twentieth century, followed by 30 years of decline (1995, 2000). Following an international collaborative research effort spurred by Putnam's findings, the

Organization of Economic Cooperation and Development (OECD, 2001) adopted a working definition of social capital as "networks together with shared norms, values and understandings that facilitate co-operation within and among groups."

The first empirical linkage between social capital and subjective well-being came soon after, when Putnam found, using subjective well-being data from DDB surveys, that individuals reported higher levels of happiness when their own levels of social capital were higher, but also when the average level of social capital of their fellow state residents was higher. He contrasted these positive spillovers of social capital to his comparable finding that individuals were happier when their own incomes were higher, but less happy when average state income was higher (Putnam, 2001; also see Chapter 6). There has been a subsequent explosion of scholarly and policy interest in social capital (surveyed by Halpern, 2005), with a much smaller number of studies investigating the effects of social capital on well-being (Helliwell, 2001, 2003; Helliwell & Putnam, 2004). For instance, Helliwell (2007) showed that social capital factors predicted both life satisfaction and suicide rates in similar ways in a broad cross-nation sample. Similarly, Diener and Tov (2007) found that variables such as lack of corruption and safety predicted national levels of life satisfaction and positive emotions. There is also an important parallel epidemiological literature of much longer standing (e.g., Berkman & Syme, 1979) that links social-capital-like variables to subsequent health outcomes.

How might policy makers increase social capital within their societies? Halpern (2005) suggests that there are strategies at the local, regional, and societal levels that can help in this respect. He suggests that at the micro or local level, programs designed to organize and fund volunteering can be useful, and volunteering is one manifestation of social capital. For example, volunteer mentors for teenagers not only can help prevent the adolescents from delinquent behavior, but the volunteering builds community networks and ties. Verlet and Devos (2007) suggest that the way local governments can best enhance well-being is to implement policies that foster strong social relationships. Policies aimed at social integration and support can encourage neighborhood interaction, community volunteering, and social trust.

Policies that enhance social interaction can be enacted. For example, zoning regulations can be used to encourage building of common areas for neighborhoods, and building codes can encourage the orientation of residences so that people encounter their neighbors. Communal green spaces, mandated by zoning regulations, can aid community cohesion and social interaction among neighbors (Kuo, Sullivan, Coley, & Brunson, 1998), and experiments have shown (Zelenski, 2007) that walking through a natural area increases well-being in comparison to traveling to the same location via an indoor route.

Trust can be increased by making government more transparent and by requiring businesses to do likewise. Trust can also be enhanced by severe penalties for fraud and corruption. Local, state, and national governments can create policies that promote and reward community involvement and volunteering. Naturally, all such policies need to be discussed in a democratic way, and must fit the context of the society. The point here is simply that social capital needs to be encouraged by policy makers, and that measures of subjective well-being can be useful in assessing progress in this domain.

Because social capital is essential to well-being, it behooves policy makers to consider it carefully when they formulate policies. Politicians need to work to maintain the trust of the public, and policies at the local level that bring people together in cooperative settings are likely to enhance social capital.

Building and Maintaining Trust

Trust has sometimes been seen as a part of social capital, and sometimes as a consequence of its presence, but in either case there is striking evidence of the importance of trust in the determination of well-being. This importance flows both directly and indirectly, as various aspects of trust have been found to be instrumental in the achievement of activities that themselves help to support well-being (e.g., good government and an efficient economy). But the importance of trust for well-being goes beyond its major instrumental roles, as several measures of trust have been found to have positive links to subjective well-being even after levels of material well-being have been taken into account (Helliwell & Putnam, 2004).

When studying the link between assessments of trust and subjective well-being, there is a possibility that optimism or some other variable might affect both assessments, giving rise to a spurious positive correlation between life satisfaction and trust. Thus, it is important to show that trust is in fact related to important outcomes that would not necessarily be expected to be associated with additional factors such as optimism. In an example of such a demonstration, Knack (2001) used data from 15 nations to examine the correlation between average self-reported social trust (as assessed by the survey question "Generally speaking, would you say that most people can be trusted, or that you can't be too careful in dealing with people?") and a behavioral measure. Researchers intentionally dropped 20 wallets in each nation and then tracked return rates. Knack found that the correlation between average trust and the average return rate was .65. Norway and Denmark usually rank at or near the top in survey measures of social trust, and all of the experimentally dropped wallets were returned in those countries.

Subsequent surveys have included measures of trust in several domains: trust in neighbors, in the police, in co-workers, in management, and in strangers. For instance, respondents can be asked how likely they think it would be that a lost wallet would be returned if found by a neighbor, a police officer, or a stranger. These distinct trust ratings give rise to very different patterns of response across individuals, across neighborhoods, and across countries. Therefore, it is possible that different effects will emerge when using trust in different domains to explain life satisfaction at the individual level. Data from the Gallup World Poll show that the relative trustworthiness of the police and neighbors differs systematically across countries. Similarly, Canadian data have shown that differences in life satisfaction among neighborhoods are strongly correlated with differences in the extent to which people trust their neighbors. The same data show very much smaller differences among neighborhoods with respect to the extent to which the police are trusted.

By systematically tracking both life satisfaction and trust, researchers and policy makers can investigate the policy decisions that might affect the climate of trust in a community. For instance, Putnam (2007) examined differences in trust among 30,000 Americans and found that trust in neighbors was systematically higher in stable communities than in unstable communities. A variety of individual-level characteristics (including age, education, whether a person owned or rented, the length of time the person lived in the community, and even ethnicity) predicted feelings of trust. In addition, various community-level predictors (including poverty rate, crime rates, and degree of homogeneity) also emerged as being important.

This last finding—that the homogeneity of a community is positively associated with the trust that individuals within that community report—has received much attention, because at first glance it suggests that diversity might have negative effects. But Putnam's conclusion is not that diversity itself is negative, but that individual and policy efforts are needed to enable people to become more comfortable with diversity. He suggested that to some extent, this is likely to occur simply with the passage of time as cultures, marriages, and ethnicities become more mixed. Therefore, he hypothesized that the most helpful policies would be those that help provide places and spaces for individuals to develop a "more capacious sense of 'we,' a reconstruction of diversity that does not bleach out ethnic specificities, but creates overarching identities . . . that do not trigger the allergic 'hunker down' reaction" (Putnam, 2007).

Putnam presented some evidence that his analysis of trust has parallel implications for the explanation of differences in subjective well-being. This is no surprise, given the strong role that trust differences play in explaining differences in subjective well-being. In the final section of this chapter we shall consider how specific policy-oriented experiments can use well-being data to evaluate alternative ways of building and maintaining trust.

City Life

A large and increasing portion of the world's population is living in urban areas, so it is natural for architects, city planners, and others to ask what characterizes cities that are more able to sustain life satisfaction. Where there are large samples of life satisfaction data, geo-coded to show where people live, it is possible to assess well-being even at the neighborhood level. This permits researchers to investigate the characteristics of more successful neighborhoods, towns, and cities, to see what lessons there are to be learned, as shown in the preceding section of this chapter. Because such data are not yet available in most countries, well-being analysis of city life has thus far been based mainly on broad comparisons between city and urban life, and on data gathered relating to how satisfied people are with different aspects of life in their cities.

Manchin (2007) reported on satisfaction in European cities using the Gallup Organization's Soul of the City project. He then divided European cities into those that are doing well versus poorly in city satisfaction, and also into those with rising and falling levels of satisfaction. In some cities (e.g., Helsinki) there were high levels of urban satisfaction, whereas in other cities (e.g., Madrid) there were low levels of general satisfaction. In addition, the researcher reported on the city satisfaction of old and young people, and the degree to which people perceive the city as attractive to innovative people. Manchin also inquired as to the desirability of the city as a tourist destination. London, Barcelona, Paris, and Rome were viewed as the most desirable cities to visit.

What predicts satisfaction with one's city? Respondents categorized as belonging to the *creative class* were attracted by factors such as beauty, having other talented people around, and the efficiency of services, and were less influenced by factors such as sports, noise levels, and the price of housing. In the most satisfied cities, people were most satisfied if they felt the city was a good place for immigrants, minorities, and people with disabilities. In cities with low levels of satisfaction, people tended to like their city more if they felt safe, and if there were good hospitals, public transportation, and cinemas.

Ong (2008) also used the Gallup World Poll data to analyze well-being in cities, and considered a number of variables that might affect the quality of urban life. For example, he created a law and order index based on reports of crime victimization, but also based on confidence in the police and feeling safe. On this index Singapore scored very high and Moscow scored low. Ong also created a work index that reflects not only whether people have a job, but also whether they have satisfying work where they can use their personal talents. Montreal scored high and Karachi scored low. People in Montreal were also very satisfied with their standard of living, as were Singaporeans.

Ong also created a well-being index based on people's life satisfaction and positive feelings. Moscow scored low on this index while Montreal and Los Angeles scored high. He found that people in these two cities were very likely to report being treated with respect and as having experienced enjoyment the day before. Ong reports that higher well-being is associated with better health, citizen engagement, productivity at work, economic development, political stability, and lower brain drain.

Social indicators such as crime rates and employment can help to identify strengths and problems. These may provide lessons for planners and city governments, as well as for employers, employees, and potential visitors and migrants. A study of city satisfaction conducted by Kansas City, Missouri, in the United States provides a good illustration of how municipalities can assess citizen satisfaction in order to help improve urban life. In 2006 the City Auditor's Office of Kansas City issued the results of its third survey of citizens, in which respondents in the municipal area reported on their overall city satisfaction, and satisfaction with specific aspects of city services. The intent of the survey was to examine residents' general views on whether Kansas City is a good place to live and work, and on various aspects of the city services and facilities. As part of the report, Kansas City was compared to 21 other Midwestern communities, and 13 other large cities such as Denver and Houston.

Not only did the audit uncover the fact that the residents of Kansas City were in most cases below average in their city satisfaction ratings, they also discovered which categories were highest (e.g., street lighting and fire protection) and which were lowest (e.g., maintenance). Because most services that cities provide are bundled together and paid for by property taxes, however, it may be hard to discern, in the absence of life satisfaction data, which services are providing good value in relation to their underlying cost. Thus, a more comprehensive measure in urban areas could indicate both general well-being and satisfaction with specific aspects of the area.

Thus, life satisfaction measures at the local level, as well as measures of satisfaction with specific services, can be used to provide best-practice examples for others to emulate. Public access to these data would help people to know more about the quality of life when choosing their destinations. More importantly, research explaining the factors leading to higher life satisfaction could help individuals and communities to provide better lives for themselves and others.

Social Experiments

Much of the policy analysis we have reported in this volume is based on correlations between life satisfaction and various aspects of individual and community circumstances. Sometimes it is possible to take advantage of so-called natural experiments, where policies or rules change in some jurisdictions but not in others. As results accumulate, there will be increasing interest. In turn, this could encourage the use of more explicitly experimental methods to assess the consequences of alternative policy options. There is a considerable history of experimental methods being used to consider the economic consequences of alternative ways of designing and delivering unemployment relief and income assistance. There is no reason why such techniques could not also be used to assess the impact of policy decisions on well-being outcomes.

When it comes to assessing policies related to social capital, the experimental method is in its preliminary stages. As described above, Putnam's U.S. social capital benchmark survey measured existing levels of trust and social capital in many participating communities. Putnam and Feldstein (2003) reported on a number of community-level policies and programs designed to build social capital.

Two further developments are needed to provide stronger evidence about the effectiveness of policy efforts to improve the social context of well-being. First, and most obviously, systematic assessments of life satisfaction, social capital, and other relevant features of the social context need to be measured before and after policy experiments are undertaken. Second, it will be important to establish control groups so as to provide a clearly defined comparison against which to assess the consequences of policy experiments. A recent Canadian policy study provides examples of how experimental methods can be used to measure and assess the well-being consequences of policies aimed at improving social capital at the individual and community levels.

The Community Employment Innovation Project (CEIP, Gyarmati et al., 2008) is a project that was funded by Canadian federal and provincial governments. It offered communities the chance to design and administer programs by which recipients of employment insurance or income assistance were offered jobs. Participating communities formed boards to select and manage community development projects, using both volunteers and employees paid for by CEIP. The employees themselves were a mixture of previous recipients of employment assistance and employment assurance. The assignment of individual participants either to CEIP employment or to the control group was random, so that the effects of the intervention could be clearly identified. The labor market and social capital consequences for the individual participants were then converted to a common basis using weights derived from life satisfaction equations, making use of survey data obtained from all individual participants at the end of the project.

The CEIP employment periods extended for up to 36 months, and outcomes were followed for another 2 years. The social capital consequences for participants were a significant part of the total benefits, as the size and structure of their social networks changed in ways that the analysis showed was likely to have led to increased life satisfaction. The study unfortunately did not include life satisfaction assessment at the beginning and during the course of the project, so that standard experimental assessments of the life satisfaction effects were not possible.

For the community-level effects, the experimental method had to be slightly different, as each participating community chose its own pace and mix of activities, and the selection of comparable control communities was performed by matching rather than by random assignment. Community-level surveys were conducted at the beginning and end of the CEIP program, with life satisfaction data collected only in the final survey. The life satisfaction data were again used to estimate equations for the likely determinants of well-being, and the resulting weights were used for the cost–benefit analysis of the social capital and other community-level effects.

One helpful aspect of allowing each community to choose the pace and structure of its own programs in the CEIP program was that there were different types of programs selected, and these differences proved to match differences in the pattern of outcomes. For example, there were significant community-level increases in social trust (as represented by answers to questions about the likelihood of lost wallets being returned if found by a neighbor) among young people in those communities that specialized in programs for youth, and better health and social integration for older residents in those communities placing more emphasis on program for seniors. In both cases these effects were still apparent in surveys conducted up to two years after the end of the program. When well-being measures are combined with experimentation, they will provide a powerful method for improving the quality of life of communities.

Together, these examples show that variables related to social context and social capital have enormous promise in terms of using well-being measures to guide policy decisions. Well-being results clearly show that social variables such as these are related to well-being, and many policies that are already in existence are designed to affect these factors. Thus, by including more systematic assessment of the social variables and well-being itself, more precise policies can be tailored to unique community goals. Ultimately, by focusing on the effects of social variables on well-being, broader improvements within communities can be made.

Section IV

Implementing the Measures

Chapter 12

Existing Surveys

In 2003, the U.S. General Accounting Office (GAO), along with the National Academies' Institute of Health, sponsored a meeting to discuss the prospect of developing a system of national indicators for the United States. The discussion focused on the goals of such indicators, the possible measures that could be included, and the existing systems that could be used as models (GAO, 2003). The conclusions that this group reached serve as a useful starting point for a discussion of existing attempts to obtain national indicators of subjective well-being. Although the indicators that participants discussed did not explicitly focus on the constructs that we have described in this book, the goals of these systems are quite similar to the goals we have set forth. Furthermore, the measures that are already in place within these systems provide a model for how subjective indicators of well-being could be incorporated into existing systems.

It would be inaccurate to say that the stated goal of the GAO meeting was to develop measures of well-being. However, a perusal of its report shows that this goal is inherent in almost any attempt to measure a broad set of indicators regarding the conditions of a city, region, or nation. For instance, in its review, the GAO concluded that one of the two primary characteristics that appears to be common among existing comprehensive indicator systems is "creating an overall picture of how a community (or region, nation, etc.) is doing" (2003, p. 15). This comprehensive picture of how an area is doing is quite similar to the broad definition of well-being that guides our own ideas about national indicators of well-being. The second primary characteristic that is common to all systems is that these indicators would be able to show the "interconnectedness of various key information areas" (p. 15). In other words, these indicators should reflect the trade-offs that exist when different lower-level goals are pursued. As we have noted, the concept of well-being also serves this goal (for a discussion of the ways that well-being measures can help address these trade-offs, see Dolan & Peasgood, 2006).

Notably, most of the systems that the GAO report reviewed explicitly cited acquiring information about the "well-being" of the city, region, or nation as a primary goal of the indicators. Yet, few of the existing measures were subjective in nature. And, more importantly, it appears that none of the indicator systems included an overall subjective evaluation of well-being. Thus, the problems that face existing list-based attempts to assess well-being (including concerns about which factors should be included, how they should be weighted, and how they should be aggregated) are also major issues for these existing strategies for assessing national and regional indicators.

There is nonetheless much that can be learned from the GAO report. The challenges that immediately come to mind when considering the implementation of subjective indicators are often the same as for indicators that rely purely on objective measures. Namely, organizers must decide which measures to use and how to acquire the information that will form the basis of the indicator system. Can measures that are already in use simply be collected in a central repository, or must new assessment programs be created? How will the measures be aggregated? Who will pay for an entirely new set of measures? The GAO report concluded that national indicators could be "built on the foundation of information from our federal statistical system (i.e., official statistics), administrative records, as well as a variety of private sources" (p. 6). In other words, national indicators of well-being need not consist of new, dedicated resources that are designed solely to assess well-being (though such resources can certainly help). Rather, they can build upon existing resources.

Fortunately, although no system exists for tracking national or regional well-being, numerous studies provide relevant information. A system of national indicators could collect data from these existing studies, or even contract with ongoing studies to incorporate additional questions or more systematic measurements to provide the data for a comprehensive system of indicators. In this chapter, we discuss some of the studies that are in place that could be used as models for a system of national indicators, or those which could even provide the basic data for such systems. We also discuss the characteristics that vary across studies that might be considered when designing future measurement strategies.

It is important to note at the outset that there are probably hundreds of studies that have recruited samples that are representative of a regional or national population and that have asked respondents to report on constructs that are at least somewhat related to well-being. Most are likely to be specialized studies conducted by groups of researchers who are focused on answering narrow questions. However, a small number of studies go beyond these goals, either by incorporating methodological features that are particularly useful for policy purposes or by collecting a broad range of measures in a more systematic fashion.

For instance, there are a few long-running cross-sectional studies that include well-being measures repeatedly in surveys that are administered to large nationally representative samples. These cross-sectional studies do not follow a single sample of citizens over time; rather, they take repeated snapshots using new samples at each occasion. Other studies recruit large representative samples and follow the same sample for many years. Both types of studies can track the well-being of a region or nation over time, but each has unique strengths and weaknesses. For instance, longitudinal panel studies allow for a closer examination of the processes that underlie changes in well-being, but they are expensive and often suffer from high rates of attrition. This may lead to questions about the representativeness of the remaining samples. Survey researchers are quite sophisticated, however, in their ability to identify the types of people who tend to drop out of surveys and to correct for their influence using complicated weighting schemes.

In addition to these within-nation studies, a small number of studies systematically address cross-national differences by administering the same questions to nationally representative samples from many different nations. Occasionally, these surveys are conducted repeatedly over time. These studies can address questions about the effects of nation-level characteristics on well-being. In the following sections, we review examples of specific efforts to understand the well-being of regions or nations using these different methodological techniques.

Cross-Sectional Studies

Single-shot cross-sectional studies with measures of well-being provide useful information about the state of a city, region, or nation at a particular point in time. If such studies incorporate well-being information, they can be used to address questions that might ultimately have policy implications. However, the most useful of these will have methodological characteristics that distinguish them in important ways. For instance, a few studies have very large sample sizes that allow for comparisons among specific demographic groups or residents of specific regions. When questions arise about specific subgroups, for example, unemployed Hispanic women, the samples are usually not large enough in the broadly representative samples.

Barrington-Leigh and Helliwell (2008) used three such studies to address questions about the effect of income comparisons on well-being judgments. Specifically, they used data from three very large cross-sectional studies, all of which had information about life satisfaction. The Equality, Security, and Community (ESC) survey recruited a nationally representative sample of over 6,500 Canadians. In addition to answering a variety of questions about the conditions of their lives and their attitudes, respondents were presented with a single item that read: "All things considered, how satisfied are you with a life as a whole these days?" The Ethnic Diversity Survey (EDS) was a much larger study of over 42,000 Canadians. Again, respondents were asked a single question about their life satisfaction as a whole. Finally, the Canadian General Social Survey (GSS) is a multiwave study that began in 1985. Each wave has a core set of demographic variables, but distinct modules are assessed in different years (with some repeats, which allows for trend analyses). The seventeenth wave included a module about life satisfaction, and this module also included a single item about satisfaction with life as a whole. Almost 25,000 Canadians responded to this survey.

By combining subjective reports of well-being with census data, Barrington-Leigh and Helliwell (2008) could examine the separable effects of a person's income from the effects of the average income of his or her neighborhood on the well-being that the person reports. As described in more detail in Chapter 6, although personal income was positively associated with life satisfaction, the income of one's neighbors was sometimes negatively associated with satisfaction (these results depended on the specific comparison group that was chosen). Research like this has important implications for our understanding of how general economic conditions affect well-being, and thus studies like the ESC, EDS, and GSS can play an important role in guiding policy.

Furthermore, although these are relatively simple cross-sectional designs, the very large sample sizes allow for regional comparisons. Barrington-Leigh and Helliwell (2008) focused on the income of regions and neighborhoods; but these are not the only variables that could be examined. Any number of aggregated city or regional variables could be assessed, and an examination of the predictive utility of this information could provide some insight into the factors that policy makers can affect that also play a role in general levels of well-being.

Data like those used by Barrington-Leigh and Helliwell (2008) are useful primarily because of their size—the fact that over 75,000 people responded to life satisfaction questions means that many fine-grained analyses can be conducted. However, there are also some limitations of such studies. Most notably, the picture that one gets is a static one. We cannot determine how various predictors change, which means that we cannot confirm whether these changes, in turn, affect well-being. It is true that information from the various studies that exist could be aggregated and tracked to get a relatively clear picture of well-being over time (and there are some efforts toward this goal; see Veenhoven's World Database of Happiness). However, locating and acquiring data from individual studies is difficult. In addition, different studies may use different measures, sampling strategies, and methodologies, which can make cross-study comparisons difficult. Therefore, a more efficient and methodologically sound procedure is to rely on studies that assess well-being in similar representative samples repeatedly over time. Such studies are often relatively standardized in their sampling strategies and measurement approaches. Thus, meaningful comparisons can be drawn across various waves of the study.

One of the most widely used data sets in the social sciences is the National Opinion Research Center's GSS (Davis & Smith, 2007). Since 1972, the GSS has recruited large, nationally representative samples of Americans on an annual or biannual basis and administered a variety of survey questions to these samples. The survey itself consists of a standard core of demographic, behavioral, and attitudinal questions, along with some specialized topic modules that have been assessed on a less frequent basis (or even just once). Most notably, in every wave the GSS included the item "Taken all together, how would you say things are these days—would you say that you are very happy, pretty happy, or not too happy?" In addition, the study has included measures of satisfaction with specific domains of life, including satisfaction with health, family life, financial situation, friendships, job, and hobbies.

The general happiness item included in the GSS is not ideal. The use of a three-point scale limits the response options that are available for participants, and thus this measure may not be as sensitive to differences and changes in external conditions as other measures. Nevertheless, this scale (along with the domain satisfaction ratings) can be used to address policy-related questions. For instance, in an influential piece, Easterlin (1995; also see Myers, 2000) analyzed trends in the happiness questionnaire from 1972 to 1991, a time when per capita gross domestic product (GDP) rose considerably. The famous Easterlin paradox that resulted from his analysis was that even though income is associated with happiness within a nation at any one point in time, rising incomes are not associated with a corresponding rise in happiness. Easterlin argued that because people compare their material position to that of the people around them, happiness will not change when the income of all individuals rise. Although Easterlin's conclusions are now disputed, results from studies like the GSS mean that such important debates can be resolved.

Others have used data from the GSS to address questions about within-sample associations between policy-relevant demographic characteristics and well-being outcomes. For instance, Myers (1999) used the GSS to show that married people are consistently happier than people who are single, separated, divorced, or widowed. More interestingly, researchers can investigate whether these links between demographic characteristics and well-being change over time. For instance, Glenn and Weaver (1988) concluded that the effect of marital status has declined over time, though Lucas and Dyrenforth (2006) showed that this result does not hold when a larger number of years are analyzed. Although developing policy from such findings is clearly fraught with value issues, policies designed to encourage marriage (e.g., tax breaks, laws making divorce difficult) can at least be informed by the empirical links between marital status and happiness, along with knowledge about how these links have changed over time.

Studies like the GSS can also be used to track differences in well-being among various groups that might be affected differently by policy decisions. For instance, concerns about racial discrimination have led to policies designed to address disparities among various racial and ethnic groups. But have these policies made a difference? Were they needed in the first place? Clearly, a measure of life satisfaction cannot answer all of these questions, but the information these measures provide is surely relevant. Figure 12.1 shows life satisfaction in the GSS plotted against time for blacks and whites separately. Perhaps not surprisingly, blacks report lower levels of happiness in every wave of the GSS, which points to the fact that the racial discrimination and income difference that exist likely do have an effect on overall well-being. However, the situation is improving, with happiness levels among blacks increasing consistently from 1972 to 2006. This shows that the measure included in the GSS is sensitive to population-level changes, and that perhaps the attention that has been placed on improving conditions for blacks has made a difference (though, of course, there are many other factors that likely also play a role). Other studies have additional methodological benefits but include questions that may not map perfectly on to the constructs of well-being that we have described here. However, they are worth considering, because they serve as models for future studies examining well-being, and because organizers of ongoing studies could be convinced to add a few measures that explicitly focus on

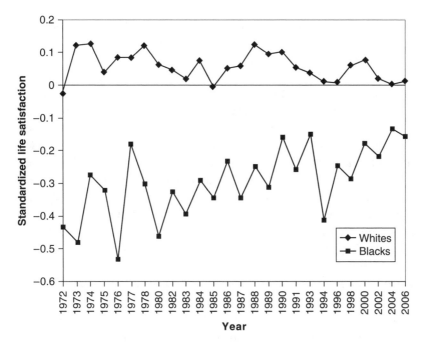

Figure 12.1 Average Happiness Scores by Year for Whites and Blacks in the General Social Survey.

well-being, and for very little cost. One of the most impressive efforts is the U.S. Center for Disease Control Prevention's (CDC) Behavioral Risk Factor Surveillance System (BRFSS). Since 1993, over two million adults in the United States have been surveyed about their health status. As part of this effort, respondents are asked a core set of health-related quality-of-life questions, one of which focuses on *mentally healthy days*. This measure asks respondents the following question about their mental health: "Now thinking about your *mental health*, which includes stress, depression, and problems with emotions, for how many days during the past 30 days was your mental health not good?"

Because the sample size of the BRFSS is so large, the number of mentally healthy days per month can be compared across distinct groups with varying characteristics. This not only allows the CDC to target groups who are susceptible to mental health problems, but it could potentially allow researchers to determine whether targeted policies actually have any effect, by comparing scores either over time (the survey is conducted yearly) or across regions with differing policies. For instance, Moriarty, Zack, Zahran, and Kobau (2006) reported that when average county-level unhealthy days (a construct that is broader than the mentally unhealthy days variable described above) was examined, 89% of the variance in this measure could be explained by nine community health status indicators. Thus, it is possible that this county-level information could reveal important causal factors in the health status of the residents. Similarly, Moriarty et al. reported that the number of mentally unhealthy days has increased from 8.4 in 1993 to 10.2 in 2003. With the rich source of data available from the BRFSS, potential explanations for this pattern could be examined.

Studies like those reviewed here show that there already exist numerous large-scale studies where the demographic characteristics, attitudes, and health statuses of residents of various nations are being tracked. A few have included measures that serve the purposes described in this book, and these resources have already been taken advantage of to address questions with important policy implications. It is also clear, however, that additional studies are needed, and well-being measures could easily be included in many existing studies. For instance, the Current Population Survey is a monthly survey of about 50,000 households in the United States that is conducted by the Bureau of the Census and the Bureau of Labor Statistics. The focus of this study is on employment variables including earnings, hours of work, and a variety of job characteristics. Adding a single question on life satisfaction could quickly, easily, and relatively affordably provide critical answers to many of the policy-related questions that we have introduced in this book.

Fortunately, some progress in this respect is being made. For example, in cooperation with Healthways, a health care provider, the Gallup Organization has begun the Gallup–Healthways Well-Being Index. This survey assesses health and well-being (including subjective indicators of well-being) among a random sample of 1,000 participants each and every day of the week. This survey should give an unprecedented look at the ways that well-being changes over time within a population. Furthermore, with such a large sample size, many fine-grained analyses can be conducted by examining differences in well-being among people with varying demographic characteristics, employment characteristics, or health statuses. Thus, as more well-being measures are added, the value that these surveys can bring may convince other survey organizers to add to their core sets of questions. Or, as the Gallup–Healthways survey shows, the value may be confirmed by the extent to which organizations are willing to pay to make the data available.

Cross-National Studies

Large-sample cross-sectional studies conducted within a single nation at a single point in time are useful for drawing conclusions about the state of well-being at that time. The addition of yearly administrations allows researchers and policy makers to track well-being over time and to assess the effect of changing circumstances on well-being. However, additional methodological features of studies can add to the questions that can be addressed in unique ways. For instance, because institutions and life circumstances may differ more dramatically across nations than across regions or cities within a nation, it would be useful to be able to compare the well-being of various nations. There are methodological concerns that arise when making these comparisons, but many would agree that having this information available is useful. Unfortunately, if different measures and different sampling strategies are used across countries, then drawing conclusions about the national differences in well-being becomes quite difficult. Therefore, it is important to conduct systematic cross-national studies with similar methodologies when attempting to answer questions about cross-national differences. Fortunately, a small number of studies that can be used to accomplish this goal currently exist.

For instance, the European Social Survey (ESS) is an ongoing research project organized and initially funded by the European Science Foundation to assess attitudes and values across the European nations. The study, which includes respondents from between 22 and 26 nations in each wave, began in 2002 and is currently in its fourth wave of data collection. Over 1,500 respondents from each nation are sampled (800 for countries with populations under two million) in each wave of administration. Participants are asked a variety of questions, including a single-item life satisfaction measure in each wave of assessment. In addition, in 2006, a 50-item Personal and Social Well-being module was included to assess a broad range of well-being-related constructs.

Panel A of Figure 12.2 shows average life satisfaction scores for the 23 nations included in the 2004 wave of the ESS. As can be seen, life satisfaction scores vary considerably across these nations. For instance, the average life satisfaction among Ukrainians was 4.28, four points below the average life satisfaction of the Danes. In Denmark, the vast majority of respondents (83.1%) reported scores on the 0 to 10 scale of 8, 9, or 10, whereas in the Ukraine, just 11.4% of respondents reported satisfaction scores this high. These differences are quite large, and future research can focus on the living conditions and governmental policies that are associated with these substantial differences in overall satisfaction with life. For instance, Panel B of Figure 12.2 depicts average life satisfaction scores against the per capita GDP of the nation. Consistent with numerous other cross-national studies (e.g., Stevenson & Wolfers, 2008, Deaton, 2008; Helliwell, 2008), the correlation is a very strong .84, showing that economic factors play a very strong role in the well-being of these nations.

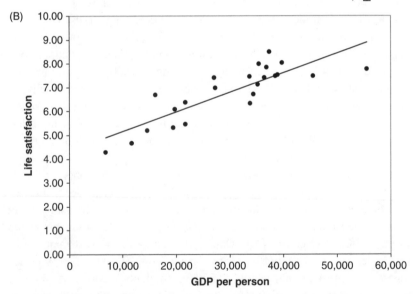

Figure 12.2 Panel A: Average Life Satisfaction by Nation in the European Social Survey; Panel B: Average Life Satisfaction plotted against gross domestic product.

Additional work using the ESS (combined with other information about the nations in question) could be used to further clarify what exactly it is about GDP that contributes to the well-being of the various nations. In addition, additional indicators could be added to a regression equation to determine what factors beyond GDP predict the well-being of these nations.

Although the ESS is an impressive study aimed at understanding the attitudes of Europeans, it is not the first nor the largest cross-national study of its kind. Beginning in the 1970s, the European Commission began tracking various attitude measures over time in the Eurobarometer studies. These studies are conducted twice a year using nationally representative samples from a variety of European nations. In many waves, questions about life satisfaction and overall happiness were administered. Like the ESS, data from the Eurobarometer studies can be used to compare well-being among nations. And like the GSS, the Eurobarometer studies can be used to track changes over time. For instance, Stevenson and Wolfers (2008) used data from the Eurobarometer to show that life satisfaction ratings increased more in nations that had stronger economic growth.

Similarly, the World Values Survey (WVS; www.worldvaluessurvey.org), along with the European Values Survey that preceded it, assesses attitudes and values (along with demographic characteristics) from respondents from 88 nations and regions around the world. Large representative samples were recruited from each nation or region, which allows for comparisons between nations (though sampling strategies do differ somewhat from region to region). This survey has been administered in five waves, with the first being conducted in 1981, and the most recent in 2005-2007. Thus, both cross-national and cross-temporal analyses can be conducted. Because the WVS includes a wide variety of questions about attitudes and values, a considerable number of psychological questions can be answered using the data. Notably, the study has included a 4-point happiness scale and a 10-point life satisfaction scale, along with numerous questions about domain satisfaction and the experience of emotions. These data can be used to rank nations on their happiness, similar to what we showed in Figure 12.2, but with a larger sample of nations. Average well-being scores can then be linked with nation-level characteristics to identify the factors that appear to be responsible for the differences that emerge.

Recently, Inglehart, Foa, Peterson, and Welzel (2008) used data from the five waves of the WVS to address Easterlin's (1974, 1995) contention that rising incomes do not lead to corresponding increases in happiness. They showed that in 46 of the 51 nations for which time series data were available, happiness rose over time. More importantly, they could link these changes in happiness both to changes in objective conditions (assessed using traditional economic indicators) and to changes in values that might result from the changes in objective conditions. Specifically, Inglehart et al. suggested that economic development, increased democratization, and increasing acceptance of diversity were associated with increases in feelings of free choice. In turn, these feelings of freedom were associated with increased levels of happiness.

Results like this are quite important for those interested in using well-being measures for policy purposes. One of the major obstacles to the implementation of systematic subjective assessment programs has been the suggestion that happiness does not change. This idea has been refuted at the individual level (Diener, Lucas, & Scollon, 2006), but until recently, there have been very little large-scale data with which to address this issue at a national level. The WVS shows that cross-national surveys can be useful in this regard. When tracking well-being over time in many nations, trends do emerge, and these trends can be reliably linked to changes in the characteristics of the nations. Although the policy implications are not always immediately obvious, it is easy to see ways that analyses such as those presented in Inglehart et al.'s paper could guide policy decisions.

The WVS is just the beginning of what we believe is a trend toward increasingly systematic assessment of well-being across countries and time. As more of these studies are conducted, more results like those described by Inglehart et al. (2008) will emerge. As a result, it will be more difficult to ignore the value of these assessments. For example, the largest effort toward understanding national differences in well-being is the Gallup Organization's World Poll. This study has acquired representative samples from more than 130 nations around the world, representing 95% of the world's adult population. Like the WVS, the World Poll includes items representing a variety of topics including health, work, religion, engagement, and—most importantly for our purposes—subjective reports of well-being. These measures can be used to rank nations, and again, characteristics of those nations can be used to identify factors that might be responsible for high or low well-being.

Although the Gallup World Poll is too new to have been used in many published studies, results are beginning to emerge. Consistent with the studies described above, these results show that national income plays an important role in average well-being—probably a larger role than has been found in the past. It also appears to be the case that at least in this very large sample of nations, the effect of income does not disappear once basic needs are met. Deaton (2008), Helliwell (2008), and Stevenson and Wolfers (2008) all found a linear association between the log of income and the life satisfaction in the Gallup ladder data, both within and across countries.

This high degree of cross-country correlation between average incomes and life satisfaction has convinced some previous skeptics to take life satisfaction data more seriously as genuine measures of well-being. However, that same high correlation might tempt others to ask what would be the point in measuring life satisfaction once it has been shown to move closely with income, since income is already being tracked. One way of answering this question is to see if there are important aspects of life satisfaction that are tapped into by quite different surveys (and are hence not just artifacts of a particular set of questions) but not captured by average per capita incomes. To do this, we took the Gallup and WVS national average measures of life satisfaction for 75 overlapping countries, extracted entirely the variation explained by differences in per capita incomes, and then tested whether the remaining life satisfaction differences from one survey could be used to explain international differences in life satisfaction measured by the other survey. The results provided striking evidence that the two measures of life satisfaction were both tapping into something beyond and above what can be represented by per capita incomes. For the WVS data, for example, 41% of the cross-country variations in life satisfaction can be explained by differences in real per capita incomes, and this rises to 60% when the Gallup residual is added to the equation (Helliwell, 2008). Thus there is important information about the quality of life, as captured by national average responses to life satisfaction, that go well beyond what can be explained by differences in per capita incomes. Furthermore, life expectancy in nations predicts the reported well-being in them beyond income, indicating that monetary measures do not fully capture the systematic variance in the well-being measures.

Helliwell, Huang, and Harris (2009) have shown that this result is not merely attributable to national differences in mood or response styles, because when the same basic equation is fitted to each of the Gallup countries, the results show considerable consistency across countries, with a common set of noneconomic and economic variables having consistent and systematic support from the life satisfaction data. Within and across countries, the life satisfaction data appear to tell coherent stories about the quality of life in ways that permit both economic and noneconomic aspects of life to be consistently assessed.

Other researchers have investigated the difference in results that emerge when different well-being measures are assessed. For instance, Diener, Kahneman, Tov, and Arora (2008) showed that although income appears to matter for life satisfaction, it is much less strongly associated with affect-focused measures. These appear to be somewhat more strongly related to social variables such as lack of corruption and human rights. Clearly, the large size and systematic nature of the World Poll will allow many more questions to be addressed. In addition, Gallup plans to continue the poll in the future, which means that trend analyses can be conducted similar to those using the WVS, GSS, and Eurobarometer studies. We are optimistic that in 10 or 15 years, the promise of these measures will be shown when large-scale studies like these are analyzed to a greater extent.

Longitudinal Studies

Cross-sectional studies provide important information about differences that exist among individuals and regions at a single point in time. Studies that are repeated over time can show how these associations change and how changing macro-level factors are associated with changes in average levels of well-being. However, in cross-sectional studies such as those described above, the same individuals are not followed over time. This makes it somewhat difficult to draw conclusions about the processes that underlie these effects. For instance, if repeated samples of a cohort are examined over time using multiple cross-sectional studies, we may find that the percent who are married and the average level of well-being could increase as the cohort ages. However, it is impossible to conclude anything about the extent to which marriage is associated with changes in well-being in this cohort (Lucas & Clark, 2006). A better way to examine the effects of marriage (or any other factor) would be to track the same individuals over time to determine whether those who got married also experienced a lasting boost in well-being. Thus, longitudinal studies that follow the same individuals over time allow for a more precise examination of the processes that underlie changes in well-being. Although such studies are time-consuming and expensive, they have the potential to shed much light on the questions in which policy makers are most interested.

For many years, economists and sociologists have used such studies to examine the processes that underlie a variety of economic conditions and transitions. Fortunately, although well-being measures were not widespread at the time of their origination, some of the longer-running studies have included well-being measures. Most notably, the German Socio-Economic Panel (GSOEP) Study is a representative longitudinal study of private households in Germany. The study began in 1984 and at the time of this writing was in its 25th year of data collection. Over 40,000 participants have been surveyed at one point or another, with many participating for 10 years or more. The GSOEP collects considerable amounts of data on the economic conditions of the participants. In addition, from the start of the survey, and increasingly over the years, it has included additional variables on the attitudes, behaviors, and psychological characteristics of the respondents. Thus, with such a large sample followed for many years, many important questions about the lives of people in Germany can be addressed.

Most notably for the purposes of this book, the GSOEP has included in every wave of its existence a single-item question on life satisfaction. The study has also included domain satisfaction questions (the specific domains that are assessed vary from year to year), and recently the survey included a measure of affective well-being. These data have been used to answer many questions regarding the psychological processes that underlie well-being judgments. For instance, we have used GSOEP data to address questions about adaptation to marriage, divorce, widowhood, and the onset of disability. Others have focused more precisely on questions that might be of interest to policy makers. For instance, Di Tella, Haisken-DeNew, and MacCulloch (2005) examined the question of whether people adapt to changes in income (they concluded that, for the most part, people do). Still others have tracked well-being over time in various regions of Germany. For instance, Frijters, Haisken-DeNew, and Shields (2005) examined the patterns of life satisfaction in East Germany following reunification. As can be seen in Figure 12.3, there are considerable differences between West Germany and East Germany, with East German life satisfaction increasing over time, apparently closer to the higher but stable West German levels. Thus, it appears that the measures used in the GSOEP are sensitive to differences in circumstances and to changes in those circumstances over time. Although the life satisfaction measures were not widely used by economists when the decision was made to include the question in the

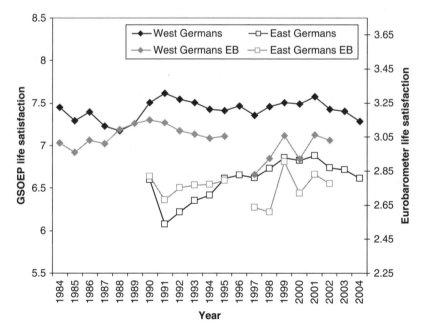

Figure 12.3 Average Life Satisfaction Scores by Year for West and East German Residents in the German Socio-Economic Panel Study (dark lines) and the Eurobarometer (light lines).

initial survey, this item is the single most analyzed item in the GSOEP data set.[1]

Other studies have modeled their design after the GSOEP. For instance, the British Household Panel Study (BHPS; Institute for Social and Economic Research, University of Essex, 2004) is an ongoing panel study focusing on social and economic change in Britain and the United Kingdom. Like the GSOEP, many of the primary goals of the study are focused on understanding changes in economic conditions. However, numerous social and attitudinal variables are assessed, and since 1996 a measure of life and domain satisfaction has been included. As with the GSOEP, the inclusion of these questions allows researchers to track well-being for specific individuals and to examine the extent to which individual-level phenomena are associated with differences and changes in well-being over time. Research using the BHPS has shown that life satisfaction measures are sensitive to changes in life circumstances such as the onset of a disability (e.g., Lucas, 2007).

More recently, the Economic and Social Research Council has proposed and begun work on a much larger study which will incorporate and greatly expand the BHPS. The U.K. Household Longitudinal Study will consist of a representative sample of 40,000 households (with an expected sample size of approximately 100,000 individuals) that will be followed yearly. As with the GSOEP and the BHPS, this new longitudinal study will incorporate standard demographic measures, along with detailed information about economic conditions. However, the stated goal of the project is to provide a broader set of indicators that can be used to address a wider variety of questions about the lives of individuals in the United Kingdom. For instance, a broader set of psychological variables will be included, and biomarker variables will be assessed. Studies like this will allow researchers to go beyond the questions that have been asked thus far. For instance, by including more direct measures of personality and by assessing well-being repeatedly over time, questions about the relative effect of set-point processes and external circumstances can be addressed.

Furthermore, as more of these studies are conducted, more interesting comparisons can be drawn. In addition to the GSOEP and the BHPS, there is an Australian household panel study (the Household, Income, and Labour Dynamics in Australia Survey (HILDA)), an American panel study (the Panel Study of Income Dynamics), and a Canadian panel study (the Survey of Labour and Income Dynamics) that have similar features

---

[1] There is an apparent testing effect in the German Socio-Economic Panel Study (Baird, Lucas, & Donnellan, 2008), whereby scores decrease with each increasing year in the study. Scores in Figure 12.3 are adjusted for this effect.

(though the latter two lack subjective measures of well-being). Organizers of these five studies have created a Cross-National Equivalent File to facilitate cross-national comparison analyses. So in addition to examining the factors that affect outcomes at a cross-sectional level, these variables can be examined and compared across time and across different nations. Not surprisingly, the organizers of these surveys often borrow from one another when revising their surveys. So as more researchers and policy makers rely on these measures, it becomes more and more likely that additional questions will be included. Furthermore, as researchers come to agree on the best measures, it is likely that these measures will be included in future surveys. Other national panel studies that include measures of subjective well-being include the Statistics Canada National Longitudinal Study of Children and Youth and the new Canadian Household Panel Survey, also run by Statistics Canada.

Longitudinal studies are important because they allow for a more detailed examination of the processes that underlie various behavioral and economic patterns. For instance, economists who are interested in predicting unemployment and reactions to unemployment may be able to use information about a person's employment history in their models. Much of this information is available in panel studies that follow individuals over time. Similarly, researchers who want to understand well-being can track what has happened over time in the lives of selected individuals to develop more informed views on adaptation and other processes that are hard to unravel using cross-sectional data. Thus, longitudinal studies that follow individuals for many years are particularly useful.

However, they also have drawbacks. Even in the studies that do an excellent job retaining participants (such as the GSOEP, BHPS, and HILDA) have some attrition. Even losing 4% or 5% of the sample in each year of administration will lead to substantial attrition over long periods of time. Weighting schemes can be used to maximize representativeness, but questions continue about those remaining in the study, and how they differ from those who drop out. On the other hand, because the investment in each person is so great, study organizers might go to greater lengths to ensure a representative sample from the outset than would organizers of a cross-sectional study. For instance, the GSOEP uses face-to-face interviewers and households are contacted by physical visits from interviewers. This may result in a different (and potentially more representative) sample than studies that rely on phone surveys, particularly with sharply declining response rates for phone surveys and the increased use of mobile phones as a primary source of communication. Thus, national accounts that rely on survey techniques will likely benefit from the incorporation of multiple methods of sampling and assessment.

What Is Left to Do?

With the existence of the studies described above, it is reasonable to ask what role a system of national accounts could fill. If organizations such as Gallup are collecting in-depth data on the well-being of a single nation over time (the Gallup–Healthways poll) along with less frequent assessments of the well-being of many nations of the world (the Gallup World Poll), what do additional systems of national indicators have to add? We believe that such a system could go beyond what exists today in several ways.

First, there are still a number of methodological limitations of existing studies. Most notably, many studies still use measures that are less than ideal. Most of the studies reviewed above have just a single item with which to assess well-being, and often (as is the case with the long-running American GSS) the specific item that is included is not the best in terms of psychometric properties. Furthermore, there is little consensus across the various study organizers about which measures to use. As a result, many of the studies reviewed above have items that are similar to one another, but not identical. This makes it difficult to compare results and build cumulative knowledge from the various studies that exist. Furthermore, the methodological differences may lead to different results, which may make it appear as though different answers emerge for the same question.

A broad system of national indicators could build on the knowledge gained from existing studies, but it would also allow for some centralization and systematization. A carefully chosen core set of measures could systematically be assessed over time and across regions. By reducing the variability in the methodology, stronger conclusions about differences could emerge. Without this centralization, researchers and policy makers may inevitably be left with a confusing picture of the well-being of those they wish to help.

This will be particularly important when comparing results from studies that vary widely in methodology. For instance, both the GSOEP (a longitudinal study) and the Eurobarometer (a cross-sectional study that is repeated yearly) could be used to track the life satisfaction of East and West Germans. As noted above, the GSOEP shows a fairly large discrepancy between the life satisfaction of those living in West Germany and those living in East Germany. As the dark lines in Figure 12.3 show, however, the gap decreased considerably following reunification in 1990. In addition, the GSOEP data suggest that West German life satisfaction increased around the time of unification, whereas East German life satisfaction declined from 1990 to 1991. There are some important similarities in the Eurobarometer data. For instance, these data also show the increase in West German life satisfaction and the decrease in East German life satisfaction from 1990 to 1991. In addition, the gap between East and West Germans closes in the Eurobarometer. However, in contrast to the results from the GSOEP, this decrease in the size of the gap appears to reflect a drop in satisfaction on the part of the West Germans. Unfortunately, it is difficult to determine why these different results emerged. At this point, the larger sample size, along with the greater number of waves of assessment in the GSOEP, might lead to greater confidence in the results that emerge from this study. But if standardized methods could be used (e.g., if an organization could conduct a longitudinal study with new refreshment samples at regular intervals), then the effect of the methods could be assessed.

A second issue is that many existing studies do not include measures at a regular enough interval to be useful for policy purposes. The largest existing study, the WVS, has been conducted only five times over an almost 30-year period. This is useful for examining broad trends, but the information that can be gained from such a study might not be precise enough to inform policy decisions. Other studies are conducted more frequently, but well-being measures are included in modules that are administered at less frequent intervals. Collecting data at the scale needed for such programs is expensive, and existing studies must accomplish many goals. Therefore, they often do not have the funds to incorporate well-being measures with the frequency that would be required to guide policy decisions. Having more centralized systems could ensure that measures were assessed at reasonable intervals.

A third problem is that some of the best existing data—like those collected by the Gallup Organization—are now proprietary. It is certainly encouraging that Gallup thinks that information about population-level well-being is important enough that they are willing to invest millions of dollars collecting the data. But private organizations will need to recoup their investment, and therefore the data will not be available to any interested party. Ideally, national indicators of well-being would provide an open and accessible source of information about how a population is doing. Although policy makers could certainly purchase access to the Gallup data, a proprietary system like this may not be ideal for policy purposes.

Another problem with existing studies is that although the sample sizes are large by existing standards, they are often not large enough to capture sufficiently large numbers of specific groups on which to draw reliable inferences. Policy questions most frequently revolve around the well-being of specific groups of citizens, such as working mothers, unemployed individuals who do not have health insurance, or those living in the vicinity of a waste deposit site. Surveys that are representative of the broad population must be extremely large to contain sufficient numbers of individuals from target groups such as these, or else targeted samples must be collected. Thus, national accounts of well-being can be designed with specific policy questions in mind, a role that is not performed by existing surveys.

Therefore, the studies that exist do not yet provide a substitute for an organized program for tracking national, regional, and especially local levels of well-being. Existing studies show that such programs are feasible, and the increasingly common analyses of these existing data for policy relevant purposes show the promise that these measures have. But existing studies also have some limitations—limitations that in many cases can be overcome with greater attention to systematic assessments that use standardized procedures and a wider variety of measures than are currently being assessed. Such programs would build on existing knowledge and help put results from existing studies in context. But they could also go much further in informing policy than current work can possibly do.

What Can We Learn from Existing Studies?

Many of the objections that can be raised about creating national accounts of well-being focus on the feasibility and utility of such accounts. The studies reviewed above show that measuring well-being could be both feasible and useful. For instance, some may object that the cost of assessing well-being would be too great to warrant an entirely new assessment project. When a new panel study was created, or repeated cross-sectional assessments were used, the cost would be significant, although substantially less that the costs involved in creating the economic and social indicators that are in place. However, future developers of national accounts could capitalize on existing assessment programs and thereby keep initial costs quite low.

There are other important reasons for adding well-being questions to a range of existing surveys rather than creating a new special-purpose survey instrument. First, a larger number of survey vehicles, and more frequent assessments would soon serve to provide sufficiently large geo-coded samples to permit the study of well-being at the local and community levels. Second, including well-being questions as part of standard modules that are used in several surveys would provide an important additional linkage across diverse surveys. Third, different host surveys would collectively provide more capacity to assess the importance of a wide range of individual and contextual factors influencing well-being. Thus the addition of a common well-being module would expand the capacity of each survey to answer questions in its own domain, while at the same time building up the size and value of the national data archives.

Numerous data collection efforts are under way already, and the results of these programs are being used to guide policy. It would not be that difficult or that expensive to add a core set of well-being questions to these ongoing efforts. To be sure, this would not be free. Surveying large representative samples costs money and is time-consuming, and organizers of such studies think carefully about each and every question that is included. Adding more question means dropping others or risking the loss of participants who do not want to be burdened with an overly long survey. However, even with these downsides, the cost of adding questions would be much less than creating a new assessment program. We think it likely that in several decades there will be standard accounts of well-being in most nations. In the meantime, existing surveys and additions to other ongoing surveys will demonstrate the usefulness of the measures to policy makers.

In cases where it is not immediately possible to add well-being measures to existing mainline official surveys, a useful start could be made by contracting with existing scientific studies to collect the data. Such studies are often searching for funding to keep their surveys going. It would be possible for government agencies that are in charge of tracking the national accounts to provide the studies with the core set of questions (along with some minimum requirements in terms of sampling strategies, and so forth), but the study organizers themselves could collect and provide the data. Again, new assessment programs are not necessarily required because of the infrastructure for data collection that currently exists.

New programs of national accounts need not be expensive. Yet as the research reviewed earlier in this chapter (and throughout this book) shows, the information that can be gained from these studies can be extremely useful. Well-being measures have already been shown to be sensitive to conditions in many ways that could inform policy decisions. In developing new national accounts of well-being, one need simply look to existing studies to find excellent models for how such studies might be undertaken. Relative to some other information that is currently being gathered, the information could be gathered quite inexpensively. Furthermore, the marginal utility of this information could be quite high—in terms of information that is systematically tracked by the government, subjective reports of well-being are quite different than what is typically assessed. Therefore, policy makers might obtain a new and very different perspective on how populations and groups are flourishing for a relatively modest price.

Chapter 13

Conclusions

Throughout this book, we have discussed a wide variety of contexts in which well-being measures could guide policy decisions. It is important to note that the well-being measures are used in quite different ways across these policy domains. In some areas the well-being measures reveal the types of environments that most enhance quality of life. In other domains, well-being measures can be used to evaluate and compare various policy alternatives. In still other policy areas, the value of the well-being measures lies in their ability to provide information on how to prevent future problems or to enhance future positive outcomes. Thus, well-being measures can help point toward broad policy directions that can raise the quality of life of a society. In some cases the measures will point to places where significant misery needs to be remedied; in other cases the measures might reveal alternatives that can enhance well-being. The large range of uses of the well-being measures is evident; they can be useful to policy makers working at the organization, city, state, national, and international levels.

In the cases we reviewed, existing data have sometimes been too sparse to support firm conclusions about the consequences of specific conditions or policies for well-being. The examples we discussed are meant to provide suggestions regarding the types of issues for which subjective well-being data could be useful. We certainly do not mean to imply that these are instances where clear conclusions can already be drawn. The evidence is preliminary, and better data are needed on most of the specific policy issues that we discussed. Systematic programs for assessing national well-being would greatly help to address such reservations because such accounts would yield much better data than we currently possess. Currently, most of the data on well-being are based on piecemeal data collected by individual investigators who are interested in their specific theoretical questions. The accounts of well-being would give a much more complete picture, and one that is purposefully aimed at answering policy questions.

It is also important to note that we do not advocate the idea that governments should intervene strongly to move society toward a primary goal of increased well-being. The proper role of governments depends on the culture and political philosophy of the citizenry, and at least in some societies, the role of government might be quite minimal. However, regardless of the level of government intervention that a society deems to be appropriate, well-being measures can help governments implement policies and actions effectively. Even if the only government role was to provide basic services such as a police force and fire protection, well-being measures could be used to help leaders provide these services in ways that were responsive to people's expectations. For those societies that desire greater intervention and social engineering from their governments, well-being measures can help there too. Such ideas are reflected in Layard's suggestion that well-being measures should be used to guide policies that lead to less work and greater income redistribution. Layard's recommendation has been interpreted by some as implying a strongly interventionist government. And although the principles that underlie this recommendation can be derived from an examination of well-being research, whether or not they are implemented must be determined by the goals, values, and desires of a society. The well-being measures can be used in much less dramatic ways; they do not always necessitate strong interventions.

One concern that we often hear when discussing the ideas presented in this book is that by focusing on well-being, governments will necessarily behave in a more controlling, paternalistic manner. For some reason, when people hear these proposals, they assume that governments that track well-being will start mandating that people feel good all the time and will force people to partake in behaviors that research shows are good for life satisfaction. We want to be clear that there is no reason to expect increased paternalism if the proposals described in this book come to fruition. Concerns about paternalism are misplaced for two principal reasons.

First, why should a shift from any current goal of government policy (e.g., to increase productivity, to improve economic growth, to develop effective health care systems, or to lower crime) to goals that consider the ultimate effects on well-being imply anything about the policies that might be used to achieve these objectives? In fact, many existing policy goals, including the goal to increase the economic health of a nation, implicitly assume that these goals will ultimately lead to higher well-being for citizens. Our proposal simply suggests that these same goals can be accomplished more effectively if levels of well-being were tracked, analyzed, and used in the decision-making process.

Second, results from major international surveys show that within and between countries, individuals highly value the freedom to develop their lives as they choose. More importantly, respondents who say that they have such freedoms tend to report greater well-being. Countries where there is a stable and trusted framework within which individuals and families have both the opportunity and the capacity to freely develop their lives are those with higher average life satisfaction. For instance, the Gallup World Poll found a high association between positive emotions and feeling free choice about how to spend one's time. Thus, in proposing that governments should track the well-being of its citizens, we recognize the importance of freedom. There is nothing about using well-being to guide policy decisions that impinges on this freedom or will make governments more paternalistic.

Timing for Implementing National Accounts of Well-Being

Is this the time for national accounts of well-being, or do we need more research and study? Economic accounts have historical roots that can be traced back at least as far as seventeenth-century England, when scholars sought to estimate the wealth of the country. Over the ensuing centuries, the measurement of economic activity has grown both in the quality of the measurements themselves and in theoretical sophistication. In the last century, efforts to quantify market production and consumption have grown dramatically in the developed nations of the world. We now have dozens of key economic measures—and hundreds of measures in total—that are systematically collected to reflect economic activity. An important point to remember is that when the first attempts at measurement began in economics, theory was not sophisticated. The increasing use of such measures allowed economic theory to be developed over time. We now have more than a rudimentary knowledge of well-being, but there is still much that is left to be learned. Systematic programs for measuring well-being will allow much more rapid development of theory. Thus, early deployment of national measures of well-being can immediately be used by policy makers, but it will also further the knowledge needed to use the accounts in increasingly effective ways. At the very least, national accounts will identify who among the citizens is suffering and who is thriving, and some policy implications of this information should be evident without a complete theory of happiness.

It should also be noted that subjective measures are already being used for several important functions even though the precise processes that underlie these judgments are not always well understood. Opinion polls already exert a strong influence on policy decisions; and subjective survey responses including consumer optimism and buying intentions are currently employed as components of economic indicators. Similarly, subjective health measures are widely collected, and these have been shown to be important predictors of longevity. These, too, already guide health policies at the national and local level.

Admittedly, there is still much to understand about subjective well-being, and we are in the early stages of creating a *science of well-being*. We need more experimental, quasi-experimental, and longitudinal studies, as well as more refined measures. There are clear limitations in our knowledge. For example, health satisfaction scores drawn from the Gallup World Poll show only a very small correlation with other indicators of the health of nations (e.g., life expectancy). For example, in the Ukraine, longevity approaches 70 years even though only about half of respondents are satisfied with their health. In contrast, in Mozambique almost 90% of respondents are satisfied with their health even though life expectancy is only about 40 years. Findings such as this raise questions about the precise factors that influence both the subjective judgments and the life expectancy values themselves. For instance, factors such as infant mortality and AIDS might reduce life expectancy without affecting the health satisfaction of those who are not affected.

In contrast to the health satisfaction findings, the association between life expectancy and the global life evaluation contained in the Ladder of Life is stronger. In this case, Mozambique falls in the expected position, with a relatively low Ladder-of-Life score that is consistent with its low life expectancy. One possibility is that health satisfaction is influenced by expectancies, including expectations regarding the quality of the health care system and those based on a respondent's age. Thus, health satisfaction might be less affected by societal longevity than is the Ladder-of-Life score. Perhaps people without fatal diseases are satisfied with their health if they live in an area where many other people have AIDS. These measurement questions do not mean that we should not institute well-being measures until we fully understand them. If this were true, then we would still not have national economic accounts.

The issue is whether we know enough about well-being to initiate systematic programs for measuring it. It should be clear from the contents of this book that the answer is "yes." The measures are sufficient to reveal some of the groups in society that are suffering, and they also tell us which groups are thriving. The measures already provide strong clues about the characteristics of nations that lead to the experience of a satisfying life for citizens, along with those that predict the opposite. The measures give clear clues about the activities and circumstances that tend to lead to ill-being and well-being. And when national accounts of well-being are instituted, our understanding of these issues will only grow.

A final consideration in terms of timing is the extent to which changing societal values make well-being more relevant as policy guides than they were in the past. People in economically developed nations now live in a *postmaterialist world* (Inglehart, 2000). Because basic needs have been met for a large proportion of the population, people are less concerned with physical goods and services and there is greater emphasis placed on personal development and experience. Thus, the increased interest in well-being research among researchers and policy makers may reflect the changing values of society. This may make it a particularly appropriate time to begin to assess well-being variables to keep pace with and tailor policy to these changing values.

It might be that centuries from now, people will look back at this time as the Dark Ages of well-being, a time in which society focused heavily on the consumption and production of market goods without determining how this activity was related to broader feelings of well-being. Imagine trying to develop economic policy without economic measures in place. Imagine a modern government trying to direct law enforcement efforts without crime statistics or attempting to budget health research money with no idea about disease prevalence. Well-being is important to most citizens in developed nations, and yet there are no systematic efforts to measure it, and therefore it receives little policy attention.

Concerns about the timing of the proposals described in this book also depend to some extent on the scope of the programs that are implemented. Systematic programs for assessing well-being need not be started from scratch. Measures might be added to existing national surveys, and this can occur immediately and with only modest cost. However, forward-thinking nations could go beyond these relatively modest efforts and institute much larger programs for assessing well-being. For instance, it would be more desirable to measure several forms of well-being with sufficient sample sizes so that distinct groups could be isolated and examined. In addition, longitudinal panel studies could be used to track well-being over time and to isolate the individual-level factors that promote or prevent well-being from occurring. Precursors of such studies now exist in nations such as Australia, Germany, and the United Kingdom.

Furthermore, many nations and international organizations such as the European Union and the Organization for Economic Cooperation and Development already assess well-being to some degree, and these efforts could be expanded. New indicators could be put in place to help policy makers study outcomes that are relevant to policies that are currently being debated. All of these initial efforts will be quite inexpensive when the potential benefits are considered. In light of the broad range of issues that will be illuminated by the well-being measures, some nations may choose to institute a full-fledged system of national well-being accounts in the near future.

Toward the Future

We have argued that the world needs systematic measures of well-being to inform the decisions of our leaders and citizens. We have also argued that we are ready to take this step. Indeed, preliminary steps are already being taken as organizations start to administer well-being questions to representative samples of respondents from broad areas of the world. Furthermore, behavioral scientists have begun use these data to determine the policy implications of specific research findings.

Should we move incrementally in small steps toward accounts of well-being, as is now occurring, or should nations and international organizations move to institute a full set of accounts of subjective well-being on an ongoing basis? The incremental steps are already in place and moving forward, and some smaller forms of national accounts of well-being already exist, for example, in the German Socio-Economic Panel Study and in the British Household Panel Study. Even though these projects are quite delimited in terms of measuring subjective well-being, the measures have proved valuable in a number of policy instances. Therefore, we feel that a bolder plan should soon be adopted by some nations. At the same time, there are of course conceptual and research questions that need to be answered. However, these same types of questions existed for economic and social indicators, and the answers to the questions were easier to formulate when the systematic measures were in place. If societies institute an ongoing panel study in which a thorough set of subjective well-being measures is included, this is certain to pay off both in terms of better policy decisions, and in terms of a better understanding of both subjective well-being and economic measures.

The costs of national systems for measuring subjective well-being are not insignificant, but neither are they enormous. For the amount of information obtained, these measures are relatively inexpensive, especially when compared to many other types of indicators. When measures are in place, the research agenda can also move forward more quickly. For example, when interventions and new policies are introduced the subjective well-being measures can be given before, during, and after the changes in a quasi-experimental way, to help evaluate the impact of the new policies.

There are a series of questions about how institutionalization of the measures will occur. For example, will demographers and economists, who hitherto often credit observable behavioral measures with more validity than subjective measures, come to embrace the measures of well-being when they examine them more carefully? On the political front, there are a number of important issues. For example, politicians will need to be convinced that well-being is an agenda that will appeal to voters. They will also need to be convinced that the well-being measures are not tied to a specific political agenda, and will not inherently favor the opposition's policy proposals. Perhaps most of all, behavioral scientists and bureaucrats need to show politicians examples where the measures of subjective well-being will help them make better decisions.

Who will be the advocates, the constituency with much to gain, who will support the measures so that they are implemented fully? It is likely that there are groups such as environmentalists or mental health professionals who will find the measures particularly attractive. However, other groups such as labor unions and business leaders are also likely to believe that the measures will reveal information that is favorable to the kinds of policies they support. It is important that citizens and politicians see that the measures will not invariably support one viewpoint or the other, and it is important that the measures are constructed in a neutral way so that they do not do so. Measures will need to be put in place so that the measurement process is relatively objective. Ultimately, the support for accounts of subjective well-being must come from the citizens and the democratic process.

How will society be different if the measures are fully in place? We do not envision that the measures will make a dramatic impact on the way societies function. It will not appear to be a society of Martians, who are unrecognizable to us today. Instead, it will simply be a society that functions more effectively in meeting human needs. Quality of life will be higher than it otherwise would have been, because policy makers and citizens will make better decisions based on more complete information. We will look back on the time when there were no subjective measures in place as we might look back on the Middle Ages as a time when economic and health measures were not in place. The societies had little way of formulating good economic or health policies because no systematic data were gathered. In this situation even the wisest leaders were largely in the dark when making decisions, just as we are in the dark now as to what will optimize the well-being of the people on earth.

In a world of systematic measures of well-being, people will make wiser choices about commuting and air pollution. Schools will be a bit safer and children a little happier. The well-being data will focus people's attention on well-being as an important outcome, and it will allow them to make sounder choices about their own well-being. Tax money too can be channeled in a somewhat more effective way. In other words, the planet will be a better place to live when the measures of subjective well-being are put in place, and when they are used by both leaders and ordinary citizens.

References

Adler, M. D. (2006). Welfare polls: A synthesis. U of Penn Law School, Public Law Working Paper No. 06-03. Available at SSRN: http://ssrn.com/abstract=885521

Ahadi, S., & Diener, E. (1989). Multiple determinants and effect size. *Journal of Personality and Social Psychology, 56*(3), 398–406.

Ahn, N. (2005). Life satisfaction among Spanish workers: Importance of intangible job characteristics. Working Papers 2005-17, FEDEA.

Ahn, N., García, J. R., & Jimeno, J. F. (2004). Cross-country differences in well-being consequences of unemployment in Europe. Working Papers 2004-11, FEDEA. (March 5, 2007).

Alfonso, V. C., Allison, D. B., Rader, D. E., & Gorman, B. S. (1996). The extended satisfaction with life scale: Development and psychometric properties. *Social Indicators Research, 38*(3), 275–301.

Andrews, F. M., & Withey, S. B. (1976). *Social indicators of well-being.* New York: Plenum Press.

Argyle, M. (1999). *Causes and correlates of happiness.* New York, NY: Russell Sage Foundation.

Asarnow; J. R., Jaycox, L. H., Duan, N., LaBorde, A. P., Rea, M. M., Murray, P., et al. (2005). Effectiveness of a quality improvement intervention for adolescent depression in primary care clinics: A randomized controlled trial. *The Journal of the American Medical Association (JAMA), 293*, 311–319.

Aspinwall, L. G. (1998). Rethinking the role of positive affect in self-regulation. *Motivation and Emotion. Special Issue: Positive Affect and Self-Regulation: I, 22*(1), 1–32.

Baird, B. M., Lucas, R. E., & Donnellan, M. B. (2008). *Life satisfaction across the lifespan: Findings from two nationally representative panel studies.* Manuscript in preparation. Michigan State University.

Barrington-Leigh, C. P., & Helliwell, J. F. (2008). *Empathy and emulation: Life satisfaction and the urban geography of comparison groups.* NBER Working Paper 14593, National Bureau of Economic Research, Inc..

Beatty, J., Covey, J., Dolan, P., Hopkins, L., Jones-Lee, M., Loomes, G., et al. (1998). On the contingent valuation of safety and the safety of contingent valuation: Part 1-caveat investigator. *Journal of Risk and Uncertainty, 17*, 5–25.

Beatty, P., Schechter, S., & Whitaker, K. (1996). Evaluating subjective health questions: Cognitive and methodological investigations. *Proceedings of the American Statistical Association, Section on Survey Research Methods.*

Becchetti, L., Castriota, S., & Giuntella, O. (2006). The effects of age and job protection on the welfare costs of inflation and unemployment: A source of ECB anti-inflation bias? Departmental Working Papers 245, Tor Vergata University, CEIS.

Bechtel, R. B., & Churchman, A. (Eds.), (2002). *Handbook of environmental psychology*. New York: Wiley.

Becker, R. A., Denby, L., McGill, R., & Wilks, A. R. (1987). Analysis of data from the places rated almanac. *The American Statistician, 41*(3), 169–186.

Beebe-Center, J. G. (1932). *Psychology of pleasantness and unpleasantness*. New York: Van Nostrad.

Berkman, L. F., & Syme, S. L. (1979). Social networks, host resistance, and mortality: A nine-year follow-up study of Almeda county residents. *American Journal of Epidemiology, 109*, 186–204.

Bird, W. (2007). *Natural Thinking: A Report by Dr. William Bird, for the Royal Society for the Protection of Birds (RSPB), Investigating the Links Between the Natural Environment, Biodiversity and Mental Health* (2nd ed.). United Kingdom: RSPB.

Blair-West, G. W., Cantor, C. H., Mellsop, G. W., & Eyeson-Annon, M. L. (1999). Lifetimes suicide risk in major depression: Sex and age determinants. *Journal of Affective Disorders, 55*, 171–178.

Bodenhausen, G. V., Kramer, G. P., & Süsser, K. (1994). Happiness and stereotypic thinking in social judgment. *Journal of Personality and Social Psychology, 66*(4), 621–632.

Boehm, J. K., & Lyubomirsky, S. (2008). Does happiness promote career success? *Journal of career assessment, 16*(1), 101–116.

Boelhouwer, J., & Stoop, I. (1999). Measuring well-being in the Netherlands: The SCP index from 1974 to 1997. *Social Indicators Research, 48*, 51–75.

Bower, G. H. (1981). Mood and memory. *American Psychologist, 36*, 129–148.

Bradburn, N. M. (1969). *The structure of psychological well being*. Chicago: Aldine.

Bradshaw, J., Hoelscher, P., & Richardson, D. (2006). An index of child well-being in the European Union. *Social Indicators Research, 80*, 133–177.

Brazier, J., & Dolan, P. (2005). Evidence of preference construction in a comparison of variants of the standard gamble method. Health economics and decision science Discussion Paper Series Ref: 05/4. School of Health and Related Research (ScHARR).

BRFSS (Behavioral Risk Factor Surveillance System). (2006). *BRFSS Annual Survey Data*. Retrieved from http://www.cdc.gov/brfss/technical_infodata/surveydata/2006.htm

Brickman, P., & Campbell, D. T. (1971). Hedonic relativism and planning the good society. In M. H. Appley (Ed.), *Adaptation level theory: A symposium*. New York: Academic Press.

Brickman, P., Coates, D., & Janoff-Bulman, R. (1978). Lottery winners and accident victims: Is happiness relative? *Journal of Personality and Social Psychology, 36*(8), 917–927.

Brzenchek, J., Ahern, K., Dominick, D., Heller, C., Gold, C., & Conway, S. (2001). *Self-reported health-related quality of life and health service utilization of Alzheimer's patients. Gerontologist, 41*(S1), 366–366.

Buunk, B. P., Collins, R. L., Taylor, S. E., VanYperen, N. W., & Dakof, G. A. (1990). The affective consequences of social comparison: Either direction has its ups and downs. *Journal of Personality and Social Psychology, 59*(6), 1238–1249.

Campbell, D. T., & Fiske, D. W. (1959). Convergent and discriminant validation by the multitrait-multimethod matrix. *Psychological Bulletin, 56*(2), 81–105.

Cantril, H. (1965). *The pattern of human concerns.* New Brunswick, NJ: Rutgers University Press.

Carver, C. S. (2003). Pleasure as a sign you can attend to something else: Placing positive feelings within a general model of affect. *Cognition & Emotion, 17*(2), 241–261.

Carver, C. S., & Scheier, M. F. (1990). Origins and functions of positive and negative affect: A control-process view. *Psychological Review, 97*(1), 19–35.

Catalano, R., Dooley, D., Novaco, R. W., Hough, R., & Wilson, G. (1993). Using ECA survey data to examine the effect of job layoffs on violent behavior. *Hospital Community Psychiatry, 44*, 874–879.

Chen, X., Rubin, K. H., & Li, B. (1995). Depressed mood in Chinese children: Relations with school performance and family environment. *Journal of Consulting and Clinical Psychology, 63*(6), 938–947.

Clark, A. E., Diener, E., Georgellis, Y., & Lucas, R. E. (2006). Lags and leads in life satisfaction: A test of the baseline hypothesis. *IZA* On-Line Discussion Paper No. 2526.

Clark, A. E, Georgellis, Y., & Sanfey, P. (1998). Job satisfaction, wage changes, and quits: Evidence from Germany. *Research in Labor Economics, 17*, 95–121.

Clark, A. E., Georgellis, Y., & Sanfey, P. (2001). Scarring: The psychological impact of past unemployment. *Economica, 68*, 221–241.

Clark, A. E., & Oswald, A. J. (1996). Satisfaction and comparison income. *Journal of Public Economics, 61*(3), 359–381.

Clements, M. L., Stanley, S. M., & Markman, H. J. (2004). Before they said "i do": Discriminating among marital outcomes over 13 years. *Journal of Marriage and the Family, 66*(3), 613–626.

Cohen, J. (1988). *Statistical power analysis for the behavioral sciences* (2nd ed.). Hillsdale, NJ: Lawrence Erlbaum.

Colbert, A. E., Mount, M. K., Harter, J. K., Witt, L. A., & Barrick, M. R. (2004). Interactive effects of personality and perceptions of the work situation on workplace deviance. *Journal of Applied Psychology, 89*, 599–609.

Coleman, J. (1990). *The foundations of social theory.* Cambridge: Harvard University Press.

Collier, C., & Christiansen, T. (1992). The State of Commute in Southern California. *Transportation Research Board 1338—Public Transit: Bus, Paratransit, and Ridesharing.* Washington, DC: Transportation Research Board, 73–81.

Costa, P. T., McCrae, R. R., & Zonderman, A. B. (1987). Environmental and dispositional influences on well-being: Longitudinal follow-up of an American national sample. *British Journal of Psychology, 78*(3), 299–306.

Crede, M., Chernyshenko, O. S., Stark, S., Dalal, R. S., & Bashshur, M. (2007). Job satisfaction as mediator: An assessment of job satisfaction's position within the nomological network. *Journal of Occupational and Organizational Psychology, 80*, 515–538.

Cropanzano, R., James, K., & Konovsky, M. A. (1993). Dispositional affectivity as a predictor of work attitudes and job performance. *Journal of Organizational Behavior, 14*, 595–606.

Crow, R., Gage, H., Hampson, S., Hart, J., Kimber, A., Storey, L., et al. (2002). The measurement of satisfaction with healthcare: Implications for practice from a systematic review of the literature. *Health Technology Assessment, 6*(32), 45-51.

Csikszentmihalyi, M. (1990). *Flow: The psychology of optimal experience.* New York: Harper & Row.

Cummings, S. M., Kropf, N. P., Cassie, K. M., & Bride, B. (2004). Evidenced based treatments for older adults. *Journal of Evidence Based Social Work: Advances in Practice, Programming, Research, and Policy, 1*, 53–81.

Cummins, R. A. (1996). The domains of life satisfaction: An attempt to order chaos. *Social Indicators Research, 38*(3), 303–328.

Davis, J. A., & Smith, T. W. (2007). *General Social Surveys, 1972–2006* [machine-readable data file] /Principal Investigator, James A. Davis; Director and Co-Principal Investigator, Tom W. Smith; Co-Principal Investigator, Peter V. Marsden; Sponsored by National Science Foundation. Chicago: National Public Opinion Research Center [producer]; Storrs, CT: The Roper Center for Public Opinion Research, University of Connecticut [distributor].

Deaton, A. (2008). Income, health, and well-being around the world: Evidence from the Gallup World Poll. *Journal of Economic Perspectives, 22*(2), 53–72.

Dickens, W. T., & Flynn, J. R. (2001). Heritability estimates versus large environmental effects: The IQ paradox resolved. *Psychological Review, 108*, 346–369.

Diener, E. (1995). A value based index for measuring national quality of life. *Social Indicators Research, 36*, 107–127.

Diener, E., Diener, M., & Diener, C. (1995). Factors predicting the subjective well-being of nations. *Journal of Personality and Social Psychology, 69*(5), 851–864.

Diener, E., Emmons, R. A., Larsen, R. J., & Griffin, S. (1985). The satisfaction with life scale. *Journal of Personality Assessment, 49*, 71–75.

Diener, E., & Fujita, F. (1997). Social comparison and subjective wellbeing. In B. P. Buunk & F. X. Gibbons (Eds.), *Health, coping, and well-being: Perspectives from social comparison theory.* Hillsdale, NJ: Lawrence Erlbaum.

Diener, E., Horwitz, J., & Emmons, R. A. (1985). Happiness of the very wealthy. *Social Indicators Research, 16*, 263–274.

Diener, E., & Iran-Nejad, A. (1986). The relationship in experience between various types of affect. *Journal of personality and social psychology, 50*(5), 1031–1038.

Diener, E., Kahneman, D., Tov, W., & Arora, R. (2008). Income's differential impact on judgments of life versus affective well-being. Paper presented at Princeton Conference, October 12th-14th, 2008.

Diener, E., Lucas, R. E., & Scollon, C. N. (2006). Beyond the hedonic treadmill: Revising the adaptation on theory of well-being. *American Psychologist, 61*(4), 305–314.

Diener, E., & Oishi, S. (2000). Money and happiness: Income and subjective well-being across nations. In E. Diener & E. M. Suh (Eds.), *Culture and subjective well-being* (pp. 185–218). Cambridge, MA: The MIT Press.

Diener, E., Sandvik, E., & Pavot, W. (1991). Happiness is the frequency, not the intensity, of positive versus negative affect. In F. Strack, M. Argyle, & N. Schwarz (Eds.), *Subjective well-being: An interdisciplinary perspective. International series in experimental social psychology* (Vol. 21, pp. 119–139). Elmsford, NY: Pergamon Press, Inc.

Diener, E., & Seligman, M. E. P. (2004). Beyond money: Toward an economy of well-being. *Psychological Science in the Public Interest, 5,* 1–31.

Diener, E., Suh, E. M., Lucas, R. E., & Smith, H. L. (1999). Subjective well-being: Three decades of progress. *Psychological Bulletin, 125,* 276–302.

Diener, E., & Tov, W. (2007). Culture and subjective well-being. In S. Kitayama & D. Cohen (Eds.), *Handbook of cultural psychology* (pp. 691–713). New York: Guilford.

Dijkers, M. (1997). Quality of life after spinal cord injury: A meta analysis of the effects of disablement components. *Spinal Cord, 35*(12), 829–840.

Dijkers, M. (1999). Correlates of life satisfaction among persons with spinal cord injury. *Archives of Physical Medicine and Rehabilitation, 80*(8), 867–876.

Di Tella, R., Haisken-DeNew, J., & MacCulloch, R. (2005 working paper). Adaptation to Income and Status in an Individual Panel. Harvard University.

Dolan, P. (2000). The measurement of health-related quality of life for use in resource allocation decisions in health care. In A. J. Culyer & J. P. Newhouse (Eds.), *Handbook of health economics*, (Vol. 1723, pp. 1738–1739). Amsterdam: Elseiver.

Dolan, P. (2007). *Finding a NICEr way to value health: From hypothetical preferences to real experiences.* SMF Foresight, The Social Market Foundation.

Dolan, P. (2008). Developing methods that really do value the 'Q' in QALY. *Health Economics, Policy and Law, 3,* 69–77.

Dolan, P., & Moore, S. (2007). From preferences to experiences: Valuing the intangible victim costs of crime. *International Review of Victimology, 14,* 265–280.

Dolan, P., & Peasgood, T. (2006 Draft). *Valuing non-market goods: Does subjective well-being offer a viable alternative to contingent valuation?* London: Tanaka School of Business.

Dolan, P., & White, M. P. (2007). How can measures of subjective well-being be used to inform public policy? *Perspectives on Psychological Science, 2,* 71–85.

Dunn, E. W., Aknin, L. B., & Norton, M. I. (2008). Spending money on others promotes happiness. *Science, 319*(5870), 1687–1688.

Dunn, E. W., Wilson, T. D., & Gilbert, D. T. (2003). Location, location, location: The misprediction of satisfaction in housing lotteries. *Personality and Social Psychology Bulletin, 29*(11), 1421–1432.

Dutton, K. A., & Brown, J. D. (1997). Global self-esteem and specific self-views as determinants of people's reactions to success and failure. *Journal of Personality and Social Psychology, 73*(1), 139–148.

Eagly, A. H., Mladinic, A., & Otto, S. (1993). Cognitive and affective bases of attitudes toward social groups and social policies. *Journal of Experimental Social Psychology, 30,* 113–137.

Easterlin, R. (1974). Does economic growth improve the human lot? Some empirical evidence. In P. A. David & M. W. Reder (Eds.), *Nations and households in economic growth: Essays in honour of Moses Abramovitz* (pp. 89–125). New York: Academic Press.

Easterlin, R. A. (1995). Will raising the incomes of all increase the happiness of all? *Journal of Economic Behavior & Organization, 27,* 35–47.

Easterlin, R. A. (2003). Explaining happiness. *Proceedings of the National Academy of Sciences of the United States of America, 100*(19), 11176–11183.

Edler, E. L., & Benyamini, Y. (1997). Self-rated health and mortality: A review of twenty-seven community studies. *Journal of Health and Social Behavior, 38,* 21–37.

Ehrhardt, J. J., Saris, W. E., & Veenhoven, R. (2000). Stability of life-satisfaction over time: Analysis of change in ranks in a national population. *Journal of Happiness Studies, 1*(2), 177–205.

Eid, M., & Diener, E. (2004). Global judgments of subjective well-being: Situational variability and long-term stability. *Social Indicators Research, 65*(3), 245–277.

Evans, G. W., & Wener, R. E. (2006). Rail commuting duration and passenger stress. *Health Psychology, 25*(3), 408–412.

Ferrer-i-Carbonell, A. (2005). Income and well-being: An empirical analysis of the comparison income effect. *Journal of Public Economics, 89*, 997–1019.

Festinger, L. (1954). A theory of social comparison processes. *Human Relations, 7*, 117–140.

Fox, N. A., & Davidson, R. J. (1986). Taste-elicited changes in facial signs of emotion and the asymmetry of brain electrical-activity in human newborns. *Neuropsychologia, 24*(3), 417–422.

Frederick, S., & Loewenstein, G. (1999). *Hedonic adaptation*. New York, NY: Russell Sage Foundation.

Fredrickson, B. L. (2003). The value of positive emotions. *American Scientist, 91*, 330–335.

Fredrickson, B. L. (2004). The broaden-and-build theory of positive emotions. *Philosophical Transactions: Biological Sciences, 359*(1449), 1367–1377.

Frey, B. S., Luechinger, S., & Stutzer, A. (2004). Valuing public goods: The life satisfaction approach. Institute for Empirical Research in Economics, University of Zurich, Working Paper Series, ISSN 1424-0459, Working Paper No. 184 (March 2004).

Frey, B. S., & Stutzer, A. (2002). *Happiness and Economics: How the economy and institutions affect human well-being*. Princeton, NJ: Princeton University Press.

Frey, B. S., & Stutzer, A. (December, 2004). Economic Consequences of Mispredicting Utility. Institute for Empirical Research in Economics (IEW) Working Paper No. 218. Available at SSRN: http://ssrn.com/abstract=639025

Frijda, N. H. (1986). *The emotions*. New York, NY: Cambridge University Press; Paris, France: Editions de la Maison des Sciences de l'Homme.

Frijters, P. (2000). Do individuals try to maximize general satisfaction? *Journal of Economic Psychology, 21*(3), 281–304.

Frijters, P., Haisken-DeNew, J.P., & Shields, M.A. (2005): Socio-economic status, health shocks, life satisfaction and mortality: Evidence from an increasing mixed proportional hazards model, Discussion Paper 496, Centre for Economic Policy Research, Australian National University.

Fujita, F., & Diener, E. (2005). Life satisfaction set point: Stability and change. *Journal of Personality and Social Psychology, 88*(1), 158–164.

Gall, G., Pagano, M. E., Desmond, M. S., Perrin, J. M., & Murphy, J. M. (2000). Utility of psychosocial screening at a school-based health center. *Journal of School Health, 70*(7), 292–298.

Gallagher-Thompson, D., Lovett, S., Rose, J., McKibbin, C., Coon, D., Futterman, A., et al. (2000). Impact of psychoeducational interventions on distressed family caregivers. *Journal of Clinical Geropsychology, 6*, 91–110.

Ganz, P.A., Lee, J.J., & Siau, J. (1991). Quality of life assessment: an independent prognostic variable for surviving lung cancer. *Cancer, 67*, 3131-3135.

Gardner, J., & Oswald, A. J. (2006). Do divorcing couples become happier by breaking up? *Journal of the Royal Statistical Society: Series A(Statistics in Society), 169*, 319–336.

Gardner, J., & Oswald, A. J. (2007). Money and mental wellbeing: A longitudinal study of medium-sized lottery wins. *Journal of Health Economics, 26*(1), 49–60.

George, J. M., & Brief, A. (1992). Feeling good—doing good: A conceptual analysis of the mood at work-organizational spontaneity relationship. *Psychological Bulletin, 112*, 310–329.

Gibbons, F. X., Benbow, C. P., & Gerrard, M. (1994). From top dog to bottom half: Social comparison strategies in response to poor performance. *Journal of Personality and Social Psychology, 67*(4), 638–652.

Gilbert, D. T. (2007). *Stumbling on happiness.* Toronto: Vintage Canada.

Gilbert, D. T., Pinel, E. C., Wilson, T. D., Blumberg, S. J., & Wheatley, T. P. (1998). Immune neglect: A source of durability bias in affective forecasting. *Journal of Personality and Social Psychology, 75*(3), 617–638.

Glenn, N. D., & Weaver, C. N. (1988). The changing relationship of marital status to reported happiness. *Journal of Marriage & the Family, 50*(2), 317–324.

Gottman, J. M., & Levenson, R. W. (2000). The timing of divorce: Predicting when a couple will divorce over a 14-year period. *Journal of Marriage and the Family, 62*(3), 737–745.

Government Accountability Office (GAO). (2003). *School vouchers: Characteristics of privately funded programs*, September 2002. (GAO-02-752).

Graham, C., Eggers, A., & Sukhtankar, S. (2004). Does happiness pay? An exploration based on panel data from Russia. *Journal of Economic Behavior and Organization, 55*, 319–342.

Grant, N., Wardle, J., & Steptoe, A. (2007). *The relationship between life satisfaction and health behavior: A cross-cultural analysis of young adults.* Unpublished paper, University College London.

Gremier, A., & Gorey, K. (1998). The effectiveness of social work with older people and their families: A meta-analysis of conference proceedings. *Social Work Research, 22*(1), 60–65.

Griffeth, R. W., Hom, P. W., & Gaertner, S. (2000). A meta-analysis of antecedents and correlates of employee turnover: Update, moderator tests, and research implications for the next millennium. *Journal of Management, 26*(3), 463–488.

Groot, W., & Maassen van den Brink, H. (2007). Optimism, pessimism and the compensating income variation of cardiovascular disease: A two-tiered quality of life stochastic frontier model. *Social Science and Medicine, 65*, 1479–1489.

Gruber, J., & Mullainathan, S. (2002). *Do cigarette taxes make smokers happier?* NBER Working Papers 8872, National Bureau of Economic Research, Inc.

Gruber, J., & Mullainathan, S. (2005). Do cigarette taxes make smokers happier? *Advances in Economic Analysis & Policy, 5*, 1412.

Gurin, G., Joseph, V., & Feld, S. (1960). *Americans view of their mental health.* New York: Basic.

Gyarmati, D., de Raaf, S., Palameta, B., Nicholson, C., & Hui, T. (2008). Encouraging Work and Supporting Communities: Final results of the Community Employment Innovation Project. Ottawa: Social Research and Demonstration Corporation.

Hagerty, M. R., Cummins, R. A., Ferriss, A. L., Land, K., Michalos, A. C., Peterson, M., et al. (2001). Quality of life indexes for national policy: Review and agenda for research. *Social Indicators Research, 55*, 1–96.

Hagerty, M. R., & Veenhoven, R. (2003). Wealth and happiness revisited—growing national income does go with greater happiness. *Social Indicators Research, 64*(1), 1–27.

Hagihara, A., Tarumi, K., Babazono, A., Nobutomo, K., & Morimoto, K. (1998). Work versus non-work predictors of job satisfaction among Japanese white-collar workers. *Journal of Occupational Health, 40*, 285–292.

Halpern, D., (2005). *Social Capital* Cambridge, Polity Press.

Han, B., & Haley, W. E. (1999). Family caregiving for patients with stroke. *Stroke, 30*, 1478–1485.

Harmon-Jones, E., & Sigelman, J. (2001). State anger and prefrontal brain activity: Evidence that insult-related relative left-prefrontal activation is associated with experienced anger and aggression. *Journal of Personality and Social Psychology, 80*(5), 797–803.

Härter, M. C., Conway, K. P., & Merikangas, K. R. (2003). Associations between anxiety disorders and physical illness. *European Archives of Psychiatry and Clinical Neuroscience, 253*(6), 313–320.

Harter, J. K., & Creglow, A. (1998). *A meta-analysis and utility analysis of the relationship between core employee perceptions and business outcomes.* Princeton, NJ: SRI/Gallup.

Harter, J. K., Schmidt, F. L., & Hayes, T. L. (2002). Business-unit-level relationship between employee satisfaction, employee engagement, and business outcomes: A meta-analysis. *Journal of Applied Psychology, 87*, 268–279.

Harter, J. K., Schmidt, F. L., & Keyes, C. L. M. (2007). Well-being in the workplace and its relationship to business outcomes: A review of the Gallup studies. In C. L. M. Keyes & J. Haidt (Eds.), *Flourishing: Positive psychology and the life well-lived* (pp. 205–224). Washington, DC: American Psychological Association.

Hartig, T., Evans, G. W., Jamner, L. D., Davis, D. S., & Garling, T. (2003). Tracking restoration in natural and urban field setting. *Journal of Environmental Psychology, 23*, 109–123.

Hartig, T., Mang, M., & Evans, G. W. (1991). Restorative effects of natural environment experience. *Environment and Behaviour, 23*, 3–26.

Haybron, D. M. (2008). Philosophy and the science of subjective well-being. In M. Eid & R. Larsen (Eds.), *The science of subjective well-being* (pp. 17–43). New York: Guilford Press.

Headey, B., Veenhoven, R., & Wearing, A. (1991). Top-down versus bottom-up theories of subjective well-being. *Social Indicators Research, 24*(1), 81–100.

Heerwagen, J. H. (1990). The psychological aspects of windows and widow design. In R. I. Selby, K. H. Anthony, J. Choi, & B. Orland (Eds.), *Proceedings of the 21st Annual Conference of the Environmental Design Research Association.* Champaign-Urbana, Illinois.

Helliwell, J. F. (2001). Social capital, the economy and well-being. In K. Banting, A. Sharpe, & F. St-Hilaire (Eds.), *The review of economic performance and social progress* (pp. 43–60). Montreal and Ottawa: Institute for Research on Public Policy and Centre for the Study of Living Standards.

Helliwell, J. F. (2003). How's life: Combining individual and national variables to explain subjective well-being. *Economic Modelling, 20*, 331–360.

Helliwell, J. F. (2007). Well-being and social capital: Does suicide pose a puzzle? *Social Indicators Research 81*, 455-496.

Helliwell, J. F. (2008). *Life satisfaction and quality of development*. NBER Working Paper 14507, National Bureau of Economic Research, Inc.

Helliwell, J. F., & Huang, H. (2008). How's your government? International evidence linking good government and well-being. *British Journal of Political Science 38*, 595-619.

Helliwell, J. F., & Huang, H. (2009). How's the job? Well-being and social capital in the workplace. *Industrial and Labor Relations Review*. Previously NBER Working Paper 11759, National Bureau of Economic Research Inc..

Helliwell, J. F., Huang, H., & Harris, A. (2009). International differences in the determinants of life satisfaction. In R. Tridip, E. Somanathan, & B. Dutta (Eds.), *New and enduring themes in development economics*. Singapore: World Scientific.

Helliwell, J. F., & Putnam, R. D. (Summer 1995). Economic growth and social capital in Italy. *Eastern Economic Journal, 21*(3), 295–307.

Helliwell, J. F., & Putnam, R. D. (2004). The social context of well-being. *Philosophical Transactions of the Royal Society of London B, 359*, 1435–1446. Reprinted in F. A. Huppert, N. Baylis, & B. Keverne (Eds.), *The science of well-being* (pp. 435–459). London: Oxford University Press, 2005.

Hennessy, C. H., Moriarty, D. G., Zack, M. M., Scherr, P. A., & Brackbill, R. (1994). Measuring health-related quality of life for public health surveillance. *Public Health Reports, 109*, 665–672.

Hills, P., & Argyle, M. (2002). The Oxford Happiness Questionnaire: A compact scale for the measurement of psychological well-being. *Personality and Individual Differences, 33*, 1073–1082.

Hooley, P. J. D., Butler, G., & Howlett, J. G. (2005). The relationship of quality of life, depression, and caregiver burden in outpatients with congestive heart failure. *Congestive Heart Failure, 11*, 303–310.

Hsee, C. K., & Zhang, J. (2004). Distinction bias: Misprediction and mischoice due to joint evaluation. *Journal of Personality and Social Psychology, 86*(5), 680–695.

Hunt, E. K., & D'Arge, R. C. (1973). On lemmings and other acquisitive animals: Propositions on consumption. *Journal of Economic Issues, 7*, 337–353.

Hygge, S., Evans, G. W., & Bullinger, M. (2002). A prospective study of some effects of aircraft noise on cognitive performance in school children. *Psychological Science, 13*, 469–474.

Iaffaldano, M. T., & Muchinsky, P. M. (1985). Job satisfaction and job performance: A meta-analysis. *Psychological Bulletin, 97*, 251–273.

Inglehart, R. (2000). Genes, culture, democracy, and happiness. In E. Diener & E. M. Suh (Eds.), *Culture and subjective well-being* (pp. 165–184). Cambridge, MA: MIT Press.

Inglehart, R. (2008). Development, freedom, and rising happiness: A global perspective (1981–2007). *Perspectives on Psychological Science, 3*, 264-285.

Inglehart, R., Foa, R., Peterson, C., & Welzel, C. (2008). Development, freedom, and rising happiness: A global perspective (1981–2007). *Perspectives on Psychological Science, 3*(4), 264–285.

Isen, A. M., & Baron, R. A. (1991). Positive affect as a factor in organizations. In L. Cummings & B. M. Staw (Eds.), *Research in organizational behavior*. Greenwich, CT: JAI Press Inc.

Jacobs, S. V., Evans, G. W., Catalano, R., & Dooley, D. (1984). Air pollution and depressive symptomatology: Exploratory analyses of intervening psychosocial factors. *Population & Environment, 7*(4), 260–272.

Judge, T. A., Thoresen, C. J., Bono, J. E., & Patton, G. K. (2001). The job satisfaction-job performance relationship: A qualitative and quantitative review. *Psychological Bulletin, 127*, 376–407.

Kahneman, D. (1999). Objective happiness. In D. Kahneman, E. Diener, & N. Schwarz (Eds.), *Well-being: The foundations of hedonic psychology* (pp. 3–25). New York, NY: Russell Sage Foundation.

Kahneman, D., Diener, E., Tov, W., Arora, R., Muller, G., & Harter, J. (2008). Quality of human life on planet earth. To be submitted to *Proceedings of the National Academy of Sciences* (PNAS).

Kahneman, D., & Krueger, A. B. (2006). Developments in the measurement of subjective well-being. *Journal of Economic Perspectives, 20*, 3–24.

Kahneman, D., Krueger, A. B., Schkade, D. A., Schwarz, N., & Stone, A. A. (2004). A survey method for characterizing daily life experience: The day reconstruction method. *Science, 306*, 1776–1780.

Kahneman, D., Krueger, A. B., Schkade, D. A., Schwarz, N., & Stone, A. A. (2006). Would you be happier if you were richer? A focusing illusion. *Science, 312*(5782), 1908–1910.

Kaplan, S. (1992). Environmental preferences in a knowledge-seeking, knowledge using organism. In J. H. Barkow, L. Cosmides, & J. Tooby (Eds.), *The adapted mind: Evolutionary psychology and the generation of culture* (pp. 581–598). New York: Oxford University Press.

Kaplan, R. (2001). *The nature of the view from home: Psychological benefits.* SAGE Publications, *http://eab.sagepub.com/cgi/content/abstract/33/4/507*

Kaplan, R., & Kaplan, S. (1989). *The experience of nature: A psychological perspective.* New York: Cambridge University Press.

Kasser, T. (2002). *The high price of materialism.* Cambridge, MA: The MIT Press.

Kasser, T., & Ryan, R. M. (1993). A dark side of the American dream: Correlates of financial success as a central life aspiration. *Journal of Personality and Social Psychology, 65*, 410–422.

Katja, R., Päivi, A. K., Marja-Terttu, T., & Pekka, L. (2002). Relationships among adolescent subjective well-being, health behavior, and school satisfaction. *Journal of School Health, 72*, 243–249.

Kessler, R. C. (2003). The impairments caused by social phobia in the general population: Implications for intervention. *Acta Psychiatrica Scandinavica, 108*(417), 19–27.

Kessler, R. C., Foster, C. L., Saunders, W. B., & Stang, P. E. (1995). Social consequences of psychiatric disorders, I: Educational attainment. *American Journal of Psychiatry, 152*, 1026–1032.

Key National Indicators Forum. (2003). *Key national indicators: Assessing the nation's position and progress.* GAO-03-672SP.

Kingdon, G. G., & Knight, J. (2007). Community, comparisons and subjective well-being in a divided society. *Journal of Economic Behavior and Organization, 64*, 69–90.

Kirkcaldy, B., & Furnham, A. (2000). Positive affectivity, psychological well-being, accident- and traffic-deaths and suicide: An international comparison. *Studia Psychologica, 42*(1–2), 97–104.

Knack, S. (2001). Trust, associational life and economic performance. In J. F. Helliwell & A. Bonikowska (Eds.), *The contribution of human and social capital to sustained economic growth and well-being.* (Ottawa: HDRC, pp.172–202: Proceedings of an OECD/HRDC conference, Quebec, March 19–21, 2000).

Knight, B., Lutzky, S., & Macofsky-Urban, F. (1993). A meta-analytic review of interventions for caregiver distress: Recommendations for future research. *The Gerontologist, 33*(2), 240–248. Layard, R. (2005). *Happiness: Lessons from a new science.* London: Penguin.

Koivumaa-Honkanen, H., Honkanen, R., Koskenvuo, M., & Kaprio, J. (2003). Self-reported happiness in life and suicide in ensuing 20 years. *Social Psychiatry and Psychiatric Epidemiology, 38*(5), 244–248.

Koivumaa-Honkanen, H., Honkanen, R., Koskenvuo, M., Viinamaki, H., & Kaprio, J. (2002). Life dissatisfaction as a predictor of fatal injury in a 20-year follow-up. *Acta Psychiatrica Scandinavica, 105*(6), 444–450.

Koivumaa-Honkanen, H., Honkanen, R., Viinamaki, H., Heikkila, K., Kaprio, J., & Koskenvuo, M. (2001). Life satisfaction and suicide: A 20-year follow-up study. *American Journal of Psychiatry, 158*(3), 433–439.

Koslowsky, M., Kluger, A. N., & Reich, M. (1995). *Commuting stress: Causes, effects, and methods of coping.* New York: Springer.

Kroh, M. (2006). An experimental evaluation of popular well-being measures. *DIW Discussion Paper.*

Kuo, F. E., & Sullivan, W. C. (2001a). Aggression and violence in the inner city: Impacts of environment and mental fatigue. *Environment & Behavior, 33*(4), 543–571.

Kuo, F. E., & Sullivan, W. C. (2001b). Environment and crime in the inner city: Does vegetation reduce crime? *Environment & Behavior, 33*(3), 343–367.

Kuo, F. E., Sullivan, W. C., Coley, R. L., & Brunson, L. (1998). Fertile ground for community: Inner-city neighborhood common spaces. *American Journal of Community Psychology, 26*(6), 823–851.

Kurth, B. M. (2005). *KIGGS: The German health survey for children and adolescents.* Berlin, Germany: Robert Koch Institut.

Kweon, B.-S., Sullivan, W. C., & Wiley, A. R. (1998). Green common spaces and the social integration of inner-city older adults. *Environment and Behavior, 30*, 832–858.

Lackner, J. M., Gudleski, G. D., Zack, M. M., Katz, L. A., Powell, C., Krasner, S., et al. (2006). Measuring health-related quality of life in patients with irritable bowel syndrome: Can less be more? *Psychosomatic Medicine, 68*, 312–320.

Lavin, T., Higgins, C., Metcalfe, O., & Jordan, A. (2006). *Health impacts of the built environment: A review.* Dublin, Ireland: The Institute of Public Health in Ireland.

Layard, R. (2005). *Happiness: Lessons from a new science.* New York: The Penguin Press.

Lazarus, R. S. (1991). *Emotion and adaptation.* New York: Oxford University Press.

Leather, P., Pygras, M., Beale, D., & Lawrence, C. (1998). Windows in the workplace: Sunlight, view, and occupational stress. *Environment and Behavior, 30*, 739–762.

Liss, S. (1991). *Nationwide personal transportation study: Early results.* Washington, DC: Office of Highway Information Management. Federal Highway Administration.

Lucas, R. E. (2005). Time does not heal all wounds: A longitudinal study of reaction and adaptation to divorce. *Psychological Science, 16*(12), 945–950.

Lucas, R. E. (2007). Long-term disability is associated with lasting changes in subjective well-being: Evidence from two nationally representative longitudinal studies. *Journal of Personality and Social Psychology, 92*(4), 717–730.

Lucas, R. E., & Clark, A. E. (2006). Do people really adapt to marriage? *Journal of Happiness Studies, 7*(4), 405–426.

Lucas, R. E., Clark, A. E., Georgellis, Y., & Diener, E. (2003). Re-examining adaptation and the setpoint model of happiness: Reactions to changes in marital status. *Journal of Personality and Social Psychology, 84,* 527-539.

Lucas, R. E., Clark, A. E., Georgellis, Y., & Diener, E. (2004). Unemployment alters the set-point for life satisfaction. *Psychological Science, 15*, 8–13.

Lucas, R. E., Diener, E., & Suh, E. (1996). Discriminant validity of well-being measures. *Journal of Personality and Social Psychology, 71*(3), 616–628.

Lucas, R. E., & Donnellan, M. B. (2007). How stable is happiness? Using the STARTS model to estimate the stability of life satisfaction. *Journal of Research in Personality, 41*(5), 1091–1098.

Lucas, R. E., & Dyrenforth, P. S. (2006). *Does the existence of social relationships matter for subjective well-being?*. New York, NY: Guilford Press.

Lucas, R. E., & Schimmack, U. (in press). Income and Well-Being: How Big Is the Gap Between the Rich and the Poor?. *Journal of Research in Personality.*

Luechinger, S. (2007). Valuing air quality using the life satisfaction approach. Unpublished manuscript, University of Zurich, Swiss Federal Institute of Technology.

Luechinger, S. & Raschky, P. A. (2007). Valuing Flood Disasters using the Life Satisfaction Approach, *Mimeo*. Institute for Empirical Research in Economics, University of Zurich.

Luttmer, E. F. P. (2005). Neighbours as negatives: Relative earnings and well-being. *Quarterly Journal of Economics, 120*, 963–1002.

Lykken, D., & Tellegen, A. (1996). Happiness is a stochastic phenomenon. *Psychological Science, 7*(3), 186–189.

Lyubomirsky, S., King, L., & Diener, E. (2005). The benefits of frequent positive affect: Does happiness lead to success? *Psychological Bulletin, 131*, 803–855.

Lyubomirsky, S., & Ross, L. (1997). Hedonic consequences of social comparison: A contrast of happy and unhappy people. *Journal of Personality and Social Psychology, 73*, 1141–1157.

Maller, C., Townsend, M., Pryor, A., Brown, P., & St. Leger, L. (2006). Healthy nature healthy people: 'Contact with nature' as an upstream health promotion intervention for populations. *Health Promotion International, 21*, 45–55; doi:10.1093/heapro/dai032. Health Promotion International Advance Access originally published online on December 22, 2005.

Manchin, R. (2007). The emotional capital and desirability of European cities. Gallup Europe. European Week of Regions and Cities, Brussels, 8–11 October 2007.

Marks, G. N., & Fleming, N. (1999). Influences and consequences of well-being among Australian young people: 1980–1995. *Social Indicators Research, 46*, 301–323.

Marmorstein, N. R., & Iacono, W. G. (2001). An investigation of female adolescent twins with both major depression and conduct disorder. *Journal of the American Academy of Child & Adolescent Psychiatry, 40*(3), 299–306.

McClellan, W.M., Anson, C., Birkeli, K., & Tuttle, E. (1991). Functional status and quality of life: Predictors of early mortality among patients entering treatment for end- stage renal disease. *Journal of Clinical Epidemiology, 44,* 83–89.

McGrath, R. E., & Meyer, G. J. (2006). When effect sizes disagree: The case of "r" and "d." *Psychological Methods, 11*, 386–401.

Messick, S. (1995). Validity of psychological-assessment—Validation of inferences from persons responses and performances as scientific inquiry into score meaning. *American Psychologist, 50*(9), 741–749.

Michalos, A. C. (1985). Multiple discrepancies theory (Mdt). *Social Indicators Research, 16*(4), 347–413.

Mittelman, M. S., Ferris, S. H., Steinberg, G., Shulman, E., Mackell, J. A, Ambinder, A., et al. (1993). An intervention that delays institutionalization of Alzheimer's disease patients: Treatment of spouse-caregivers. *The Gerontologist, 33*, 730–740.

Moore, E. O. (1981). A prison environment's effect on health care service demands. *Journal of Environmental Systems, 11*, 17–34.

Moriarty, D., Zack, M. M., & Kobau, R. (2003). The centers for disease control and prevention's healthy days measures—Population tracking of perceived physical and mental health over time. *Health and Quality of Life Outcomes, 1*(1), 1–37.

Moriarty, D., Zack, M., Zahran, H., & Kobau, R. (November, 2006). The importance of tracking subjective health—Measuring the perceived physical and mental health of U.S. adults 1993–2005. Paper presented at the National Science Foundation Meeting on Science Policy and Well-Being. Arlington, Virginia.

Morris, N. (2003). Health, well-being and open space: Literature review. OPENspace: The research centre for inclusive access to outdoor environments (www.openspace.eca.ac.uk/pdf/healthwellbeing.pdf).

Mossey, J, M., & Shapiro, E. (1982). Self-rated health: A predictor of mortality among the elderly. *American Journal of Public Health, 72*, 800–808.

Murphy, G., Athanasou, J., & King, N. (2002). Job satisfaction and organizational citizenship behaviour: A study of Australian human-service professionals. *Journal of Managerial Psychology, 17*, 287–297.

Myers, D. G. (1999). *Close relationships and quality of life.* New York, NY: Russell Sage Foundation.

Myers, D. G. (2000). The funds, friends, and faith of happy people. *American Psychologist, 55*(1), 56–67.

Nakazato, N., Schimmack, U., & Oishi, S. (2008). Moving, objective characteristics of dwellings, dwelling satisfaction, and life satisfaction. Manuscript in preparation.

Neisser, U., Boodoo, G., Bouchard, T. J., Boykin, A. W., Broday, N., Ceci, S. J., et al. (1996). Intelligence: Knowns and unknowns. *American Psychologist, 51*, 77–101.

Nickerson, C., Schwarz, N., & Diener, E. (2007). Financial aspirations, financial success, and overall life satisfaction: Who? And how? *Journal of Happiness Studies, 8*, 467–515.

Nickerson, C., Schwarz, N., Diener, E., & Kahneman, D. (2003). Zeroing in on the dark side of the American Dream: A closer look at the negative consequences of the goal for financial success. *Psychological Science, 14*, 531–536.

Novaco, R. W. (1992). Automobile driving and aggressive behavior. In M. Wachs & M. Crawford (Eds.), *The car and the city: The automobile, the built environment, and daily urban life* (pp. 234–247). Ann Arbor: University of Michigan Press.

Novaco, R. W., & Collier, C. (1994). Commuting stress, ridesharing, and gender: Analyses from the 1993 state of the commute study in Southern California. *Transportation Board Research, 1433*, 170–176.

Novaco, R. W., Kliewer, W., & Broquet, A. (1991). Home environmental consequences of commute travel impedance. *American Journal of Community Psychology, 19*(6), 881–909.

Novaco, R. W., Stokols, D., & Milanesi, L. (1990). Objective and subjective dimensions of travel impedance as determinants of commuting stress. *American Journal of Community Psychology, 18*, 231–257.

Nowlis, V. (1965). Research with mood adjective checklist. In S. Thompkins & C. Isard (Eds.), *Affect, cognition, and personality.* New York: Springer.

OECD. (2001). *The well-being of nations: The role of human and social capital.* Paris: Organization for Economic Cooperation and Development.

Oishi, S., Diener, E., & Lucas, R. E. (2007). Optimal level of well-being: Can people be too happy? *Perspectives on Psychological Science, 2*, 346–360.

Oishi, S., Schimmack, U., Diener, E., & Suh, E. M. (1998). The measurement of values and individualism-collectivism. *Personality and Social Psychology Bulletin, 24*(11), 1177–1189.

Ong, P. (2008). Soul of the city: Where does Singapore stand? A white paper by Gallup Singapore for Ministry of National Development (MND). Singapore: Gallup Organization.

Organ, D. W. (1988). *Organizational citizenship behavior: The good soldier syndrome.* Lexington, MA: Lexington Books.

Ôunpuu, S., Chambers, L. W., Patterson, C., Chan, D., & Yusuf, S. (2001). Validity of the US behavioral risk factor surveillance system's health related quality of life survey tool in a group of older Canadians. *Chronic Diseases in Canada, 22*, 93-101.

Pakenham, K. I., Chiu, J., Bursnall, S., Cannon, T., & Okochi, M. (2006). The psychosocial impact of caregiving on young people who have a parent with an illness or disability: Comparisons between young caregivers and noncaregivers. *Rehabilitation Psychology, 51*, 113–126.

Parsons, R., Tassinary, L. G., Ulrich, R. S., Hebl, M. R., & Grossman-Alexander, M. (1998). The view from the road: Implications for stress recovery and immunization. *Journal of Environmental Psychology, 18*(2), 113–140.

Paul, K. I. (2005). *The negative mental health effect of unemployment: Meta-analyses of cross-sectional and longitudinal data.* Unpublished doctoral dissertation, Universität Erlangen-Nürnberg, Germany.

Pavot, W., & Diener, E. (1993). Review of the Satisfaction with Life Scale. *Psychological Assessment, 5*, 164-172.

Peak, T., Toseland, R., & Banks, S. (1995). The impact of a spouse-caregiver support group on care recipient health care costs. *Journal of Aging and Health, 7*(3), 427–449.

Peasgood, T. (2007). Does well-being depend upon our choice of measurement instrument? Delivered at British Household Panel Survey (BHPS) conference, University of Essex, Colchester, UK, July 5–7, 2007.

Pelled, L. H., & Xin, K. R. (1999). Down and out: An investigation of the relationship between mood and employee withdrawal behavior. *Journal of Management, 25*(6), 875–895.

Perlman, M., & Marietta, M. (2005). The politics of social accounting: Public goals and the evolution of the national accounts in Germany, the United Kingdom and the United States. *Review of Political Economy, 17*(2), 211–230.

Petty, M. M., McGee, G. W., & Cavender, J. W. (1984). A meta-analysis of the relationships between individual job satisfaction and individual performance. *The Academy of Management Review, 9*(4), 712–721.

Pisarski, A. E. (1987). *Commuting in America.* Westport, CT: Eno Foundation for Transportation Research.

Pressman, S. D., & Cohen, S. (2005). Does positive affect influence health? *Psychological Bulletin, 131*(6), 925–971.

Prizmic, Z., & Kaliterna-Lipovcan, L. J. (2008). Differential predictors of specific affects in a representative sample of Croatian citizens. Presented at 4th European Conference on Positive Psychology, Opatija, Croatia, July 1–4, 2008. Book of abstracts. p 215.

Putnam, R. D. (1993). *Making democracy work: Civic traditions in modern Italy.* Princeton: Princeton University Press.

Putnam, R. D. (1995). Tuning in, tuning out: The strange disappearance of social capital in America. *Political Science and Politics, 28,* 664–683.

Putnam, R. D. (2000). *Bowling alone: The collapse and revival of American community.* New York: Simon & Schuster.

Putnam, R. D. (2001). Social capital—Measurement and consequences. In J. F. Helliwell & A. Bonikowska (Eds.), *The contribution of human and social capital to sustained economic growth and well-being* (pp. 117–135). Ottawa: HDRC. Proceedings of an OECD/HRDC conference, Quebec, March 19–21, 2000.

Putnam, R. D. (2007). *E Pluribus Unum*: Diversity and community in the twenty-first century. The 2006 Johan Skytte prize lecture. *Scandinavian Political Studies, 30*(2), 137–174.

Putnam, R. D., & Feldstein, L. M. (2003). *Better together: Restoring the American community.* New York: Simon & Schuster.

Rayo, L., & Becker, G. S. (2007). Evolutionary efficiency and happiness. *Journal of Political Economy, 115,* 302–337.

Reschovsky, C. (2004). *Journey to Work: 2000.* Washington, DC: U.S. Census Bureau.

Robbins, L. (1938). Interpersonal comparisons of utility: A comment. *Economic Journal, 48,* 635–641.

Roberts, B. W., & DelVecchio, W. F. (2000). The rank-order consistency of personality traits from childhood to old age: A quantitative review of longitudinal studies. *Psychological Bulletin, 126*(1), 3–25.

Robie, C., Ryan, A. M., Schmieder, R. A., Parra, L. F., & Smith, P. C. (1998). The relation between job level and job satisfaction. *Group & Organization Management, 23*(4), 470–495.

Robinson, A. (1991). Lung cancer, the motor vehicle, and its subtle influence on bodily functions. *Medical Hypotheses, 28,* 39–43.

Rockett, J. R., & Thomas, B. M. (1999). Reliability and sensitivity of suicide certification in higher-income countries. *Suicide and Life Threatening Behavior, 29*(2), 141–149.

Rohde, C. L. E., & Kendle, A. D. (1994). *Report to English Nature—Human Well-being, Natural Landscapes and Wildlife in Urban Areas. A Review.* University of Reading, Department of Horticulture and Landscape and the Research Institute for the Care of the Elderly, Bath.

Ruggeri, M., Warner, R., Bisoffi, G., & Fontecedro, L. (2001). Subjective and objective dimensions of quality of life in psychiatric patients: A factor analytical approach. The South Verona Outcome Project 4. *British Journal of Psychiatry, 178,* 258–275.

Rumsfeld, J.S., MaWhinney, S., McCarthy, M., Shroyer, A.L.W., VillaNeuva, C.B., O'Brien, M., Moritz, T.E., Henderson, W.G., Grover, F.L., Sethi, G.K., & Hammermeister, K.E. (1999).Health-related quality of life as a predictor of mortality following coronary artery bypass graft surgery. *Journal of the American Medical Association, 281,* 1298–1303.

Rutter, M. L. (1997). Nature-nurture integration: The example of antisocial behavior. *American Psychologist, 52*, 390–398.

Salmivalli, C., & Isaacs, J. (2005). Prospective relations among victimization, rejection, friendlessness, and children's self- and peer-perceptions. *Child Development, 76*(6), 1161–1171.

Salvatori, A. (June, 2007). *Employment protection legislation and workers' wellbeing: Evidence on job and satisfaction.* Paper presented at the International Conference on Policies for Happiness, Certosa di Pontignano, Siena, Italy.

Sans-Corrales, M., Pujol-Ribera, E., Gené-Badia, J., Pasarin-Rua, M. I., Iglesias-Pérez, B., & Casajuana-Brunet, J. (2006). Family medicine attributes related to satisfaction, health and costs. *Family Practice*, February 3, 2006, pp. 1–9.

Sapolsky, R. M. (1994). *Why zebras don't get ulcers: A guide to stress, stress related diseases, and coping.* New York: W.H. Freeman.

Saris, W. E., Van Wijk, T., & Scherpenzeel, A. (1998). Validity and reliability of subjective social indicators—The effect of different measures of association. *Social Indicators Research, 45*(1–3), 173–199.

Sawyer, M. G., Kosky, R. J., Graetz, B. W., Arney, F., Zubrick, S. R., & Baghurst, P. (2000). The national survey of mental health and wellbeing: The child and adolescent component. *Australian and New Zealand Journal of Psychiatry, 34*, 214–220.

Schachter, S. S., & Singer, J. E. (1962). Cognitive, social and physiological determinants of emotional state. *Psychological Review, 69*, 379–399.

Schimmack, U. (1997). The Berlin everyday language mood inventory (BELMI): Toward the content valid assessment of moods/Das Berliner-Alltagssprachliche-Stimmungs-Inventar (BASTI): Ein Vorschlag zur kontentvaliden Erfassung von Stimmungen. *Diagnostica, 43*(2), 150–173.

Schimmack, U. (2003). Affect measurement in experience sampling research. *Journal of Happiness Studies, 4*(1), 79–106.

Schimmack, U. (2008). Measuring wellbeing in the German Socio-Economic Panel. Journal of Applied Social Science Studies, in press.

Schimmack, U. (2009). Measuring wellbeing in the German Socio-Economic Panel. *Journal of Applied Social Science Studies, 2.*

Schimmack, U., & Crites, S. L., Jr. (2005). The structure of affect. In D. AlbarracÃn, B. T. Johnson, & M. P. Zanna (Eds.), *The handbook of attitudes* (pp. 397–435). Mahwah, NJ: Lawrence Erlbaum Associates, Publishers.

Schimmack, U., Diener, E., & Oishi, S. (2002). Life-satisfaction is a momentary judgment and a stable personality characteristic: The use of chronically accessible and stable sources. *Journal of Personality, 70*(3), 345–384.

Schimmack, U., & Lucas, R. E. (2008). *Environmental influences on well-being: A dyadic latent panel analysis of spousal similarity.* University of Toronto: Manuscript in preparation.

Schimmack, U., & Oishi, S. (2005). The influence of chronically and temporarily accessible information on life satisfaction judgments. *Journal of Personality and Social Psychology, 89*(3), 395–406.

Schimmack, U., Oishi, S., Furr, R. M., & Funder, D. C. (2004). Personality and life satisfaction: A facet-level analysis. *Personality and Social Psychology Bulletin, 30*(8), 1062–1075.

Schimmack, U., Radhakrishnan, P., Oishi, S., Dzokoto, V., & Ahadi, S. (2002). Culture, personality, and subjective well-being: Integrating process models of life satisfaction. *Journal of Personality and Social Psychology, 82*(4), 582–593.

Schimmack, U., Schupp, J., & Wagner, G. G. (2008). The influence of environment and personality on the affective and cognitive component of subjective well-being. *Social Indicators Research, 89*(1), 41–60.

Schimmack, U., Wagner, G. G., Krause, P., & Schupp, J. (In press). An experimental panel study of shortterm stability of well-being indicators. *Social Indicators Research.*

Schmidt, F. L., & Hunter, J. E. (1996). Measurement error in psychological research: Lessons from 26 research scenarios. *Psychological Methods, 1*(2), 199–223.

Schneider, B., Hanges, P. J., Smith, D. B., & Salvaggio, A. N. (2003). Which comes first: Employee attitudes or organizational financial and market performance? *Journal of Applied Psychology, 88*, 836–851.

Schneider, L., & Schimmack, U. (In press). A meta-analysis of self-informant correlations of well-being measures. *Social Indicators Research.*

Schreckenberg, D., & Meis, M. (2007) Effects of aircraft noise on noise annoyance and quality of life around Frankfurt Airport. Final abridged report. Available from: http://www.verkehrslaermwirkung.de

Schwartz, S. H. (1992). Universals in the content and structure of values: Theoretical advances and empirical tests in 20 countries. *Advances in Experimental Social Psychology, 25*, 1–65.

Schwarz, N., & Clore, G. L. (1983). Mood, misattribution, and judgments of well-being: Informative and directive functions of affective states. *Journal of Personality and Social Psychology, 45*, 513–523.

Schwarz, N., Kahneman, D., & Xu, J. (2008). Global and episodic reports of hedonic experience. In R. Belli, F. P. Stafford, & D. F. Alwin (Eds.), *Calendar and time diary methods in life course research.* Thousand Oaks, CA: Sage.

Schwarz, N., & Strack, F. (1999). Reports of subjective well-being: Judgmental processes and their methodological implications. In D. Kahneman, E. Diener, & N. Schwarz (Eds.), *Well-being: The foundations of hedonic psychology* (pp. 61–84). New York, NY: Russell Sage Foundation.

Sen, A. (1990). Development as capability expansion. In K. Griffin & J. Knight (Eds.), *Human development and the international development strategy for the 1990s.* London: Macmillan.

Shore, L. M., & Martin, H. J. (1989). Job satisfaction and organizational commitment in relation to work performance and turnover intentions. *Human Relations, 42*, 625–638.

Singer, J., Lundberg, U., & Frankenhaeuser, M. (1978). Stress on the train: A study of urban commuting. *Advances in Environmental Psychology, 1*, 41–56.

Smit, D. J. A., Posthuma, D., Boomsma, D. I., & De Geus, E. J. C. (2007). The relation between frontal EEG asymmetry and the risk for anxiety and depression. *Biological Psychology, 74*(1), 26–33.

Smith, S., & Razzell, P. (1975). *The pool winners.* London: Caliban.

Spencer, A. (2006). Mental health screening for kids: A movement in the making. *State health Notes, National Conference of State Legislators.* March 20, 2006, 27(463). Columbia University TeenScreen Program: Mental health check-ups for youth. (TeenScreen.org).

Staw, B. M., & Barsade, S. G. (1993). Affect and managerial performance: A test of the sadder-but-wiser vs. happier-and-smarter hypotheses. *Administrative Science Quarterly, 38,* 304–331.

Steger, M. F., Kashdan, T. B., & Oishi, S. (2007). Being good by doing good: Daily eudaimonic activity and well-being. *Journal of Research in Personality, 42*(1), 22–42.

Stein, M. B., & Kean, Y. M. (2000). Disability and quality of life in social phobia: Epidemiologic findings. *American Journal of Psychiatry, 157*(10), 1606–1613.

Stevenson, B., & Wolfers, J. (2008). Economic growth and subjective well-being: Reassessing the Easterlin paradox. Available at SSRN: http://ssrn.com/abstract= 1121237

Stokols, D., & Novaco, R. W. (1981). Transportation and well-being: An ecological perspective. In I. Altman, J. F. Wohlwill & P. B. Everett (Eds.), *Transportation and behavior, 5, Human Behavior and Environment: Advances in theory and research.* New York: Plenum Press.

Stubbe, J. H., Posthuma, D., Boomsma, D. I., & De Geus, E. J. C. (2005). Heritability of life satisfaction in adults: A twin-family study. *Psychological Medicine, 35*(11), 1581–1588.

Stutzer, A. (2004). The role of income aspirations in individual happiness. *Journal of Economic Behavior and Organization, 54,* 89–109.

Stutzer, A., & Frey, B. S. (2007a). Commuting and life satisfaction in Germany. *Informationen zur Raumentwicklung, 2/3,* 179–189.

Stutzer, A., & Frey, B. S. (Eds.), (2007b). *Economics and psychology. A promising new cross-disciplinary field.* Cambridge, MA: MIT Press.

Stutzer, A., & Frey, B. S. (2008). Stress that doesn't pay: The commuting paradox. *Scandinavian Journal of Economics, 110*(2), 339–366.

Sumner, L. W. (1995). The subjectivity of welfare. *Ethics, 105*(4), 764–790.

Sumner, L. W. (1996). Welfare, happiness, and ethics. Oxford: Claredon Press.

Talbot, J. F., & Kaplan, R. (1991). The benefits of nearby nature for elderly apartment residents. *International Journal of Aging and Human Development, 33,* 119–130.

Tennessen, C. M., & Cimprich, B. E. (1995). Views to nature: Effects on attention. *Journal of Environmental Psychology, 15,* 77–85.

Tett, R. P., & Meyer, J. P. (1993). Job-satisfaction, organizational commitment, turnover intention, and turnover: Path analyses based on metaanalytic findings. *Personnel Psychology, 46*(2), 259–293.

Thaler, R. H., & Sunstein, C. R. (2003). Libertarian paternalism. *American Economic Review, 93*(2) 175–179.

Toseland, R., & McCallion, P. (1997). Trends in caregiving intervention research. *Social Work Research, 21*(3), 154–164.

Tov, W., Ng, W., Diener, E., Kesebir, P., & Harter, J. (in press). The social and economic context of peace and happiness. In R. S. Wyer, Jr., C.-y. Chiu, & Y.-y. Hong (Eds.), *Understanding culture: Theory, research, and application.*

Ulrich, R. S. (1979). Visual landscapes and psychological well-being. *Landscape Research, 4,* 17–19.

Ulrich, R. S. (1984). View through a window may influence recovery from surgery. *Science, 224,* 420–421.

Ulrich, R. S. (2002). Health benefits of gardens in hospitals. Paper presented at the meeting of the International Exhibition Floridade, Haarlemmermeer, Netherlands, April 4–October 20, 2002. (http://www.plants-in-buildings.com/documents/symposium-ulrich_000.pdf)

Ulrich, R., Simons, R. F., Losito, E., Fiorito, E., Miles, M. A., & Zelson, M. (1991). Stress recovery during exposure to natural and urban environments. *Journal of Environmental Psychology, 11*, 201–230.

Urry, H. L., Nitschke, J. B., Dolski, I., Jackson, D. C., Dalton, K. M., Mueller, C. J., et al. (2004). Making a life worth living—Neural correlates of well-being. *Psychological Science, 15*(6), 367–372.

USA General Social Survey. (2008). Social change reports. Retrieved from *http://www.norc.org/*

Van Praag, B. M. S., & Baarsma, B. E. (2005). Using happiness surveys to value intangibles: The case of airport noise. *The Economic Journal, 115*, 224–246.

Van Praag, B., & Ferrer-I-Carbonell, A. (2004). *Happiness quantified: A satisfaction calculus approach*. New York: Oxford University Press.

Veenhoven, R. (1991). Is happiness relative? *Social Indicators Research, 24*(1), 1–34.

Vemuri, A. W., & Costanza, R. (2006). The role of human, social, built, and natural capital in explaining life satisfaction at the country level: Toward a national well-being index (NWI). *Ecological Economics, 58*, 119–133.

Verlet, D., & Devos, C. (2007). Can local governments enhance the subjective well-being of their citizens? International Conference: *Policies for Happiness*. Siena, Certose di Pontignano, June 14–17.

Verme, P. (2007). Happiness and freedom. Unpublished paper, University of Turin.

Visser-Meily, A., Post, M., Schepers, V., & Lindeman, E. (2005). Spouses' quality of life 1 year after stroke: Prediction at the start of clinical rehabilitation. *Cerebrovascular Diseases, 20*, 443–448.

Walker, S. S., & Schimmack, U. (2008). Validity of a happiness implicit association test as a measure of subjective well-being. *Journal of Research in Personality, 42*, 490–497.

Wanous, J. P., & Hudy, M. J. (2001). Single-item reliability: A replication and extension. *Organizational Research Methods, 4*(4), 361–375.

Warr, P. (2007). *Work, Happiness and Unhappiness*. Mahwah, NJ: Lawrence Erlbaum Associates.

Warren, S., Kerr, J. R., Smith, D., Godkin, D., & Schalm, C. (2003).The impact of adult day programs on family caregivers of elderly relatives. *Journal of Community Health Nursing, 20*, 209–221.

Watson, D. (1988). The vicissitudes of mood measurement: Effects of varying descriptors, time frames, and response formats on measures of positive and negative affect. *Journal of Personality and Social Psychology, 55*(1), 128–141.

Watson, D., Clark, L. A., & Tellegen, A. (1988). Development and validation of brief measures of positive and negative affect: The PANAS scales. *Journal of Personality and Social Psychology, 54*(6), 1063–1070.

Weaver, C. N. (1977). Relationships among pay, race, sex, occupational prestige, supervision, work autonomy, and job satisfaction in a national sample. *Personnel Psychology, 30*(3), 437–445.

Weitoft, G. R., & Rosen, M. (2005). Is perceived nervousness and anxiety a predictor of premature mortality and severe morbidity? A longitudinal follow up of the Swedish survey of living conditions. *Journal of Epidemiology and Community Health, 59*(9), 794–798.

Wells, N. M., & Evans, G. W. (2003). Nearby nature; a buffer of life stress among rural children. *Environment and Behaviour, 35*, 311–330.

Welsch, H. (2006). Environment and happiness: Valuation of air pollution using life satisfaction data. *Ecological Economics, 58*, 801–813.

Wener, R. E., Evans, G. W., Phillips, D., & Nadler, N. (2003). Running for the 7:45: The effects of public transit improvements on commuter stress. *Transportation, 30*, 203–220.

White, R., & Heerwagen, J. (1998). Nature and mental health: Biophilia and bioiphobia. In A. Lundberg (Ed.), *Environment and mental health* (pp. 175–192). London: Lawrence Erlbaum.

White, S. M, & Rotton, J. (1998). Type of commute, behavioral aftereffects, and cardiovascular activity: A field experiment. *Environment and Behavior, 30*(6), 763–780.

Williams, M. L., McDaniel, M. A., & Nguyen, N. T. (2006). Meta-analysis of the antecedents and consequences of pay level satisfaction. *Journal of Applied Psychology, 91*(2), 392–413.

Wilson, W. (1967). Correlates of avowed happiness. *Psychological Bulletin, 67*, 294–406.

Winkelmann, L., & Winkelmann, R. (1998). Why are the unemployed so unhappy? Evidence from panel data. *Economica, 65*(257), 1–15.

The World Health Organization (1948). Official Records of the World Health Organization (No. 2, p. 100). Retrieved from *http://www.who.int/en/*

The World Health Organization (WHO). (2008). Retrieved from *http://www.who.int/research/en/*

Woodward, L. J., & Fergusson, D. M. (2001). Life course outcomes of young people with anxiety disorders in adolescence. *Journal of the American Academy of Child & Adolescent Psychiatry, 40*(9), 1086–1093.

Wright, T. A., & Bonett, D. G. (2007). Job satisfaction and psychological well-being as nonadditive predictors of workplace turnover. *Journal of Management, 33*, 141–160.

Wright, T. A., & Staw, B. M. (1999). Affect and favorable work outcomes: Two longitudinal tests of the happy-productive worker thesis. *Journal of Organizational Behavior, 20*, 1–23.

Zelenski, J. M. (September, 2007). Talk to me, talk to the trees: Personality and happiness. Invited paper presented at the Canadian Institute for Advanced Research program meeting on Social Interactions, Identity, and Well-Being (SIIWB). Ottawa, ON.

Index

Accident prevention program studies,
  43–44
  Adaptation, 98–109. *See also*
    Aspiration spiral
  effects of major life events, 103
  heritability studies, 99–102
  ideas in support of, 99
  of lottery winners, 87, 103
  preferences vs. hedonic adaptation,
    108–109
  role of, 98–99
  to spinal-cord injuries, 104–105
  to temperature (example), 107
  unemployment, 106
  within-person life satisfaction change,
    105–106
Adolescents. *See* Checkups for school
  children
Affective indicators of well-being, 15–19
Affective revolution in psychology
    (1980s), 16
Ahadi, S., 115
Ahn, N., 163–164
AIDS, 66, 211
Air pollution
  life satisfaction valuation approach,
    157–158
  revealed preference approach, 41

subjective well-being and, 158
  valuation difficulties, 49
Airport noise, 147–150
  economic impact study limitations,
    147–148
  life satisfaction assessments, 148–149
  subjective well-being assessment, 148
Alzheimer's disease, 137, 139, 144
Arora, R., 199
Asarnow, J. R., 141
Aspiration spiral, 109–110
AWB indicators, 79, 80, 91

Babazono, A., 151
Barrick, M. R., 166
Barrington-Leigh, C. P., 113, 114,
    190, 191
Beatty, J., 43–44
Bechtel, R. B., 150
Beck Depression Inventory, 138
Becker, R. A., 29, 32–33
Behavioral (misconduct) fines, 53–54
Behavioral genetic studies, 100–101
Behavioral Risk Factor Surveillance
    System (BRFSS), 193–194
Behaviorism, rise of (1930s), 15
Biases, 17, 19, 28, 57, 97–98

Biophilia hypothesis (Bird), 155
Bird, W., 155
Bisoffi, G., 143
Blumberg, S. J., 43
Bonett, D. G., 166
Bono, J. E., 165
Bradburn, N. M., 79
Bradshaw, J., 141
Brickman, P., 87, 103
Broaden-and-build theory
        (Frederickson), 64, 125
Brzenchek, J., 144
Bullinger, M., 150
Butler, G., 138

Canadian Household Panel
        Survey, 203
Caregiving burden, 138–139
Caste system of India, 120
Catalano, R., 157, 164
Cavender, J. W., 165
Center for Disease Control (CDC/U.S.),
        143, 193
Checkups for school children, 140–142
Chen, X., 141
Child and Adolescent Component of the
        National Survey of Mental Health
        and Well-Being, 141
Churchman, A., 150
Citizens (people)
    adaptation issues, 98–109
    choice improvement/informed
        voting, 63
    compensation for government actions
        on, 51–52
    elimination of misery of, 59–60
    evaluative judgments of life, 19–20
    GNP and, 36
    group identifications of, 122
    individual cravings of, 32–33
    involvement in indicator creation, 34
    manipulation by policy makers,
        121–122
    organizational citizenship, 167
    overestimation of life satisfaction, 151
    proper role of government, 209
    social indicators for evaluation of,
        23–24
    taxation issues, 171

terrorism's impact on, 50
    well-being and behavior of, 56, 64,
        127, 180
City life, 179–181
Clark, A. E., 161, 162
Coates, D., 87, 103
Colbert, A. E., 166
Coleman, J., 175
Collier, C., 151
Community Employment Innovation
        Project (CEIP), 181–182
Commuting, 150–154
    impacts of, 150
    potential externalities, 151
    public vs. solo, 154
    well-being consequence studies,
        151–153
Compensating differentials, 49
Construct validation, 19, 84
Consumer Sentiment Index, 122
Content validity, 78–80, 84
Contingent valuation method, 42
Convergent validity, 80–82, 84
Conway, K. P., 144
Costanza, R., 155
Creglow, A., 167–168
Cross-National Equivalent File, 203
Culture wars, 60–61
Cummings, S. M., 139
Current Population Survey (U.S.),
        36, 194

Day Reconstruction Method (DRM),
        152, 153
Deaton, A., 198
Debate resolution, 58–59
Denby, L., 29
Depression
    of adolescents and children, 140–142
    air quality (L.A.) association, 157
    cardiac problem association, 144
    caregiving burden and, 139
    importance of, to policy makers, 158
    suicide association, 89, 95
    WHO estimates, 66
Desmond, M. S., 142
Devos, C., 176
Diener, E., 91, 97, 115, 125, 161,
        176, 199

Dijkers, M., 104
Disability (people with) studies, 104–105
Discrepancy theories, 110
Discriminant validity, 83–84
Di Tella, R., 87, 201
Divorce and life satisfaction, 88–89
Dolan, P., 23–24, 45, 48, 50, 137
Domains of social indicators, 5, 25t,
        26–30, 32, 33, 91–93
Dooley, D., 157, 164

Easterlin, R., 85
Economic analyses, enhancement of
    compensating for government actions,
        51–52
    evaluating/improving public
        goods/services, 52
    externalities assessment, 48–49
    fines/compensation for lost welfare,
        52–54
    valuing nonmarket goods, services,
        costs, 49–50
Economic approaches to quality of life,
        34–40, 35t. *See also* Gross
        domestic product
    beneficial vs. detrimental products,
        39–40
    externalities (secondary effects), 39
    goods/service, gray vs. black market,
        38
    income/expenditure calculations,
        35–37
    limitations of, 40
    nonincluded constructs, 37
    nonmarket goods, valuation of, 41–45
Economic well-being (measures), 11–15,
        13f, 25, 48, 97
Education (social indicator), 30–31
Emotions. *See* Negative emotions;
        Positive emotions
Employee well-being, 55–57, 115
Eurobarometer studies, 197, 204
European Community Household Panel
        survey, 163–164
European Social Survey (ESS), 195–197
Evans, G. W., 150, 153, 156, 157
Experimenting society, 61–62
Externalities (secondary effects), 39
    commuting, 151, 158

described, 39
    of economic activities, assessment of,
        48–49, 173
    environmental, 41
    of material consumption, 114
    negative, 38–39, 114
    positive, 114

Face validity, 77–78, 84
Ferrer-i-Carbonell, A., 148, 173
Fines and compensation, for lost welfare,
        52–54
Fleming, N., 162
Foa, R., 197 ·
Fontecedro, L., 143
Food and Drug Administration (U.S.), 42
Forum on Key Indicators, 24, 28, 34
Frederick, S., 98
Frey, B. S., 49, 152, 162
Fritjers, P., 201

Gall, G., 142
Gallagher-Thomspon, D., 139
Gallup-Healthways Well-Being Index,
        194, 204
Gallup World Poll, 48, 60, 172, 180
General Accounting Office (GAO), 24,
        26
Georgellis, Y., 161, 162
German Socio-Economic Panel Study
        (GSOEP), 15, 102, 152, 161–162,
        200–205
Gilbert, D. T., 43
Goods (public) and services
    evaluation/improvement of, 52
    gray vs. black market, 38
    inclusion/non-inclusion in national
        accounts, 37
    quality-of-life influence of, 48–49
    societal values and, 212
    valuation methods, 41–43
Good society, 23–24, 60–62
Gorey, K., 139
Governmental/organization effectiveness,
        improvement of
    good society, advancing definition of,
        60–62
    groups experiencing misery, 59–60
    informed voting, 63

mental health, 66
personal choice improvements, 63
refining policy concepts, 62–63
resolving difficult debates, 58–59
setting/justifying policy default
    options, 57–58
subjective well-being (as goal), 63–66
trade-offs/multiple factor evaluation,
    54–55
workplace/domicile characteristics,
    55–57
Great Depression (U.S./1930s), 36
Gremier, A., 139
Groot, W., 136–137
Gross domestic product (GDP), 3, 4,
    26t, 35t
    concerns about usefulness of, 75
    correlation to well-being, 12,
        15, 86
    defined, 36
    freedom of choice measures, 48
    as gauge of societal progress, 4
    paid employees vs. volunteers, 37

Hagerty, M. R., 34
Hagihara, A., 151
Haisken-DeNew, J. P., 87, 201
Haley, W. E., 139
Halpern, D., 176
Han, B., 139
Hanges, P. J., 166
Happiness Adjusted Life Years (HALY)
    measure, 136–137
Harris, A., 199
Harter, J. K., 166, 167–168
Härter, M. C., 144
Hate crime legislation, 58
Hayes, T. L., 168
Health and well-being (policy examples)
    caregiving burden, 137–140
    checkups for school children,
        140–142
    health spending, 133–137
    subjective health, 143–145
Hedonic adaptation, 98–109. See also
    Adaptation
Hedonism, 18, 123–124
Helliwell, J. F., 113, 114, 190, 191, 198,
    199

Heritability of well-being, 100–102
Hoelscher, P., 141
Homicide rates (social indicator), 33
Hooley, P. J. D., 138
Hough, R., 164
Household, Income, and Labour
    Dynamics in Australia Survey,
    202–203
Household Longitudinal Study (U.K.),
    202
Housing, ideal (characteristic
    identification), 55–57
Howlett, J. G., 138
Huang, H., 199
Human Development Index (UN), 9, 25,
    32, 78
Hygge, S., 150

Iaffaldano, M. T., 165
Immoral behavior, condoning of,
    126–127
Income (economic indicator), 3, 4, 5, 12.
    See also German Socio-Economic
    Panel Study; Human
    Development Index
    disposable, 13
    employment/unemployment,
        115–116
    global calculations, 35
    options resulting from, 14
    reason for moving beyond, 97
Income distribution/structure of income
    taxes, 171–174
Information (irrelevant) information
    captured by subjective
    well-being, 119–120
Inglehart, R., 197–198
Institute of Health (National Academies),
    31

Jacobs, S. V., 157
Janoff-Bulman, R., 87, 103
Jimeno, J. F., 163–164
Job satisfaction, 14, 55, 99–100, 162,
    164–167
Judge, T. A., 165
Judgments (evaluative)
    cognitive judgments, 123, 127
    of depression/suicide, 89

Judgments (*continued*)
  examination of biases in, 19 (*See also* Construct validation)
  of global life satisfaction, 19–20, 47, 72–73, 81, 85, 128
  of income (effects of), 190
  of relationships, 88
  relative vs. absolute, 99, 111, 112
  responsiveness to external circumstances, 95–96
  self-judgments of well-being, 158
  of social comparison, 110
  underlying psychological processes, 201, 211
  willingness-to pay, 44

Kahneman, D., 152, 199
Kaplan, S., 155–156
Katja, R., 141
Keyes, C. L. M., 168
KIGGS (German Health Interview and Examination Survey) report, 133–134
King, L., 125
Kingdon, G. G., 114
Knack, S., 177–178
Knight, J., 114, 139
Kobau, R., 193
Koivumaa-Honkanen, H., 89–90
Krueger, A. B., 152
Kuo, F. E., 155
Kweon, B.-S., 155

Lackner, J. M., 145
Ladder of Life scale (global life evaluation), 48, 211
Layard, Richard, 171
Li, B., 141
Libertarian paternalism, 57–58
Life/life circumstances
  evaluative judgments of, 19–20
  question of mattering, 114–116
Life satisfaction (global happiness) measures. *See also* Air pollution; Airport noise; Caregiving burden; Commuting; Parks and green spaces
  of children, 141
  city life, 180–181

employment/unemployment, 115–116
environment correlation, 54
five-item scale assessment, 69
income correlation, 48, 49, 53, 87, 94
inconsequence of trivialities, 120
influence of public goods/services, 52
information gathering surveys, 36
married vs. divorced/widowed people, 88
national wealth correlation, 85–86
pro-social behavior correlation, 63
reliability issues, 72–73, 77
self-ratings of, 81, 82
spousal death/divorce correlation, 88–89
suicide/behavior choice correlation, 91
terrorism correlation, 49–50
Living Conditions Index (Netherlands), 27
Longevity (social indicator), 3, 25t
  genetic factor, 101
  increases in industrialized nations, 133
  Ladder of Life scale correlation, 48, 211
  optimal level determination, 31
  public health measures evaluation, 211
  self-rating predictive measures, 144
Lottery winner happiness study, 87, 103
Lowenstein, G., 98
Lucas, R. E., 105, 116, 161, 162–163
Luechinger, S., 49, 157–158, 170
Lutzky, S., 139
Lyubomirsky, S., 111, 125

MacCulloch, R., 87, 201
Macofsky-Urban, F., 139
Manipulation of subjective well-being, 120–122
Marietta, M, 35–36
Marja-Terttu, T., 141
Marks, G. N., 162
Married couples vs. divorced/widowed people, 88–89
McCallion, P., 139
McGee, G. W., 165
McGill, R., 29
Meis, M., 149

Mental health, 66
  of children, monitoring needs,
    140–142
  employment problems and, 162–163
  gamble vs. well-being approach, 137
  quality-of-life survey about, 193
  studies (reviewed by Pavot/Diener), 91
Merikangas, K. R., 144
Michalos, A. C., 110
Minorities, 58, 117, 121, 179
Misery of groups, identification of, 59–60
Mittelman, M. S., 139
Money and well-being, 84–87
Moore, S., 45
Moriarty, D., 144–145, 193, 194
Morimoto, K., 151
Mount, M. K., 166
Muchinsky, P. M., 165
Murphy, J. M., 142

Nadler, N., 153
National Academies' Institute of Health,
    31
National-level well-being, 48
National Longitudinal Study of Children
    and Youth, 203
National Survey of Mental Health and
    Well-Being, 141
Natural disasters and risk sharing,
    169–171
Nature. *See* Parks and green spaces
Negative emotions, 17, 100, 125, 152
New Freedom Commission on Mental
    Health (U.S.), 140, 150
Nobutomo, K., 151
Novaco, R. W., 151, 164

Objections to well-being measures, 6
  adaptability, 98–109
  constructs, 95–96
  creating national accounts of
    well-being, 219
  irrelevancy of self-evaluation, 120
  screening school children for mental
    health, 142
  utilitarianism vs. subjective
    definitions, 126–127
Objective measures of well-being. *See
  also* Economic well-being

(measures); Gross domestic
    product (GDP); Social indicators
  attempts at identification of, 30
  Forum on Key National Indicators
    meeting, 24
  GAO report, 188
  limitations of, 130
  objectivity, defined, 9–11
  physical health component, 9
  vs. subjective measures, 3, 17, 31,
    118–120, 143
"On top of the world" affect measure
    (Bradburn), 79
Organizational citizenship, 167
Organization effectiveness. *See*
    Governmental/organization
    effectiveness, improvement of
Organization for Economic Cooperation
    and Development (OECD), 176,
    212–213
Oxford Happiness Scale, 78–79
Oxford Poverty and Human Development
    Initiative (OPHDI), 25, 28

Pagano, M. E., 142
Päivi, A. K., 141
Parks and green spaces, 154–157. *See
    also* Biophilia hypothesis;
    Restoration hypothesis
  benefits of contact with nature,
    154–156
  natural capital studies, 155–157
Patton, G. K., 165
Paul, K. I., 163
Pavot, W., 91
Peasgood, T., 50, 152
Pekka, L., 141
People. *See* Citizens (people)
Perlman, M, 35–36
Perrin, J. M., 142
Peterson, C., 197
Petty, M. M., 165
Phillips, D., 153
Physical health, 9
Pinel, E. C., 43
Policy examples
  air pollution, 157–158
  airport noise, 147–150
  commuting, 150–154

Policy examples (*continued*)
    parks and green spaces, 154–157
    social context of well-being, 175–183
Policy makers
    choices provided (to citizens) by,
        57–58, 63
    cost-benefit analysis challenges, 49
    health spending decisions, 133–137
    need for aids in making decisions, 3–5,
        7, 48, 63
    problem-solving debates by, 61
    trade-offs evaluation, 51–52, 54–55
    well-being indicators used by, 3, 6, 7,
        34, 47, 48–49
    well-being result manipulations,
        121–122
Positive emotions, 16
    "broaden-and-build" theory, 64
    during commuting, 152
    freedom of time association, 210
    ideas about functions of, 124
    mundane levels/frequency, 79
    during nature walks, 156
    prediction of (factors), 176
    pursuit of, vs. negative emotions, 17
    studies of, 125, 128
Preference realization, monetary
    indicators of, 11–15
Psychological Heisenberg principle, 6666
Psychologists
    affective revolution (1980s), 16–18
    happiness vs. well-being, 8–9
    individuals vs. group focus, 70, 175
    life satisfaction five-term scale, 69
    well-being measures gathered by, 5,
        165
    work outcomes/job satisfaction
        studies, 166–167
Putnam, R. D., 114, 175–176, 178

Quality Adjusted Life Years (QALY)
    measure, 42, 136
Quality-of-life indicators
    Becker (et al) study of, 32–33
    described, 23–24
    economic approach to, 34–40, 35t

Raschky, P. A., 170
Razzell, P., 87

Relationships and well-being, 87–89
Reliability of well-being measures,
    68–74
    cognitive vs. affective well-being, 73
    comparison of effect size across
        studies, 70
    effects of (illustration), 71
    examination/determination of, 71–72
    random error variances, 69–70
    response categories determination,
        73–74
    studies of, 70–72, 74
    variances of (process-related), 72–73
Religious participation/spirituality, 28
Restoration hypothesis (Bird), 155
Revealed preference approach (to
        nonmarket goods valuation)
    environmental evaluation, 41
    health-related market behavior, 135
    housing prices, air pollution
        evaluation, 158
    limitations of, 50
    natural disaster (floods) evaluation,
        170
    noise pollution evaluation, 148–149
Richardson, D., 141
Risk-transfer mechanism, 169
Robbins, L., 16
Role of well-being measures, 96–98
Roosevelt, Eleanor, 124
Rosen, M., 91
Ross, L., 111
Rubin, K. H., 141
Ruggeri, M., 143
Rutter, Michael, 100–101

Salvaggio, A. N., 166
Salvatori, A., 164
Sanfey, P., 162
Schimmack, U., 81, 87, 116
Schmidt, F. L., 167–168
Schneider, B., 166
Schreckenberg, D., 149
Schwartz, S. H., 25
Schwarz, N., 97
Scientific advancement, lack of benefits
    from, 117
Self-reports/judgments of well-being, 16,
    19, 26, 147, 165

convergent validity and correlation of,
    80–81
criticisms of, 67, 121, 122
health-related quality of life, 143–145
self-administered questionnaires, 74
social trust vs. behavioral measures,
    177–178
stressful events, 156
suicide association, 89
weather association, 120
Seligman, M.E.P, 37, 97
Sen, A., 25, 26
Shields, M. A., 201
Smith, D. B., 166
Smith, S., 87
Social comparison, 110–114
    contrast effects (in early models), 111
    described, 110
    downward vs. upward comparisons,
        111–112
    naturalistic studies, 114
    in realistic change scenarios, 113
Social context, importance of, 175–177
Social experiments, 181–183
Social indicators, 23–34, 26t. See also
        Forum on Key Indicators; Human
        Development Index
    collection vs. non-collection of, 28–29
    convergence with well-being
        measures, 48
    described, 23–24
    domain inclusion determinations,
        26–30
    identification methodologies,
        24–25
    information integration, 32–33
    international comparisons, 25t
    interpretation requirements, 34
    limitations of, 26, 28, 33
    measurement problems with, 30–32
    reason for development of, 37
    selected proposed measures, 24t
Social phobias, 141
Soul of the City project, 179
Spencer, A., 142
Spinal-cord injuries, 104–105
Standard gamble hypotheticals
        approach (to nonmarket goods
        valuation), 42

Staw, B. M., 167
Stevenson, B., 197, 198
Stokols, D., 151
Strack, F., 97
Studies, 81
    accident prevention programs,
        43–44
    adaptation, 99
    airport noise, 148–149
    assessment of trust-subjective
        well-being, 177–178
    behavioral genetics, 100–101
    commuting, 151–153
    cross-national, 194–199
    depression, 89
    determined-ashamed vs.happy-sad, 79
    effects of major life
        events, 103
    heritability, 99–102
    income, 14, 75, 86, 87
    issues of reliability, 70–72, 74
    longitudinal, 200–203
    lottery winners, 87, 103
    natural capital studies, 155–157
    people with spinal-cord injuries,
        104–105
    positive emotions, 125, 128
    reported vs. experiences state, 91
    social comparisons, 113–114
    wealth of nations, 48, 85
    well-being judgments, 120
    within-person life satisfaction change,
        105–106
Studies, cross-national, 194–199
    Eurobarometer studies, 197, 204
    European Social Survey, 195
    Gallup World Poll, 198–199
    World Values Survey, 197–198
Studies, cross-sectional, 189–194
    Behavioral Risk Factor Surveillance
        System, 193–194
    Current Population Survey, 194
    Equality, Security and Community
        survey, 190
    Ethnic Diversity Survey, 190
    Gallup-Healthways Well-Being Index,
        194, 204
    General Social Survey, 190,
        191–192

Studies, longitudinal, 200–203
British Household Panel Study, 202
Canadian Household Panel Survey, 203
German Socio-Economic Panel Study, 15, 102, 152, 161–162, 200–205
Household, Income, and Labour Dynamics in Australia Survey, 202–203
Household Longitudinal Study, 202
National Longitudinal Study of Children and Youth, 203
Survey of Labour and Income Dynamics, 202–203
Stutzer, A., 49, 162
Subjective health, 143–145
health-related quality of life, 143
longevity/survival self-ratings, 144
quality of life measures, 143–144
Subjective well-being (measures). *See also* Social indicators
adequacy/legitimacy concerns, 6
air pollution and, 158
convergence with economic/social indicators, 48
definition, 9–11
depression and, 163
as a good thing (question), 123–126
immoral behavior condoned by, 126–127
importance/relevance of, 46–47
international indicators, 25t
irrelevant information captured by, 119–120
as its own goal, 63–66
lack of technology/scientific advance benefits, 117
limitation of, 120
manipulation of, 120–122
measurement of, 11–20
affective indicators, 15–19
life, evaluative judgments of, 19–20
monetary indicators, 11–15
objective measures vs., 3, 17, 31, 118–120, 143
problems revealed by, 4
reliability/validity concerns, 5–6
strengths of, 47

susceptibility to aspiration spiral, 109–110
Suicide/suicide rates (social indicator), 30, 89–91, 140–141, 142
Sullivan, W. C., 155
Survey of Labour and Income Dynamics (Canada), 202–203

Talbot, J. F., 155–156
Tarumi, K., 151
Taxation differentials, impact of, 59–60
Tax policies, 171–174
Technology, lack of benefits from, 117
TeenScreen program, 142
Terrorism, life satisfaction correlation, 49–50
Toseland, R., 139
Tov, W., 176, 199
Trust, building and maintaining, 177–179
Twin studies (heritability of well-being), 99–100

Unemployment, 115–116, 160–165
increased community violence, 164
scarring effect, 162
white vs. blue collar workers, 163
United Kingdom, 14, 35–36, 152, 156, 202, 212
United Nations, 25
United States
commuting study, 150
Current Population Survey, 36, 194
Great Depression, 36
hate crime legislation, 58
health status survey, 206
national accounting system, 35–36
New Freedom Commission on Mental Health, 140
United States General Accounting Office (GAO), 31

Validity of well-being measures, 74–77
domain satisfaction/behavior change, 91–93
as evaluative judgment, 75
married vs. divorced/widowed people, 88–89
money and well-being, 84–87
range of, 76–77

rejection of subjective measures,
75–76
relationships and well-being, 87–89
types of
construct validation, 19, 84
content validity, 78–80, 84
convergent validity, 80–82, 84
discriminant validity, 83–84
face validity, 77–78, 84
Valuation of nonmarket goods, 41–45
contingent valuation approach, 42
Quality Adjusted Life Years, 42
revealed preference approach, 41
and services/costs, 49–50
standard gamble hypotheticals
approach, 42
willingness-to-pay approach, 42, 43
van den Brink, H., 136–137
Van Praag, B., 148, 173
Vemuri, A. W., 155
Verlet, D., 176
Verme, P., 48

Warner, R., 143
Wealth of nation studies, 48, 85
Weitoft, G. R., 91
Well-being
definition of, 8–20
global differences, 101
money and, 84–87
national accounts timing
implementation, 210–213
need for subjective indicators of, 3–5
relationships and, 87–89
subjective/objective definitions
vs. subjective/objective indicators,
10
vs. happiness, 8
Well-being measures. *See also*
Objections to well-being
measures; Objective measures of
well-being; Subjective well-being
(measures)
goal/role of, 96–98

intuitive vs. counterintuitive
construction, 97–98
reliability, 68–74
usage determination, 127–128
validity, 74–77
construct validation, 19, 84
content validity, 78–80, 84
convergent validity, 80–82, 84
discriminant validity, 83–84
face validity, 77–78, 84
Wells, N. M., 156
Welsch, H., 157
Welzel, C., 197
Wener, R. E., 153
Wheatley, T. P., 43
White, M. P., 23–24, 48
Wiley, A. R., 155
Wilks, A. R., 29
Willingness-to-pay approach (to
nonmarket goods valuation), 42,
43
Wilson, G., 164
Wilson, T. D., 43
Wilson, W., 81
Winkelmann, L., 162
Within-person changes, 67, 105–106,
162–163
Witt, L. A., 166
Wolfers, J., 197, 198
Workplace well-being, 165–168. *See also*
Job satisfaction
World Database of Happiness
(Veenhoven), 191
World Health Organization (WHO), 66,
133–134, 143
World Values Survey, 48, 60,
198–199
Wright, T. A., 166, 167

Zack, M. M., 193
Zahran, H., 193